G000167058

Online Public Relations

A Handbook for Practitioners

James L. Horton

QUORUM BOOKS
Westport, Connecticut • London

Library of Congress Cataloging-in-Publication Data

Horton, James L.
Online public relations : a handbook for practitioners / James L. Horton.
p. cm.
Includes bibliographical references and index.
ISBN 1-56720-406-6 (alk. paper)
1. Public relations—Handbooks, manuals, etc. 2. Corporations—Public relations—Handbooks, manuals, etc. I. Title.

HD59.H598 2001
659.2′0285—dc21   2001016131

British Library Cataloguing in Publication Data is available.

Library of Congress Catalog Card Number: 2001016131
ISBN: 1-56720-406-6

First published in 2001

Quorum Books, 88 Post Road West, Westport, CT 06881
An imprint of Greenwood Publishing Group, Inc.
www.quorumbooks.com

Printed in the United States of America

The paper used in this book complies with the
Permanent Paper Standard issued by the National
Information Standards Organization (Z39.48–1984).
10 9 8 7 6 5 4 3 2 1

Every reasonable effort has been made to trace the owners of copyright materials
in this book, but in some instances this has proven impossible. The author and
publisher will be glad to receive information leading to more complete acknowl-
edgments in subsequent printings of the book, and in the meantime extend their
apologies for any omissions.

For Sara Patricia Horton
and
My Parents
Edward Joseph Horton
Claudine Henrietta Horton

Contents

Preface

WHAT YOU SHOULD KNOW
BEFORE READING THIS BOOK

The objective of this handbook is to help public relations practitioners use online media to serve clients better, faster, and less expensively. It is written for practitioners who need quick explanations that they can use immediately, and it is designed to be a handbook that sits on your desk or a nearby shelf where you grab it as you need it.

This presents a challenge. Online technology and applications are massive and mysterious. Even online technicians do not know every element of the electronic maze that comprises online media. This book attempts to clarify thickets of jargon that appear to have little bearing on the work of public relations practitioners but somehow keep popping up to confuse issues. The goal is to strive to provide explanations that are useful to you in your work.

The book has been divided into sections:

- Online technologies
- Online information dissemination and retrieval
- Ways to use online to build relationships with individuals and publics
- Industry sources online

Sections are broken into short explanations that you can read quickly like using a dictionary or encyclopedia. We strive to make entries practical so that you can get back to work with the least amount of interruption.

Each entry

- Defines a topic.
- Tells how it fits into public relations and why you should know it.
- Discusses who uses it.
- Suggests why it should be used to communicate more effectively.
- Suggests appropriate uses and gives pointers how to use it tactically.

Online media, especially the Internet, have changed public relations and the public relations practitioner's job. Organizations are online. Vendors are online. Customers are online. Shareholders, critics, competitors, employees, local communities, municipalities, state and federal government agencies are online.

You probably use online media today in some capacity, even if just for e-mail. In fact, most PR practitioners cannot function now without e-mail to maintain contact within their organizations, with vendors and others. E-mail has had an extraordinary impact on PR. Those of us from the days of faxes and surface mail have trouble remembering how we used to operate. Indeed, those of us old enough to recall days before faxes find it nearly impossible to believe that we could have worked in PR at such a leisurely pace. On the other hand, speed threatens some basic values of PR, especially when practitioners become more enamored with rapid response than with accuracy and well-thought-out counsel.

Throughout this book, we strive to use simple language and to avoid burying you in "geek speak," but online media are technology, and buried in the jargon of technology are opportunities for those who understand them and use them creatively. You use technology daily, although you might not think about it. Anything that requires a mechanical process of some kind has technology in it—a pencil, a telephone, word processing, a fax machine, a camera, books, magazines, and the like—and you know enough about the technology of those media to work with them. Think of online as a new pencil, and you need to know enough about this pencil to write with it.

Although the Internet is not even a decade old as a practical PR medium, it has been in existence since the late 1960s. There are plenty of places to read about its thirty-year overnight success story, the rise of the Web and of e-commerce. We recommend that you consult the following Web site, where the history of the Internet is discussed in detail: http://www.isoc.org/guest/zakon/Internet/History. Robert Zakon has compiled comprehensive facts and statistics. It is less easy to find the history of commercial online services, such as America OnLine (AOL) and CompuServe, but their success paralleled the growth of the Internet in importance. In fact, at one time in the 1980s and early 1990s, they were more important than the Internet for public relations practitioners. It was only later that commercial services connected to and were largely absorbed by the Internet.

One topic we will not discuss in this book is the size of the Internet and online media. Whatever we write will be out of date instantly because of the furious growth of online. Online users today number in the hundreds of millions and pages of information in the billions. There are places to get updated statistics. Try: http://www.cyberatlas.com or http://www.lcweb.loc.gov/global/internet/inet-stats. html. The Library of Congress maintains the second site, and it is a compendium.

Rarely, perhaps never, has a medium grown as quickly as online, once the Web was developed. Think of phonographs, movies, radio and television. The Web in its short life already has outstripped most of them, and perhaps all of them in terms of the number of sites and pages of content that it carries. And the stunning part of the Internet is that it shows no signs of slowing down.

A second topic that we will not discuss is online demographics. These too are changing so rapidly that anything in print is dated instantly. We know that the Internet started as a hangout for well-educated and relatively affluent men and now is equally weighted between males and females with educational and income characteristics that are rapidly approaching national averages. On the other hand, the percentage of minorities, of country usage, of e-commerce, and so on, change by the hour. Still, online services do not serve everyone. Millions—and perhaps, billions—have no access to it, and may not for years, if ever. It is up to public relations practitioners to find out if their target audiences have access to online services.

We suggest the following places to get updated demographic information: http://www.dir.yahoo.com/Computers_and_Internet/ Internet/Statistics_and_Demographics. Several useful sites are listed there. You might also try http://www.nua.ie. This firm tracks worldwide Internet trends.

One last point that you the PR practitioner should remember about online media is that they are mostly uncontrolled arenas of speech, with the good and ill that such uncontrolled speech allows. Services such as AOL and CompuServe have some safeguards, and depending on where they are, some government controls. The Internet, for the most part, does not, even though governments worldwide try to impose control especially in the area of copyrights, false news reports, and some kinds of pornography. However, you should be aware of the unedited nature of online media and their impact for good and ill on corporate reputation.

With that, let's move forward. Chapter 1 frames online media in the context of corporate communications.

For PR practitioners looking for additional texts about online PR, we suggest that you look at the following works:

- Holtz, Shel, *Public Relations on the Net* (New York: Amacom, 1999) 332pp. ISBN 0-8144-7987 -1
- Middlebert, Don, *Winning PR in the Wired World: Powerful Communications Strategies for the Noisy Digital Space.* (New York: McGraw-Hill, 2001) 235 pp., ISBN 0-07-136342-4
- O'Keefe, Steve, *Publicity on the Internet* (New York: John Wiley & Sons, Inc., 1997) 401 pp. ISBN 0-471-16175-6
- Sherwin, Gregory R. and Emily N. Avila, *Connecting Online: Creating a Successful Image on the Internet.* (Grants Pass, Oregon: The Oasis Press, 1997) 450 pp. ISBN 1-55571-403-X

As with everything written about online media, these works are dated to some extent. In "Internet Time," anything written yesterday is old, but the books do provide a base from which readers can better understand online media.

Several people were instrumental in encouraging me to write this book. Among them was my editor, Eric Valentine, who urged me on when I had vowed not to lose any more weekends at the computer. My wife and daughter showed utmost patience while I sat for months in my office pecking at the keyboard. My father and my wife, both better writers than I, labored through hundreds of pages of manuscript to point out omissions and errors. Peter Shinbach, APR of The Birmingham Group, added extraordinary insight and brought me down to earth where I needed it. Mike Millican of Robert Marston and Associates, Inc.; Dr. Michael McGraw of Seton Hall University, and George Wolfe of US Trust all read the manuscript at various stages and provided valuable insight. Others too numerous to mention helped in clarifying concepts and ideas over the months. To all, thank you.

As always, any errors in the text are mine alone, and I am grateful when readers point them out.

Online Media

Online media are tools for information distribution and retrieval, for entertainment, and for relationship building with individuals and audiences. Traditional print and electronic media—newspapers, phones, phonographs, movies, radios, TVs—perform the same function. The differences between online and traditional media lie in matters of degree. Whereas traditional media tend more toward mass, one-way distribution of information, online tends more to individualized two-way distribution. In that respect, online media are closer to direct marketing.

Online media consist of networks of computers, some of which hold content and most of which are agents for content retrieval and interaction with other computers and software applications. Networks are not new. The universal telephone system built in the United States during the twentieth century was the first great network, and today the bulk of computer networking still relies on its millions of miles of cable and tens of thousands of switches.

The technical difference between traditional and online media is that online media can carry just about anything, and hence they are more flexible than any other medium except face-to-face communication. Virtually every communications technology has been influenced by or subsumed into online. Online media transport data, text, images, animated images, databases, audio, video and more. Most importantly, they allow two-way conversation. We can converse with individuals anywhere in the world at any time using multiple media. This is a feat that newspapers, telephones, radios, and TV either cannot do or cannot achieve as economically as online.

Online media complement and supplement public relations. They do not replace the work of relating to internal and external audiences, nor do they replace media that we use today. They expand the power of persuasion and interaction with new media tools. This is a point that public relations practitioners need to remember. The principles of persuasion, credibility, and communication do not change, and one does not enter a world in which one must relearn everything. Many, if not all, of the crafts that PR practitioners learn in formal and on-the-job training still apply online, but the emphasis is different enough that one can feel like a stranger in a foreign land.

Consider one example—the newsletter. The newsletter was until recently a printed publication with its own guidelines for content, writing, formatting, and design. The newsletter today is largely electronic and sent by e-mail with its own guidelines for content, writing, formatting, and design depending on the e-mail format that you use. In addition, e-mail newsletters can embed sound and video, and connections that take one out of the newsletter to Web sites, information databases, to phone calls or online chat rooms. Suddenly, the humble newsletter has become a medium with communications potential far exceeding the original low-cost, easy-to-produce paper-based vehicle for getting news out. It is understandable that traditional PR practitioners are nervous and online enthusiasts overstate their case that online media are completely different.

Online media have enormous reach worldwide, and their reach continues to grow rapidly. An analogue to online's near-universal and individualized delivery—a postal delivery system—is slow and cumbersome by comparison. People can visit you instantly online from anywhere. And, they do. For example, the author developed and runs a Web site for public relations practitioners (http://www.online-pr.com) that welcomes PR practitioners from the United States, from the United Kingdom, from India, Hong Kong, Australia, Saudi Arabia, South Africa, Venezuela, and points in between. No other medium that communicators use has that instant and far-flung reach. That said, online may never have the reach of global postal systems. It requires an infrastructure of technologies that are not yet widespread in many countries, and it may take decades before any Rwandan tending cattle in Africa can e-mail any Brazilian fishing along the Amazon. But even the largest newspapers do not come close to the reach of online, nor do the largest TV or radio networks.

One factor that remains the same between online and traditional media is the matter of choice. Users choose the online content they wish to have and not publishers. Users choose content in newspapers and on TV and radio and not editors or producers. No one has to come to your Web site, and if a visitor does stop by, he or she does not have to stay long. No one has to buy a newspaper or turn on the TV or radio, and if the person does, he or she does not have to linger long. Here again, it is a matter of degree. There are millions of Web sites, and, by comparison, hundreds of TV channels. There are hundreds of millions of e-mail addresses and by comparison, only one newspaper in most U.S. cities. It is harder to gain a large audience online because of the millions of channels to choose from, and it is easy to leave. A click of the mouse and one is gone. On the other hand, in a 500-channel TV universe, the click of a remote control is not much different except for one thing. A user can not only click away online, but he or she can talk back, unlike in television.

Curiously, while users choose content, online publishers do not have to follow users' preferences. The reason for this is economics. It is cheap to get online by comparison with print or video production. The cost of computers, modems, and Internet connections has plunged to a point where nearly all levels of society can afford to create and publish content. Millions of Web sites exist because someone created them without much expectation of anyone, other than the publisher, using them. There are as well thousands of "living dead" sites built for events long past that have never been taken down. Because of online's inexpensive distribution, commercial, corporate, personal, and "living dead" sites exist side by side in cyberspace. This creates overwhelming clutter and potential for distraction. The term "surfing" recognizes the propensity for online media to lead users from one spot to the next without a reference point for return. This presents a continuing challenge. Content must be informative and entertaining, or both, to keep users from leaving a site. PR practitioners must work harder online and define audiences more accurately.

Communities of interest online are amazing in their diversity from health to butterflies to nuclear physics to doll collecting to fitness and thousands more topics. Online communities span the earth. They have no boundaries and as a result, they have changed the way organizations communicate. Traditional media have never had that kind of reach. What is said in Singapore echoes online in Alabama, and what is whispered in Boston is overheard online in Rome. Ideas and information leap boundaries, and they do not require the intermediary of a journalist or editor to make the jump. Chinese activists in the United States can denounce the government of China in e-mail to Shanghai. Web sites in Middle Europe appeal for help from immigrant populations in other countries. When the government of Australia outlawed Web-based pornography sites, Australian pornographers shifted their content to U.S.-based computers. Anyone clicking on a local Australian site was transferred immediately to the United States. The author worked with a major electronics manufacturer that discovered product introductions in Japan were discussed within hours in online newsgroups reaching the United States, United Kingdom, Finland, and New

Zealand. Online public relations practitioners must think both globally and locally at the same time.

Secondly, online PR practitioners must think in terms of source credibility more than in the past. There is a huge benefit to information gatekeepers—reporters, editors, producers, and others who independently gather and process information. They check information for accuracy and credibility and save users the time of vetting information on their own. They distill information to what is important and save users from wading through heaps of irrelevant gossip and half-truths. Many online newsgroups, chat rooms, and Web sites are filled with trash, and in the middle of the trash, there might be a kernel of truth. The danger is that users mistake trash for truth and lies for facts. This has always been a part of the public relations challenge. There are individual editors, reporters, and producers in traditional media that one cannot trust to report accurately, but online has hundreds, or thousands, of them, and they reach journalists in traditional media who keep up with newsgroups and chat rooms. Hoping that a reporter will not know about that semihidden embarrassing incident that the corporation has stumbled into is less realistic now. More than likely, the reporter is calling about the incident. A responsible journalist today will have visited a company's Web site, looked into online databases, and visited online bulletin boards before calling the PR department.

One fact that PR practitioners can count on when working online is that people are people for good and ill. Human behavior has not changed with the invention and spread of online media. Online amplifies individuals and broadcasts their quirks for others to see. Public relations practitioners entering the online world should not expect monsters that Renaissance cartographers drew on maps where geography was unknown. What they will find are mixtures of cultures and beliefs, ideas and opinions that are more diverse than what they ordinarily deal with.

Before online, because of the limitations of traditional media, one could assume an audience with similar characteristics—a mass audience. Since online, one cannot assume a mass audience. Fringe groups can gain a following online as easily as balanced critics can. Strange ideas can take root and mutate with alarming speed. The online public relations practitioner deals with them in much the same ways as in traditional public relations—with facts and openness. But, rather than send one press release to all audiences, one may need to work much more with tailored messages to individuals and small communities of interest.

Interactivity is a key difference between online and traditional media. It is not one that is fully understood either. Online publishers like TheStreet.com, MSNBC, and Slashdot.org have taken advantage of it by promoting interaction among journalists, between journalists and readers, and among readers. Thus, at the end of articles, one finds a link to e-mail one's response directly to the reporter who wrote the story. One finds story ranking software. With a click, one can tell a publisher whether a story was of interest and how much. One finds newsgroups where journalists talk to each other while readers look on. One finds newsgroups where readers and journalists talk together. One finds links that let readers e-mail stories to other readers with a message. One finds news stories where a topic is posed and readers contribute their collective wisdom to amplify the topic.

These experiments are exciting because they can draw users closer to the organization. They are challenging because journalists can no longer maintain distance from readers. They are also incomplete because we don't know what works and what doesn't, nor how interaction will change online publishing. Public relations practitioners for the most part have not engaged in interactive experiments for a number of reasons. The key one is that PR departments are understaffed and do not have the time to interact with individuals to the extent that they need or would like to do. Eventually, public relations will get involved, or interactive response will be placed elsewhere, such as customer service departments. And if the latter action happens, public relations will be diminished.

Interactivity highlights the primary challenge to public relations practitioners—and indeed, to anyone working online. Online media are at the beginning of their development. Little is known about them. We are like early printers—Gutenberg, Manutius, or Caxton—who could not foresee the great publishing houses of centuries later. We barely understand the transforming power of online media and only time will tell their impact. Online media await writers, artists, engineers, thinkers, implementers, activists, politicians, and others to find their full power. Enthusiasm for online media today is the flush of experimentation, of pushing back technical limits and seeing the new tricks that online media can play. It is an intoxicating experience. Five years from today, we may use online differently than we do now, and ten or twenty years from today, even more differently. But, online is so prevalent already that PR practitioners dare not hang back and wait until the medium has settled into mature forms.

As time passes, we will better understand the power and limits of online media. We will discover that they are better than some media that PR practitioners have long used. We will learn that they are not as good for other forms of communication. Individuals will still read books and newspapers, watch television, go to movies, listen to radio, and peruse brochures. *Dot-com* companies recognize this with radio and television advertising blitzes beseeching individuals to click to their sites. Publishers of online media need traditional media and vice versa. This should comfort public relations practitioners transitioning from traditional to online media, and it should disturb practitioners who work solely online. Successful use of online media requires an integrated approach.

Online media tools do not guarantee communications success: Tools can be used well or badly. Giving a person a pencil does not make him Shakespeare, nor does a camera make one a great photographer like Ansel Adams. Media are craft skills, and public relations practitioners are craftspeople and message managers. They know some communications crafts well and organize specialists to implement other crafts.

Online media are so adaptable and complex that they are essentially collaborative, and PR practitioners will find themselves working with other groups more often than not. For example, on large Web sites few communicators do everything required—writing, designing, coding, maintenance, and measurement. Online media are closer to filmmaking where writers, producers, directors, designers, talent, editors, and technology blend in a mix of art and science. Public relations practitioners strive to understand enough of online media to use them effectively. They learn rules and grammars, denotations and connotations, and technologies that produce information, translate it, and distribute it online. This is not that much different from the way PR practitioners employ traditional media. Few practitioners design their own brochures, run their own printing presses, and stitch pages together in a bindery. They direct craft specialists who do these jobs. The practitioners know enough of the rules and grammars, denotations and connotations, and technologies of printing to get the job done.

The key for public relations practitioners is to remember the purpose of communication. They should avoid getting so wrapped in technology and creativity that they forget what a medium is to do. Letting online technologies dictate messages is already too evident. Try http://www.webpagesthatsuck.com for examples of Web pages where creativity and technology overwhelm content.

In the end, results count. Was a message communicated or not? Was an audience persuaded or not? Was a crisis contained or not? Effective communication translates meaning to action whether in print, radio, television, or online. It depends on audience receptivity and persuasion because some information remains unknown. Persuasive techniques support communication and do not supplant it. However, online media with their near-universal and individualized reach complicate effective communication. Online, PR practitioners must deal with people of different cultures, beliefs, and worldviews, whereas in the past it was easier to hide behind limitations of traditional media. The hard and disappointing fact is that sometimes no matter how one communicates online, the intended individual is not listening or is incapable of understanding and is not shy about speaking out. This is no different than it ever was, but online makes lack of understanding immediate in chat rooms where conspiracy theorists debate your organization's evil deeds, in newsgroups where employees express outrage over the benefits plan, and in e-mail that enumerates peccadilloes of your leaders. Online reminds PR practitioners that communication is, and always has been, hard and chancy work. Most communications programs are closer to baseball batting averages. A total of three hits out of ten at bats is good performance and four out of ten is a ticket to the hall of fame.

Online media are bound by the same principles of corporate communication as all other media. They strive for the following:

- Simplicity
- Timeliness
- Openness
- Definition
- Flexibility
- Individuality
- Meaningfulness
- Measurability

Simplicity is the sharp focus of messages and media on the ideas and themes that support the survival and success of an organization. It is difficult to achieve because simple communication strives to control all verbal and nonverbal communications resources. It seeks to unify two-way communications in the most effective ways to translate meaning into action. Online media provide powerful tools to achieve simplicity, especially in internal corporate communication, where Intranets are breaking down traditional walls to information dissemination. On the other hand, the tools only work as well as the practitioners who use them. Hence, the need for public relations practitioners to become familiar with online techniques.

Timeliness strives to provide information that a person needs when he or she needs it in order to influence decisions and actions and keep them consistent with an organization's goals. Online media reduce the time needed to transmit messages and elicit feedback. The downside to such media is that they put pressure on the organization and public relations practitioner to deliver information. And here, organizations too often fail. Materials on Web pages are outdated or simply in error. Requests go unanswered. E-mail becomes a way to hide rather than to communicate in a timely fashion. Modern public relations was founded on serving journalists who work under deadline pressure. Online takes public relations back to the future, except that timeliness applies to all communications and not just to media relations.

Openness means that information collected anywhere can be communicated anywhere in any direction to support or complete actions that ensure an organization's survival and success. Online media are boundary jumpers, but they do not ensure openness. Paradoxically, an open technology organization can be a closed communication organization, because the entity withholds information from individuals who need it. A prime contributor to closed communication is the "need-to-know" philosophy. In "need-to-know" organizations, managers decide what information an individual should have to do his or her task. The managers frequently give individuals too little information to understand links among tasks and a sense of a whole process. Errors that result are sometimes monumental, as the nation's intelligence agencies can attest. Public relations practitioners should be in the lead in calling for openness and explaining why it is important to the survival and success of organizations.

Definition defines purposeful communication. It determines who communicates what messages through which media to message receivers inside and outside an organization in order to support organizational survival and success. Definition starts outside an organization with key customers and constituencies and progresses to the inside. Definition is not a one-time act. It is continuous because key individuals who influence the survival and success of an organization change constantly and their concerns change as well.

Unfortunately, the near-universal reach of online media makes definition difficult and chaos a norm. PR practitioners should lead a continuous effort to define organizational spokespersons online, the messages that spokespersons can communicate credibly and individuals they should address. There is one question that PR practitioners should help answer: "Who in this organization is credible to this key customer or constituency at this time?" If it is a benefits question, it might be the benefits administrator, the head of human relations, or even the CEO. If it is a question of company direction, it might be the CEO, the chief information officer (CIO), or the chief financial officer (CFO). It depends on the individual who is seeking information.

Flexibility means that organizations adapt messages, media, and audiences as needed to survive and succeed. An organization avoids committing itself so heavily to any one medium, message, or audience that it has no recourse. The customers that drive growth today might not be the same customers tomorrow. The constituencies that are key to company survival today may differ tomorrow. As a result, organizations strive for wiggle room in their choices of messages, media, and audiences without changing core goals and key ideas that drive the organization.

Because online media are flexible and interactive, they reflect change more quickly than traditional media do. Managers working online have a term for this—*Internet Time*. Internet time refers to shifts that occur in hours rather than days and days rather than months or years. Organizations that once moved glacially now rage like flooding rivers and are driven by fear that one misstep can compromise survival and success. There is a new understanding of serendipity, fortuitous connections, and unfortunate outcomes that pose opportunities and threats.

But the flexibility of online is dangerous, and managers who get lost in responding to change can lose focus on what an organization does. Here is where PR practitioners can serve as reminders of the core business principles and messages in support of the CEO. For example, Amazon.com is flexible in building Web pages that respond to individual customer requests for books, electronics, and a host of other goods. On the other hand, Amazon.com learned early on that it needed to deliver the right product to the right customer at the right time day after day in order to fulfill customer demands. Flexibility in communications means that Amazon can encompass new customers and their needs individually, but it does not change Amazon's goal to pick, package, and deliver products in a timely fashion in order to remain a money-making business.

Individuality means that communications persuade one person at a time and not groups. Individuals accept group norms and act in groups but remain individuals. Public relations practitioners think about media as mass distribution because the PR industry was born and grew up during mass marketing of newspapers, radio, and television programs. Online media, on the other hand, are individual and interactive, even when presented in a mass media format. Individuality may well be the hardest concept for practitioners to accept in online PR, even though technologists have provided ways to customize or personalize media. For example, MyYahoo! lets you choose the content and layout of your Yahoo! entry page into the Web. Yahoo!'s individualized Web page lets me find what I want when I want it in the way I want it even though I am one of 45 million visitors a month. Many public relations practitioners are not used to this level of interaction, and think it a burden to distribute general messages in individualized packages. It may take an entirely new generation of PR practitioners to overcome the bias toward mass media thinking.

Meaningful communication defines messages whose intent and purposes are clear. Ideally, every message has one meaning, one subtext, and one intent, but this is never the case. Message recipients derive multiple meanings and subtexts from every message. Communicators are forced to emphasize the explicit intent of a message and to combat meanings and subtexts that harm intent. Meaningful messages encompass the intent and purpose of a message sender; the capacities, psychology, and culture of the message-receiver; the mutual interest or activity that underlies a message; and the place and time in which a message is sent. A meaningful message may be elaborate or one word like a stop sign. Public relations practitioners work hard to develop and express meaningful messages. They know how difficult it is to do, but what they may not realize is how online has changed the task.

Online media allow for terse or complex messages, but the near universality of online tends to push one toward elaboration in which a message-sender makes context and reasons for a message specific. This happens because the message-sender does not know the ultimate recipients of even a simple e-mail. E-mail is easily forwarded to others and loses its original context. Web pages start with the understanding that they are reaching a broad range of individuals because Web pages are published for anyone to read. Yet, here too, the task has added challenges. For example, should a Web page be in multiple languages? Web users speak many languages and content is more meaningful in a user's native tongue. PR practitioners should examine online content continuously for its meaningfulness to key message recipients and be ready to adjust content and presentation accordingly.

Measurable communication determines whether a message contributes to or detracts from an organization's survival and success. There is no neutral communication, because all message sending uses resources and competes for attention. Messages with no or little value waste time and money. Measurement is the only way to estimate what communication works. It is a controversial topic among public relations practitioners. Many believe that their work cannot be measured, but that is not true any longer, if it ever was. (The ultimate measurement, of course, is whether an organization's internal and external constituencies believe in the organization's viability and prospects for success. Public relations practitioners can always measure that.)

Online media are measurable. On a continuum, e-mail is the least calculable and Web pages the most. Because e-mail can be mass-mailed, forwarded, and made anonymous, tracking e-mail's source and impact is difficult. An organization can never know absolutely who has seen its messages and who not. On the other hand, e-mail can be set up so that the sender knows that it has been opened at a recipient's box, even if the sender does not know who actually read the e-mail.

Web sites, on the other hand, are different. One does not go to a Web site unless one chooses to do so. However, once that person arrives, movement through the Web site can be tracked precisely. One's journey through the site can provide close measurements to Web developers about what content is of interest and what not. Web page measurement is in its infancy, but it is already more sophisticated than measurement used for traditional media, such as magazines, television, and radio.

SUMMARY

Public relations practitioners should understand that online media serve all the many tasks and types of content in organizational communication. Online media are the closest an organization can come to one channel carrying all forms of communication. However, online media are crafts that require positioning, development, execution, management, and integration with other media. They are powerful and robust, but like all media, they can overwhelm messages if not used correctly.

Today, PR practitioners combine traditional PR and online skills in their work. They communicate internally and externally using online. They release information online, such as press releases, announcements, and media contact letters. They find information online. They monitor news, individual and group opinions about their organizations, products, and services online. They communicate through online media to respond to and manage crises. They market organizations' products and services online. They send direct and mass messages online. They engage with target individuals and build relationships online. They target audiences precisely online, whether media, local communities, consumers, shareholders and investors, employees, government and civic leaders, critics and activists, or voters. They maintain a presence twenty-four hours a day, seven days a week online. They cross geographic and cultural boundaries online. They form alliances with other organizations online to further the interests of both entities.

PR practitioners also know that online is still far from perfect. For example, they know that it is hard to find people online and for them to find you because there is no central directory for e-mail or Web pages. They recognize that online does not replace other media, especially face-to-face communication. They are aware that although online is nearly universal, it does not reach everyone, and in some countries, it barely reaches anyone. They know that the volume of online communication can overwhelm messages, and there is no guarantee of audience interest in any message, even when well presented. They understand that online media are insecure and always will be, and they accept that they must contend with other voices online that can have the same strength as theirs, for good and ill. Finally, they understand that online media are emerging technologies and that they are like pioneers of telephone, radio, and television. They dream of what is to come, and many of their visions are in error.

Online PR today is both exhilarating and frustrating with enormous benefits that have been realized already in its short life. There is much more to come for adventurous practitioners willing to get involved.

2

Online Terminology

Every technology has a language, and to use that technology, you need to know some of its lingo. For example, pica, em, en, and point are units of measurement in printing. If you have ever printed a brochure, you have bumped into them.

There is arrogance within any fraternity that knows this jargon. The brothers of a craft assume that you know it too, and they will not treat you as an equal unless you do. Many terms are common sense, and once you see what is referred to, you have no trouble remembering them. Some terms are difficult, and you will find that even technologists do not always understand or use them correctly.

This chapter is a starter list of terms. It is not exhaustive. If you are looking for in-depth discussions or definitions of technological terms, try a site such as `http://www.netlingo.com` or `http://www.whatis.techtarget.com` where you will find hundreds of terms. There are several encyclopedia and Web reference sites too, including `http://www.webreference.com` and `http://www.webopaedia.com`. Like all things on the Web, the list of acronyms grows daily as technology changes. Some terms fall out of usage while others emerge. It is the author's hope that the terms in this chapter will give you a starting point when you need to translate what the technologists are talking about.

One final note: The chapter is structured so that you can dip into a topic and leave. You don't have to read the chapter from beginning to end.

ADOBE ACROBAT®

This is software that lets you convert a document to a type of picture file, called a **Portable Document Format (PDF)** that can be read by any kind of computer anywhere. It was developed by Adobe Systems Incorporated (http://www.adobe.com/), a company that builds software for Web and print publishing, including graphic design, imaging, dynamic media, and tools to build Web pages.

Adobe Acrobat Reader, a free piece of software from Adobe Systems Incorporated, lets you open and read the Portable Document Format. The beauty of Adobe Acrobat for public relations is that it preserves fonts, formatting, colors, and graphics of any document that you wish to convert, such as a brochure or annual report. In fact, many companies publish annual reports and brochures online using Adobe Acrobat. That way, they do not have to develop a separate online design, and publications are available for investors, customers, and others to read and/or retrieve (download) at will. PDF files print correctly on any printer, so anyone with a color or black-and-white printer can reproduce your publication as you designed it. According to Adobe Systems Incorporated, more than 40 million people have installed Acrobat Reader on their computers, and many sites provide a direct link to the page where you can get the reader. You should provide a link, too, if you use the software. The downside of Adobe Acrobat files is that they can be large, and large files can open slowly. An impatient person will move on rather than wait. Secondly, it is far from certain that Adobe Acrobat will remain a standard. Standards change over time.

If you have print publications, consider putting them on your Web page in Adobe Acrobat. Next, consider whether you should print publications at all if your organization and its constituencies are mostly online. If that is the case, start with an online design that can be printed directly from the screen.

ANIMATION

Online animation is no different from a cartoon that you watch on TV, or a movie. It is a series of still images superimposed on one another quickly so that they seem to move.

Animation is easy to do online, and there are many forms. You have seen animated stills on Web pages. Envelopes come out of mailboxes. A cartoon figure waves at you. Eyes bug out of a photo. There are tens of thousands of such images and new ones created daily. There are libraries of animated images for free and for sale online. Several software programs let one animate and play images from simple to highly complex, full multimedia games and presentations. One of the most common is the **Macromedia Shockwave Player** that plays back complex animations and a similar piece of software called the **Macromedia Flash Player**. Both are from Macromedia, Inc. (http://www.

macromedia.com/), a company that builds software to help professional Web developers create animated Web sites.

Animation is a basic tool in effective communications. For example, text crawlers move across a Web site like a stock ticker to deliver announcements and news. Animated diagrams explain processes better than still drawings do. Flashing icons alert one to urgent announcements. Blinking icons let you know that updated information has been placed on a page.

There is one rule to remember about animation: Tie it directly and tightly to the communication objective. Overuse of animation is frequent online. It is distracting and slows comprehension. More importantly, a huge animation file can freeze a screen while it downloads. Don't let Web designers dupe you into using animation because "it's cool."

APPLICATION SERVICE PROVIDER (ASP)

Early on in computing, technicians learned how to store instructions (software) in a computer then use the software for word processing, designing, communicating, and all the other tasks that a PR practitioner does on a daily basis. This is partially why computer storage media (hard disks, floppy disks, and CD-ROMs) continue to grow in capacity. The Application Service Provider (ASP) seeks to change that by sending down over the Internet to your computer just the applications that you need at the moment. The rationale behind the ASP's approach is this:

- You don't need to pay for a large hard drive or other expensive storage media.
- You don't need to pay for software when you don't use it. You rent software as you need it.
- The ASP will keep your software up to date without you having to pay for or worry about it.
- You have a greater availability of different types of software programs at a lower over all cost.
- You can outsource much information technology administration cost.

Though this seems to be a better approach than buying software and loading it into your computer, there are downsides as well.

- Using ASP software requires high-speed access to the Internet. Otherwise, it takes much too long to download.

- Using an ASP requires you to upgrade software when an ASP upgrades. This is OK unless the software upgrade also forces you into a computer or other hardware upgrade as well because the new software has features that require new hardware.
- Security is a concern when you use software that is downloaded from the Internet, or when you store files, calendars, e-mail addresses, and more on the Internet, which some services allow you to do.
- When you outsource administration of your software, you are dependent on the company that you hand it to. If the company is reliable, you are OK. If not, you could be in trouble.
- You can rent time on powerful software, but you still need to learn how to use it and how to integrate it into company processes.

The ASP approach is part of two other concepts that are discussed frequently in relation to online—**Thin client** and **Total Cost of Owner-ship** (TCO). A thin client is a personal computer stripped to essentials and placed on either an internal network or on the Internet. The idea behind a bare-bones machine is that it costs less to buy and less to maintain over its life span, especially because software and files are stored centrally in a server or on the Internet. Information technology administrators have learned that maintenance of a personal computer and its software over its useful life span costs many times more than the machine itself. This has generated discussion about the Total Cost of Ownership of personal computers (TCO). TCO equals the sum of the purchase price for software and hardware, installation and mainte-nance costs over their lifetimes, upgrade costs, and disposal costs. For most organizations, TCO is high and technologists are seeking ways to reduce the cost.

BROADBAND

Broadband refers to the capacity of copper wire or glass fiber that delivers data. The data is made up of the 1s and 0s that make up the bits of computing and groups of 1s and 0s—such as 10011001—make up bytes. A broadband cable is a large pipe that delivers huge amounts of bits and bytes at high speed. A standard telephone line, by contrast, is a straw. Think of a water distribution system in any city. Mains are huge capacity pipes that feed into smaller diameter pipes that feed buildings and still smaller pipes that service the apartments in the building. Between large broadband pipes and skinny straws are several data pipes with different capacities for delivering bits and bytes and differ-ent price ranges. Here are a few to impress your friends.

Ultra-high-speed lines that haul enormous loads of information are **backbones**, because they are spines to which all cables of a communication network connect. These optical fiber cables run at speeds greater than 2.5 billion bits per second—soon to rise to more than 6 trillion bits per second. By contrast, a **Digital Subscriber Line** (DSL) connecting to a computer can run in the range of 1.5 million bits per second, whereas a **cable modem,** which also connects directly to a computer, can receive and send greater than 500,000 bits per second. Compare this to a telephone **modem**, a device that hooks to a regular telephone line to deliver data. On a good day, it transmits 64,000 bits per second. Other terms that you might hear are **T1** (1.54 million bits per second) and **T3** (44.736 million bits per second). To further confuse you, the term used to describe the number of bits per second that a standard telephone line carries is **baud** (a term left over from the days of the telegraph). The fastest modem runs at 64,000 baud.

What is important to remember? Fast is better. The faster that data can enter a computer, the easier it is to get large files and to run multimedia, such as animations, movies, audio, video, and the like.

Unfortunately, the *slowest* **common denominator** rules online media design. One should not transmit data any faster than the slowest user can handle it. In the United States, the *slowest* common denominator is changing as cable modems and Digital Subscriber Lines are installed, but even so, it will be several years before the majority of the United States enjoys high-speed service, and other countries are further behind. If a Web page targets individuals in locales with a slow communications system, avoid large files and multimedia. Knowing the speed of data delivery that target users can handle is a basic online consideration.

A point to remember: Web designers work with high-speed connections. They can forget that others do not enjoy the same speed that they have. Hence, they build applications that are too big for users with modems. PR practitioners may need to remind Web designers of the speed limits in which they operate.

BROWSER

A browser started as simple software that you load into your computer in order to read formatted text on the Internet. It has rapidly grown into a complex tool with more functions than a Swiss Army knife. Before browser software came along, it was difficult to format text on the Internet with different types of fonts, borders, photos, and illustrations. (Commercial services like AmericaOnline (AOL) could do it, but they were built differently.) Today's browsers are versatile and a key to success of the World Wide Web. They are also large programs that take up a lot of space on your computer.

A Web page arrives at your computer wrapped in formatting codes, called **Hyper Text Markup Language (HTML),** that tell the browser the color of the page, the type of font to use, where to place text, where to place images, and so on. The browser assembles the page that you view from the formatting codes. This is close to what a word processor does. The text page that you see in a word processing program uses hidden formatting language. In the early days of personal computing, this language was visible, and in fact, users had to enter some of the format codes manually.

Here is an illustration of what HTML formatting codes look like (you do not need to know what any of this code means):

```
<table border="3" width="90%" height="1" cellspacing="0"
bordercolorlight="#FFFFFF" bordercolordark="#FFFFFF"
bgcolor="#000080">
<tr>
 <td width="100%" height="34" bgcolor="#000080"
bordercolor="#FFFFFF" bordercolorlight="#FFFFFF"
bordercolordark="#FFFFFF"><p align="center"><font
face="Times New Roman" color="#FFFFFF"><big><big><big>
<big>Online Public Relations</big></big></big></big>
</font></td>
</tr>
<tr>
 <td width="100%" height="1" bgcolor="#FFFFFF"
bordercolor="#FFFFFF" bordercolorlight="#000080"
bordercolordark="#000080"><font face="Times New Roman"
color="#FF0000"><big><big><big><big><p align="center">
</big></big></big></big></font><small><font face="Arial"
color="#000080"><strong>Last update<small> </small><! —
Webbot bot="Timestamp" S-Type="EDITED" S-Format="%m/%d/%y"
startspan —>01/25/00<!—Webbot bot="Timestamp" endspan i-
checksum="12302" —></strong></font></small></td>
</tr>
</table>
</center></div><div align="center"><center>
<table border="1" width="90%" bordercolor="#FFFFFF">
<tr>
 <td width="1-%"><p align="center"><font face="Arial"
size="2" color="#000080"><strong>Online
 Public Relations is dedicated to helping you<br>
 deliver better, faster and less-expensive online PR.
</strong></font></td>
</tr>
</table>
```

Here is how a browser renders the HTML formatting codes that you just read into a Web page.

Online Public Relations

Last update 01/25/00

Online Public Relations is dedicated to helping you
deliver better, faster and less-expensive online PR.

At this point, a professor might ask, "Any questions?" What has happened to browsers since their invention is astonishing. Today, they are used to find, retrieve, view, and send information on the Internet. Browsers include

- E-mail.
- Newsgroup readers. (We'll write more about this later.)
- Multimedia players for video, sound, and animated images.
- Conferencing so that users in different locales can meet in real time.
- Plug-in software and applets that let you perform functions that a browser does not do. (An **applet** is a little software application that works with a browser; a **plug-in** is a software application that fits into a Web browser like an electric plug into a socket. Adobe's Acrobat reader [See Adobe Acrobat] is a plug-in.)
- Chat—where you can type messages to another in real time.
- Security software.
- Lists of sites to which you wish to return.
- Pages of sites that you have previously visited.
- A way to read hypertext in formatted pages.

There is more packed into a browser than what is listed here, but this gives you the idea.

Two browsers have overwhelming market share. **Microsoft**® **Internet Explorer** (http://www.microsoft.com) and **Netscape Navigator** (http://www.netscape.com/). Both load into your computer, but they are not totally compatible, so a Web page built for one might not work completely, or as well, on the other. This happened because both Microsoft and Netscape put their own software applications into their browsers. In addition, earlier versions of these two browsers, and browsers from developers other than Microsoft and Netscape, cannot handle all the applications that Explorer or Navigator use today.

What are the points that PR practitioners should take from this?

- Use the most recent version of a browser. The most recent version of a browser will have all the functions that the developers are putting into Web pages.

- Use the browser with the greatest market share. Web page developers build pages to accommodate the browser with the greatest market share.
- Test new Web pages against both Microsoft and Netscape browsers to see how they look. Make adjustments if there are serious differences, or build two versions of a page—one for Explorer and one for Navigator.
- Make sure that your target audience is not using an earlier browser that cannot handle functions that you intend to use.

Incompatibilities are fewer now. In the early days of the Web—around 1995—Web developers would specify the browser you should use. Now, Web developers pretest browser compatibility, or openly exclude older browsers because a majority of users have changed to a newer version. This also forces users with older versions to get newer ones.

A PR practitioner's job is to make sure that a medium communicates effectively to target individuals and audiences. You need to make sure that your Web page can be read by those you want to reach. Before launching a Web site, have the Web developers show the page in Explorer and Navigator and in old and new versions of these browsers. Also, have the developers explain how they are accommodating users with different kinds and vintages of browsers.

CHAT

Chat is live messaging technology. You write to someone and get a response back from that person immediately. Text flows between two computers without stopping. Online chat often uses a **channel,** a location online where one finds others interested in the same topic. You might also use a **meeting room**—a secured or hidden channel—where you can write privately one-to-one or to a targeted group. A version of live messaging technology is called **white boarding.** You write on a board that looks like a white chalkboard, or on a computer screen, using a computer mouse as a pencil, and the viewer at the other end sees what was written.

Chat programs come with many features, including

- Multiplatform support: Programs work on computers using Microsoft Windows or Apple Macintosh operating systems without difficulty.
- Moderated chatting: One person is in charge.
- News.
- Calendars and scheduling.

- Voice messages.
- An answering machine.
- Message history.
- Security provisions.
- Buddy lists, which help one see when friends are online.
- Directory searches to find others with similar interests.
- File transfers.
- Notification that someone wants to chat with you.

Chat has grown explosively, particularly on the commercial service, AOL. On the Internet, there are several chat programs, including Internet Relay Chat (IRC), AOL Instant Messenger, The Palace, Talk City, and ICQ. Chat is an accepted and frequently used tool for work, customer contact, and publicity. Celebrity chats promote movies, records, television shows, and other entertainment. Workers use chat to coordinate with colleagues and clients. Companies use chat to help customers on e-commerce Web sites.

Chat has good and bad features. Although immediacy is beneficial, chat can annoy if chat requests continue to pop up while you are concentrating. Chat with more than one person needs a moderator. Otherwise, it becomes a confused series of partial messages tumbling over one another. Chats with large groups do not work at all and are more of a promotional ploy. When 5,000 people wait in a chat room to talk to a movie star, at best 10 of them will get to submit a question. The rest watch. Large-scale chats often use a person who screens questions and one who writes responses.

An allied version of chat technology is the **real-time Web presentation.** The real-time web presentation allows one to show PowerPoint slide presentations and other types of files—spreadsheets and graphics—in real time on the Web without traveling to a distant location. Real-time presentation services, such as WebEx (http://www.webex .com), provide features that include whiteboards, annotation tools, polling and voting, chat, Internet telephone (also called Voice over Internet Protocol, or VoIP), and Web tours. These services also provide address books, calendars, and document storage. The immediate benefit to the PR practitioner is that it can cut down on flying everyone in for a presentation or, conversely, placing speakers on extended and tiring road shows. Wall Street adapted this technology quickly because of the timesaving it provides in giving financial presentations to audiences in multiple locations.

COMPRESSION

Compression packs data into a smaller physical space. Think of a trash compactor in a kitchen. Compression does not appear to connect to any work that PR practitioners do. But, in fact, it does. It underlies virtually everything online. Compression is necessary to save space and time when sending data across a network or storing it. Images, audio and video, text, and data files are compressed. Some applications, such as video, would not be possible without squeezing image and sound data into a size that a network and slow computer connections can handle. You do not need to know how compression is done, but it is good to remember how much space compression can save. A text file, for example, can be squeezed to just 50 percent of its size.

There are several tools that you will encounter to compress then decompress files, such as **WinZip, PKZIP,** and **BinHex,** if you are a Macintosh user. (Once a file is compressed, you can't read it until you decompress it.) If you are a PC user and want to use only one program, choose WinZip because it decompresses the others. For Macintosh users, **StuffIt** is popular.

Compression has one other advantage. Compressed documents survive trips online better than uncompressed documents for a variety of technical reasons. Sometimes documents attached to e-mail will be scrambled in transmission and arrive useless. This is maddening when one is on deadline. If the person on the other end can handle a compressed document, send it that way for safety.

DISPLAY MODE

The easiest way to explain display mode is to point out that the same Web page on two different computer screens may look different. On one the type is large and the page seems to push out the side of the screen. On the other, the text is small and the page seems to squeeze toward the center. This happens because computers can show data on screens at different levels of resolution and color.

To begin, a computer's monitor projects an image on the screen in tiny dots called picture elements, or **pixels.** The French impressionist painter, George Seurat, created landscapes out of dots of paint that blended together to form a scene. A computer does the same thing electronically. Pixels come in various tiny sizes, and the smallest create a high-resolution image. Pixels describe the color that shows at the exact spot where the pixel glows on a screen. They do this by mixing red, green, and blue. Pixels can render anywhere from 16 colors on a computer screen up to 16,000,000 colors depending on the power of the computer.

The earliest display technology was the Color Graphics Adaptor **(CGA).** This crude computer hardware from the early 1980s could render 4 colors and had a resolution of just 320 pixels horizontally and

200 pixels vertically. Then came the Enhanced Graphics Adaptor (**EGA**). It pushed the number of colors to 16 and resolution to 640 pixels horizontally and 350 pixels vertically. You could actually read text with an EGA adaptor, but you couldn't use it for graphic design. The EGA adaptor was superceded by the Video Graphics Array (**VGA**) that is still in use. With VGA, you have a choice of rendering 16 colors at a resolution of 640 × 480 pixels, or 256 colors at a lower resolution of 320 × 200 pixels. Next came the Extended Graphics Array (**XGA**) that gives a choice of 16,000,000 colors in a resolution of 800 × 600 pixels or a higher resolution of 1,024 × 768 pixels in 65,536 colors. Today, the Super Video Graphics Array (**SVGA**) handles up to 16,000,000 colors but allows variable screen resolutions based on the size of a computer monitor.

You do not have to remember much of this, but if you design a Web page in 16,000,000 colors, and someone looks at it with a monitor set to 65,536 colors, that person is not going to see the design in the same way. Check online displays at various resolutions to make sure that a design does not fall apart when resolution is changed.

Most computer users do not understand pixels or resolution and rarely change the original computer settings. Hence, it is a good rule of thumb to design Web pages using the most common display mode to have the best chance of communicating to the largest number of target individuals without difficulty.

E-MAIL TECHNOLOGY

To many, online is e-mail. E-mail, the transmission of text messages and attached files, so dominates online media that businesses cease to function when e-mail goes down and many journalists will not accept publicity approaches in any other way. E-mail is the earliest form of online communication, and it has an array of applications, some of which we will discuss.

E-mail started out as different types, but it merged in the 1990s into interconnected systems. Early on, some e-mail systems linked departments or companies but did not communicate externally. Other e-mail systems, such as the commercial services America OnLine (AOL) and CompuServe, allowed one to write to individuals in other places but only if you and they were on AOL or CompuServe. The rise of the Internet forced all these systems to link together, but they are not the same technically or in what you can do with them. Today, these systems use Internet standards to exchange messages. Internet standards are a detailed series of rules for how to format e-mail and send it from place to place. However, e-mail exchanges among different e-mail systems do not always work as well as they should and, for example, files attached to e-mail can get scrambled in transmission.

Internet-based e-mail messages are broken into parts. The top part of the message is the **header.** A header has

- The date and time the message was sent.
- The name of the person to whom the message was sent.
- The name of the message sender.
- A subject line describing message contents.
- The path the message took from the sending computer to the receiving computer.

Header information is not much different from what you type on an envelope. However, you might not see the e-mail header when you open e-mail because some e-mail systems remove it like taking a letter out of an envelope and throwing the envelope away. Sometimes this is unfortunate because **path information** can provide you with clues to where an e-mail has been. For example, there are times when a client calls and asks, "Why haven't you responded to my e-mail?" My elegant answer is, "Huh? What?" I had not received the e-mail. When the message finally comes in, path information tells me where it was and, most importantly, for how long. That also tells me whose e-mail system is down. E-mail systems can be quirky and lose a letter like the post office. The author used one system that always collected messages from the Internet, but didn't always send messages out. E-mail would pile up in the electronic out box for hours.

For the most part, e-mail messages come in **ASCII** (American Standard Code for Information Interchange) text, also called plain text. ASCII is text with no formatting and just 128 characters. Other standards are slowly infiltrating, such as **Rich Text File** (RTF), that allows more than 30,000 characters, but it will take time. ASCII text limits what PR practitioners can do. We are used to formatting, even simple formatting, and ASCII requires contortions to format. However, new technologies are transforming e-mail, including applications that open links to web pages and deliver multimedia content—audio, video, and animation. These will provide new opportunities for PR practitioners when they reach general use and circulation.

The way e-mail works, how it passes messages from one point to the next and finally to a mailbox file in your computer, is complex, and you don't need to know about it. However, there are terms that we should mention. **Mailto** links in Web pages automatically start an e-mail program to let you write and send e-mail through the Web page. **Autoresponders,** also called **mailbots, infobots,** and **e-mail-on-demand,** have opened major opportunities for PR practitioners because they send a response automatically when an e-mail arrives. For example, you might get a message that tells you the person you e-mailed is out of the office and whom you should contact in that person's absence. **Listserv** is an e-mail program that automatically sends to individual names on a mailing list. For example, you wish to keep everyone up to date on an issue developing in the news. With listserv, each time you send something to the listserv e-mail box, it sends automatically to everyone else. There are thousands of listservs on the Internet. **Mime** (Multipurpose Internet Mail Extensions) e-mail lets you send attachments over the Internet, including graphics, audio, and faxes. (This can create a problem when an attachment is Mime encoded at one end but not decoded at the other end. You get a garbled message. Then, you have to use a product like **WinZip** to unscramble it (see Compression).

Once in awhile you will hear **SMTP** (Simple Mail Transfer Protocol). This is the standard that sets the rules for sending and receiving e-mail over the Internet. But, like many standards, it did not go far enough, so engineers developed still more standards that define how you get e-mail in your e-mail box. One is called **POP3** (Post Office Protocol 3) and the other **IMAP** (Interactive Mail Access Protocol). Each handles e-mail a little differently, and they are beyond what PR practitioners need to know. (However, if you wish to learn more about e-mail Internet protocols, go to `http://www.faqs.org`. Be prepared. Engineers wrote the standards for other engineers. They are not light reading.)

FILE TRANSFER PROTOCOL

How do you retrieve a file from the Internet and load it into your computer? Many sites store documents and software that individuals can download freely or at a price. This is where **File Transfer Protocol** comes in. You will hear technicians talk about **FTP**. FTP is the detailed Internet standard that defines how to exchange files between computers. You can retrieve documents and software directly from ftp sites that are repositories or from Web pages. Many sites are called **Anonymous FTP** because they allow anyone to retrieve files without identifying themselves. There are tens of thousands of anonymous ftp sites on the Internet, and specialized search engines can help you find them, such as `http://www.ftpsearch.lycos.com`. These sites carry software, games, screensavers, technical advice, and other content. Depending on where you are, you might hear one other term related to file retrieval. It is **WebNFS** (Web Network File Sharing). Sun Microsystems developed this standard for downloading files and proposed it as a general standard for the Internet.

FTP gives you the option to post large documents or programs online for others to get without contacting you personally. For example, the investor relations practitioner can offer lengthy financial analyst reports to investors and the PR practitioner can offer a free promotional game to consumers—all from a company's Web page. Application Service Providers discussed earlier also rely on FTP.

IMAGE MAPPING

Visualize a map of the world. If you click on any country, up pops pages of information about that country. The technology that lets you click on any country to get more information about it is image mapping. Image mapping is used everywhere. Consider, for example, a diagram of a company's divisions. Click on each division in the diagram to learn more about the division. Or, consider a picture of products. Click each product to find out more, or items in a room on which you can click to go to different places.

Image mapping requires an image in GIF format (see Image Technology) and a program that lets you outline sections of the image to make **hot spots.** Hot spots are regular or irregular shapes in which you can place links to other pages of information. Image mapping once required programming skill because you had to tell the computer the exact place where each hot spot is in an image. Now, it is a point-and-click exercise with a mouse.

Image mapping is a visual way to help visitors navigate online, and it adds depth of meaning that no amount of explanatory text can equal. It is particularly useful on pages that direct visitors to online content— often called **switching pages**.

Image mapping is a tool that PR practitioners can and should use frequently to make message presentation more effective.

IMAGE TECHNOLOGY

Image technology includes software and hardware that let one create and send images online. We have discussed pixels, the tiny dots that mix red, green, and blue to form a color then blend with other pixels to create a picture (see **Display Mode**). Image creation uses pixel technology. For example, **scanner** hardware converts photos to pixels. Graphic artists use pixel manipulation software to change pixels in order to add effects or take away defects. This is software such as **Adobe PhotoShop** from Adobe Systems Incorporated and **Corel Photo-Paint** from Corel Corporation.

To draw pixel images, graphic artists use software such as **Adobe Illustrator** and **CorelDraw**. These programs can create imagery as simple as stick figures or as complicated as three-dimensional landscapes. High-powered and custom-built imaging software on supercomputers has produced feature-length, computer-animated cartoons, such as *Toy Story* (1 and 2) and *Bug's Life*.

Image creation and photo manipulation are the province of graphic artists trained in art and the use of the specialized software. PR practitioners should know enough about good and bad art to determine the images that support a message versus those that do not. PR practitioners also should know how images are saved and used online, especially on Web pages, because these terms occur constantly.

There are at least twenty ways to save image files. Most methods compress images into smaller file sizes because the number of pixels needed to produce a photo, for example, is huge—millions of bits per image. Downloading even one uncompressed photo can cause a computer to choke.

There are two image file storage formats used on the Web—**GIF** and **JPEG**. GIF means Graphics Interchange Format. GIF was a proprietary method to compress and send image files developed by Unisys Corporation that has since become a standard. A GIF image is compressed using a relatively simple method, and as a result GIF files tend to be larger in size than JPEG (Joint Photographic Experts Group) files. JPEG images are compressed up to twenty-nine ways, and they throw out pixels in order to shrink an image size even more. A heavily compressed JPEG file looks like fuzzy square blocks, or **jaggies,** if blown up in size. Both GIF and JPEG files create motion by displaying a rapid sequence of still images. These are called **animated GIFs** and **progressive JPEGs** (see Animation).

To help online users with slow connections, GIF images are also **interlaced.** This means that the image is painted piecemeal from a fuzzy outline to a finished photo using seven waves of pixels to fill in blanks. Users with slow connections can get an idea of what an image is and can move on, if they want to, without waiting for the whole image. As connection speeds grow, there will be less need for interlacing.

Image technology underlies everything online because online is intensely visual. The key to imaging technology is to use it well. As a rule of thumb, use images with smaller file sizes whenever possible. Online users have itchy mouse fingers, and they will not wait for slowly appearing images without a compelling reason to do so. Plan the use of images as carefully as text and develop a close working relationship with Web page designers. There is a tendency for copywriters to pitch text over a wall to designers who make it fit. This turns into a tug-of-war between design and content. Online media should always be integrated. Designers and writers should work closely together to produce visual/textual solutions. Unfortunately, many clients do not appreciate this unity, and it is up to PR practitioners to educate them.

One last point about image technology that should be made here concerns the **digital camera**. Digital cameras do not use film. They use a light-sensitive Charge-Coupled Device (CCD), or similar technology, to record pixels directly onto photocells. The camera then stores the pixel image as a picture file. Digital cameras are widely available and affordable, and they have unlimited uses. They provide PR practitioners with a fast way to take and publish photos. The resolution of most digital cameras is not yet up to that of the finest film cameras, but for most purposes, it doesn't need to be. (This is changing rapidly. Digital cameras have reached the resolution of a 35mm camera.)

It is also common to use digital photography to give viewers a feel for ongoing events. General Motors, for example, combined digital photography and Webcams (*see* Streaming Media) to extend the reach of its exhibits at the Detroit Auto Show to online audiences while the show was going on.

INTERNET TECHNOLOGIES

Internet technologies cover an array of terms that make up the worldwide online network called the Internet. These terms all refer to **standards**, or **protocols**, that every member of the Internet must follow for the Internet to work (Given intense competition among high-tech companies, it is amazing that so many have subscribed to Internet standards).

The Internet is an electronic pipeline that hauls **packets** of information from post office to post office for delivery to a specific computer. Packets are electronic envelopes. When you send a file across the Internet, software called **Transmission Control Protocol (TCP)** cuts the file into pieces, stuffs the pieces into packets, and gives them a **sequence** number (Packet 1, Packet 2, Packet 3. . .).

Delivering each packet is the job of a second standard called **Internet Protocol (IP)** and together they form an acronym that you will hear often—**TCP/IP**. Internet Protocol addresses each data envelope before it goes into the Internet pipeline. The addressing system is large, but not large enough. There are a total of 4,294,967,296 addresses available, and addresses are numbers, not the names that you see in Web page addresses. Address numbers look like a telephone number—e.g., 209.157.22.230. Periods between each number tell the computer what to look for. The first address number (209) identifies the network on which the host computer resides. The second number (157) tells which host computer it is. The third and fourth numbers (22.30) identify subnetworks then the actual computer itself. A Zip code on an envelope works the same way.

On the Internet, there are special-purpose computers that hold millions of addresses in giant tables. These computers tell packets where to go. Other machines called **routers** are like postmen who separate letters into bins for delivery. Routers determine which local or distant bin to send a packet to. This is **packet switching.** As packets reach one computer on the Internet, they are switched to the next computer and so on until they arrive at the destination. And, if one computer knows that the next computer is bogged down, it automatically sends packets to another computer that routes them along a different path. Similarly, if your local post office knows that the regional post office is overburdened, it can send your mail to another regional post office for processing.

Packets provide an advantage for sending data. They do not have to go in any order or on the same path from one computer to another. Because each packet has an address and sequence number, it is reassembled at the other end in the right order every time. What this means as well is that smaller computers can route packets rather than giant mainframe computers because packet switching is **connectionless.** In other communications systems, such as the telephone, each time I dial, I must connect through the network to open a circuit with another phone. When computers do this, they require a lot of power to open and sustain the connection. Packets do not need an open connection.

There are other terms that you will encounter when talking about the Internet. A **node** is a point like a post office where data transmissions connect in a network, either to send packets from one computer to another or a final point where packets are delivered. A **point of presence (POP)** is the location of a **network access point** that has a unique address like that discussed earlier. An **Internet Service Provider (ISP)** provides connections to the Internet at a point of presence (POP), as does an **online service provider (OSP).** A **host** is a computer that has two-way access to other computers on the Internet. That is, it can send and receive packets, and it has its own unique address. The contents of Web pages are stored on hosts so that they can be sent on demand. There are more terms than what are listed here, but, for the most part, PR practitioners do not need to know them.

Why is any of this important? You don't need to know how the post office works to send mail. On the other hand, if you were to work closely with the post office, as a direct mail specialist does, you would need to know some terms. In online public relations, PR practitioners work with Internet technicians who use these terms.

INTERNET TRAFFIC STATISTICS

Several technologies measure the amount of traffic on the Internet. Some provide minute-to-minute measurements, some hourly, and some cumulative for months and years. The reason to know about Internet traffic is that sometimes the Internet gets overburdened and it slows down—way down. Internet traffic statistics are the radio station helicopters that whine overhead and tell you what you suspected: You're stuck, and you won't make your meeting on time. When the Internet slows down, it is not always clear why. An **Internet traffic report** (also called **Internet weather report**) tells you what is happening around the Internet.

The speed of Internet traffic is a concern to PR practitioners. It is no different than the speed of the post office in delivering letters. Using a system subject to slowdowns, or worse—breakdowns—creates risk in communications. Because the Internet continues to grow at a furious rate, it is not always possible for the physical network to keep up. In fact, one estimate is that by 2003, it will have cost $1.5 trillion to build new Internet infrastructure. One can expect slowdowns on the Internet as a normal course of business.

INTERNET 2

This is a high-speed implementation of the Internet that connects major U.S. universities. The regular Internet now carries so much traffic that leading-edge experiments carried out in universities must fight for capacity. Rather than fighting, they're switching. The speed of Internet 2 is in the range of 155 million bits per second. For comparison, the highest speed connection to a regular user's computer is 8 million bits per second. Universities will use Internet 2 for the most advanced imaging, multimedia, and supercomputing. PR practitioners working in academic environments should know about Internet 2 and take advantage of it, if possible, to help develop more effective communications techniques.

IP MULTICASTING

Multicasting is broadcasting of audio and video over the Internet to many users at the same time. Essentially, it is online radio and TV broadcasting. Most of the Internet is one person asking for files at a time, but IP multicasting allows distribution to multiple users at a time. To do this required complex engineering. In 1994, an Internet Engineering Task Force set up a network called **MBone**. This network linked together computers that could handle multicasting. The engineers also developed a way to tunnel through computers that could not handle multicasting. The MBone multicasts at 500,000 bits per second, and its actual traffic runs from 100,000 to 300,000 bits per second. It is used mostly for streaming audio (music) and video. That is, audio and video that transmit continuously across the Internet, rather than files that you download first, then play. Using the MBone network requires effort. One cannot go to any Internet Service Provider and sign up because a provider has to support the service. One needs to tell people what service providers to use in order to get MBone multicasts.

KNOWBOT

There are other terms to describe this software—for example, **intelligent agent**, **agent**, and **newsbot**. A **knowbot** gathers information for you or performs some other kind of service automatically on a preset schedule without your presence. Newsbots gather information from news sites then assemble it or provide links to stories for you. URL-Minders alert you when a Web page has changed.

Knowbots are useful for PR practitioners because they help keep a finger on the pulse of an industry, key issues, and marketplaces for which practitioners are responsible. Once you program the keywords for knowbots to search, they work day after day. The only caution about knowbot software is that it isn't flexible. Knowbots bring back exactly what you tell them to gather. If an important story is not phrased in a way that a knowbot can identify it or does not use a preprogrammed keyword, a knowbot will pass it by. In other words, do not trust knowbots completely to find everything you need to know.

LINK CHECKING TECHNOLOGY

A link checker is essential technology for Web page administration. What a link checker does is to click on each link in a Web site and make sure that it works. This includes links to other pages inside the Web site and links to pages in other Web sites somewhere else on the web. Dead links annoy users, and sites with "Error: 404: Not Found" and "Error: Host not found" messages drive users away. The challenge to Webmasters is the number of links that require checking. There can be dozens to thousands. The author's Web page, online-pr.com, has more than 2,500 links.

Links to external sites get out of date just like media mailing lists. A reporter leaves a beat and moves on. So too, Web sites close down or move to another address. The author estimates that 15 to 20 percent of the external links on his Web site break annually. Before link checking technology, checking links was painful and not done often. Since link checking technology, it is easy to keep links up to date. One such program, called **Linkbot** (http://www.watchfire.com/), dials each Web site link from its own computers using twenty or more high-speed connections. This condenses link checking from hours to minutes. Linkbot produces a detailed report of broken links and other errors.

Online PR practitioners should make sure that every Web site they are responsible for has a system for checking links. You cannot communicate when links that you depend on are broken.

MEASUREMENT TECHNOLOGY

Online has several measurement technologies, but almost all of them are for Web sites and not e-mail. Using measurement, PR practitioners can tailor messages to users' interests and preferences. This advantage, however, accrues only to those who own a Web site. When PR practitioners try to gauge readers on sites that are not their own, their measurement challenges are the same as trying to figure out who has read an article in a newspaper or magazine.

E-mail is the least measurable online medium because it can be mass-mailed, forwarded and made anonymous. One can count inbound e-mail to determine who is sending messages, as long as the message sender is identified. One can count the host from which the message came to develop statistics about the region from which e-mail was sent. But, one can never be certain where outbound e-mail ends up because it can be passed on without the original sender ever knowing that this was done. It is no different than a printed brochure that can move from one person to another.

On the other hand, to get a Web page, a computer has to send a request to the host computer where the Web site is stored. The request tells the host computer the address of the computer asking for the Web site and the specific Web page requested. The host computer then knows what to send and where. This is no different than calling someone on the phone and asking that person to mail a press kit to you. However, what the host computer does then is to store each request in a log.

Some Web site owners do not analyze Web logs because it is too expensive or because their Internet Service Provider (ISP) does not have analytical software. Instead they use a Web page counter. That is, each time a computer requests a page, counter software tallies it. You will see, for example, "This page has been visited XXXXXX times since (DATE)." Counters tell you some information like the most and least visited pages on your Web site, but not much more.

Log files, on the other hand, contain the numerical address of the computer requesting a Web page, the date and time the request was received, the page requested, and the browser and operating system used on the computer making the request. Each time a computer requests a page, it sends this information to the computer holding the Web site. In a typical online session, you might click through ten or twenty pages on a Web site and send ten to twenty requests that the host computer stores in a Web log.

Requests piled in a log file produce a trove of information that one can process using **server log analysis** software. This software sorts, catalogues, and summarizes requests. Part of the software even gets the domain names from which the request came. Rather than seeing an address number like 203.62.41.36, you see a URL like `http://www.wxyz.com`.

Here are some of the reports that server log analysis software produces:

- Site traffic by hour, day, week, month, time of day, and time of week.
- Search engines that referred individuals to a site.
- The most-used keywords that identify the site.
- Other Web sites that refer visitors and the names of those sites.
- The most visited and least visited pages on your site.
- The number of clicks on advertising banners.
- Pages where visitors enter most frequently, pages where visitors leave most frequently and pages that visitors access then leave immediately without traveling elsewhere.

PR practitioners can learn a great deal of detail about targeted individuals and audiences from such reports and can adjust messages and media as a result.

However, there is one technical element that can defeat server log analysis software. An organization can use one Internet Protocol (IP) address for many machines rather than one IP address for each machine. Unfortunately, server log analysis can only log the one IP address. Thus, for example, a company with 100 computers has one IP address. Locally, the company applies a subaddress like a department number that distinguishes each of the 100 computers. The PR practitioner can never know which of the 100 computers under the single IP address accessed the Web site. On the other hand, with software such as a **page sniffer**, one can tell whether a person has visited a page, even if a copy of that page is stored on the person's local computer. Page sniffer software is invisible code residing on a Web page that reports back to a central collection site whenever a person clicks on that page.

Another software technology called a **cookie** has added depth to measurement. A cookie is information that a Web site inserts into a file on your computer when you request a page from that site. Originally, cookies had nothing to do with measurement. They were a way for you to tell a Web site your preferences. For example, each time you visit a news site, cookie information stored on your computer tells the news site to make your name pop up and to send you just political and sports stories.

However, technologists soon figured out that cookie information could be used for detailed measurements of users' online information preferences across many Web sites, and here is how they did it. Each time a visitor with a cookie shows up at a Web site, the site logs the cookie information. Technologists collect the cookie logs from many Web sites and analyze them to build millions of user profiles that list the content each person looked at across those many sites. This has become a way to match banner advertising on Web sites to user interests. A firm called DoubleClick (http://www.doubleclick.com/) developed technology that reads the cookie information from your computer, compares it to your user profile, and displays a banner ad matched to your interests. It does this in a few thousandths of a second. Thus, if you read about autos and visit auto Web pages, the banner ad you see comes from an auto manufacturer. On the other hand, if you browse through luxury goods such as watches and jewelry, the banner ad you see comes from a jeweler.

There are other terms used frequently in Web page measurement that you also should be aware of.

- **Click:** When a person clicks on an advertising banner on a Web site.
- **Clickthrough:** Means the same as click, but emphasizes that an individual interacted with the banner ad by clicking on it to read more about a product or service.
- **Click rate:** The number of times someone clicked on a banner ad compared to the total number of visitors to the page. A good click rate is in the range of two people out of a hundred Web page visitors clicking on a banner ad.
- **Clickstream:** The path that visitors take through a Web site. This term doesn't refer to banner advertising at all and is confusing.

Web page measurement is less expensive than other research methods used in public relations, such as focus groups and surveys. However, you cannot get rid of focus groups or surveys because what Web page measurement tells you is only part of what you need to know. You can watch a person travel a Web page second by second, but you cannot know the individual's aspirations, motivations, and other psychological dimensions.

Privacy (see Chapter 3) is an issue in measurement. Some individuals fear that tying online measurement to personal behavior is spying. In fact, when DoubleClick began to gather information on individuals' names, addresses, and other personal information, the firm touched off an explosion of protest. One activist organization, The Center for Democracy and Technology (http://www.cdt.org) launched a "Websit" that called for individuals to opt out of information gathering that links cookie information to personal data.

As measurement technologies improve, online research companies will know more about individuals using online media. The concern for public relations is how to use such information without abusing it. The potential for abuse is high, particularly when practitioners driven to reach an objective decide that the end justifies the means.

MEDIUM

A medium is a means to deliver content. In online PR, the medium is the electronic envelope, or packet (see Internet Technologies) that carries content through the Internet's network. Anything that you can cut up and stuff into packets can go on the Internet. Online carries text, images, music, voice, video, animation, radio, television, software programs, and more. Hence, online PR practitioners should be ready to work in all these multimedia forms.

In addition, the packet has reduced the number of technologies that media require—for example, a printing press, a photo processing lab, a CD-ROM disc stamping machine, and so forth. Packets supplant these production vehicles and reach farther. It is easy on the Internet to read brochures from India and to listen to live radio from Germany at the same time at your desk. This is why publishers who rely on traditional technologies are concerned about the Internet. Because packets can carry everything and can go just about anywhere, the question of content ownership has become a battleground. Copyrighted music, books, images, movies, and more have been pirated and distributed online without paying for them. The Internet has made protection of intellectual property much more difficult. This is why PR practitioners should be in the lead in respecting property rights to protect the reputations of their organizations from charges of theft.

MIRROR SITE

Because the Internet or a popular Web site can bog with traffic, organizations establish more than one Web site with the same information. They place these **mirror sites** in different geographic locales and send user requests to them in order to speed response. For example, a West Coast technology company will establish mirror sites on the East Coast of the United States, in Europe, and in Japan so that visitors do not have to plow through the major highways of the Internet to get information. Updating mirror sites is a concern. For active sites with lots of changes, it is necessary to synchronize each mirror site frequently.

Companies use mirror sites as well to distribute software. For example, you will see on Microsoft's Web sites a choice of locations from which to retrieve its programs and instructions telling you to pick the location nearest to your computer. Without such mirroring, distributing large software would be impractical because the Internet could not handle the floods of data.

Web technologists will get mirroring done, but PR practitioners should know when it is needed.

MUD, MOO, MUSH, MUCK, MUSE

These terms refer to worlds existing only online. A **MUD** (also called a **MUCK**) is a multiuser dungeon or castle, or other locale where one can wander from room to room. In these rooms, one can combat creatures, learn about a topic, or visit with others. A **MOO** is a multiuser dungeon in which you design your own objects, such as an **avatar,** the visual sign that represents you. **Avatars** can be smiley face cartoons, birds, unicorns, any number of things. (The word "avatar" was taken from Hindu religion.) A **MUSH** (Multi-User Shared Hallucination) provides tools to build MUDs and MUCKs. MUSE (Multi-User Entertainment Ltd) refers to a company that specializes in building multiplayer, online computer games.

Why should a PR practitioner care about such technology? Because MUDs are a way to appeal to individuals who like to explore or learn through adventures. MUDs are primarily, but not solely, youth-oriented, and if one is attempting to reach teenagers with targeted messages, a MUD might be a creative way to reach them.

NETWORK

A network refers to any connection of two or more computers for the purpose of transferring information. You will encounter two kinds of networks frequently—local area networks (**LANs**) and wide area networks (**WANs**). A local area network is a group of computers, printers, and other devices linked together, typically in an office or building. A WAN is a network that connects a larger geographical area, such as several office buildings or a region with multiple plant locations. LANs and WANs are not part of the Internet, but they can connect to the Internet. E-mail software on a LAN sends messages to the Internet when e-mail leaves the local office environment. The LAN can also pass e-mail to a WAN, if it is going to another office building or plant location, without going on the Internet.

This is a complication for PR practitioners who think of online solely as the Internet and commercial networks such as America OnLine (AOL). But, in fact, online PR was originally practiced only on LANs and WANs, when companies first used online communication to reach employees. LANs and WANs remain network building blocks, and opportunities to use them creatively in public relations are many. For example, one might create a newsletter restricted to a LAN or WAN, or use Internet technology to build an internal Web site, called an **Intranet**, that resides only on a LAN or WAN.

Networks intertwine with one another like spaghetti in a bowl, but like pasta strands, they are not joined unless one ties each strand to the other. Before using online media in an organization, a PR practitioner needs to know how its networks are connected and what their capabilities are. For example, a network might carry e-mail but not have the capability to carry an internal Web page.

One term that you will hear when discussing LANs is **Ethernet.** Ethernet describes technologies used to hook computers, printers, scanners, and other devices together. This covers everything from wiring to wall plugs to transmission speeds and circuit boards used to connect to the Ethernet. Ethernet technology is a study unto itself, and typically a LAN administrator will qualify in building and administering Ethernets. This can mean that the LAN administrator is not familiar with Internet technologies, and the PR practitioner cannot rely on the LAN administrator to solve technical problems related to the Internet. This is one more challenge that online PR practitioners deal with.

There is a new kind of networking that PR practitioners should know about. It is called peer-to-peer (P2P). Peer to peer networking communicates directly from one desktop computer to another desktop computer. Sitting at my PC, I connect directly to you at your PC. Usually, I would communicate to a computer called a server that would then communicate to you. P2P removes the server in the middle.

There are several forms of P2P communications and some you may have used to share files with another person. Napster, the music file sharing service, Gnutella (http://www.gnutella.wego.com) and FreeNet (http://www.freenet.sourceforge.net) are three examples of P2P approaches to file-sharing networking although Napster used a central server that helped searchers find music files they wanted to swap. A collaboration software using P2P is Groove (http://

www.groove.net). It permits one to set up workgroups on the Internet where you and users you invite meet in virtual *shared spaces* with available tools, such as:

- instant messaging
- live voice
- file sharing
- pictures
- threaded discussion
- free-form drawing
- outlining
- video

Other applications have or are arriving as well, including search engines and distributed computer processing. The SETI@ home project actually ties together tens of thousands of computers to process radio transmissions from outer space in a search for extraterrestrial life. P2P is being used for social purposes in that thousands of distributed computers are being chained together to help find new drugs for AIDS and vaccines for diseases. PR practitioners can use P2P creatively to serve information to others and to chain together computers for philanthropic purposes, such as providing a company's spare processing power to deserving organizations.

PINGING

Pinging is a way to find out if an Internet address is working. A **ping** (packet Internet groper) sends a request packet to a site then waits for a response from it. This is useful when, for some reason, another site does not respond when you ask for it. There are several ways to ping another site. One way is to use the computer operating software on a PC, called MS-DOS. When your computer is online, go to the computer's MS-DOS screen and type in "ping xxx.yyy."—for example, "ping online-pr.com." Ping software immediately sends four request packs to http://www.online-pr.com and listens for four responses from the site. It tells you whether it got all packets back, the time it took to get them back, and the approximate length of a round trip from the remote site to your computer.

Pinging salves anxieties when sites appear to lock up, slow down, or otherwise misbehave. Some ping software also reports the number of connections, or **hops**, it took to reach a Web site and the time that your request packets waited at each connection. Hops along the Internet provide clues to where things are slow. For example, the Web site might be working well, but a computer between the Web site and your computer might be bogged with traffic. A hop report will show the wait time at that computer, and you then know that the problem is a busy Internet and not a broken Web site. Rather than yell at a Webmaster in frustration, you can seethe about the state of the Internet. Ordinarily, PR practitioners will not use pinging in their daily work, but it is good to know that it is there when nothing seems to work.

PROGRAMMING LANGUAGES

Programs tell a computer to do something. It takes hundreds of programs for online media to work. We define here just a few terms that you will hear in online PR work. The first is **HTML**.

Hypertext Markup Language (HTML) tells a browser how to display a page on a computer screen. It is the same as basic markup, or formatting, instructions in a word processor. Without formatting instructions, text would be one font, and it would be shoved over to the left-hand side of the screen—just like most e-mail. HTML is less flexible and powerful than the hidden formatting instructions in common word processors, such as Microsoft Word (see Browser, for an example).

In fact, HTML is an easy-to-use version of a powerful formatting language called **SGML** (Standard Graphic Markup Language). SGML is a worldwide standard that tells one how to define instructions for formatting text. Technologists developed SGML because early word processors all formatted text differently, and text could not move from one word processor to another, or even display on different computer terminals. For those who remember early days of personal computing, working with clients who used a different word processor was frustrating. Companies often kept two or three word processors in their inventories to deal with the lack of compatibility.

SGML tells how to define formatting (also called markup) instructions. It does not say what markup instructions should be, but rather, how they should be written so that any computer can understand them. This is called document type definition (**DTD**). A DTD stays at the top of a document so that any computer can figure out how to display the document properly.

SGML is complex and not used online. HTML is easier to write and is the key online programming/formatting language for the Web. The World Wide Web Consortium (http://www.w3.org) maintains HTML standards. To give you an idea of how detailed these standards are, specifications for HTML 4.01 filled more than 350 pages.

The Internet is moving toward SGML with a standard called **XML** (Extensible Markup Language). The World Wide Web Consortium maintains standards for it too. There is much excitement about XML because it allows industries to build libraries of formatting tags to describe products and services. For example, one can define a specific formatting tag for kitchen sink faucets. Then, people looking for kitchen sink faucets no longer have to search Web sites. They send out a search program to look just for the kitchen sink faucet formatting tag. The search engine brings back hundreds of types and brands of kitchen sink faucets from dozens of Web sites. This, of course, requires manufacturers to define and accept standard formatting tags, which is happening. XML is already used in banking, for automatic exchange of information, and for development of a Web code that works on mobile phones. As use of XML grows, the Web will become easier.

If you are not confused already by alphabet soup, let me add a few more terms. The first is **XHMTL.** XHMTL is a newer version of HTML that acts like XML. The industry did this because millions of Web developers like HTML and do not want to move to XML, at least not yet, and maybe never. XHMTL is a part of XML, but it looks like HTML. Call it a transition language. You will hear more and more references to "X," and eventually most Web-page coding will be in either XHTML or XML.

DHTML means Dynamic HTML. This version of HTML allows for **cascading style sheets** that keep a look and feel on every page of a Web site and **content layering**, to vary content by page. DHTML allows more animation and interaction between a Web page and user, and it provides **dynamic fonts** to get rid of an irritation that annoys Web builders and visitors. This irritation occurs when a Web page uses a text font that a visitor does not have. The visitor's Web browser then displays text in the browser's default font and that can wreck the look of a page. Dynamic fonts download the proper font with the page, so the page always displays correctly.

SHTML (Server-side Include Hypertext Markup Language) is yet one more HTML-related term. It means that the computer holding the Web page attaches something to the page each time it sends that page out. One of the most common attachments is a phrase stating the date when the page was last modified. This lets users know how up-to-date the page is.

Most PR practitioners do not work directly with HTML. They just need to know it is there and some of its features and functions. Increasingly, they—and even Web developers—use authoring software that generates HTML code while one works in a screen that looks and acts like a word processor. Popular HTML authoring tools include Allaire Corp.'s **Cold Fusion** (http://www.allaire.com/), Microsoft's **Front Page** (http://www.microsoft.com/), SoftQuad Software Inc.'s **HoTMetaL Pro** (http://www.softquad.com/). These tools are not programming languages, but they make HTML code generation and Web page building easier. They have taken the task of writing HTML away from technicians and placed it directly into the hands of content publishers. For that reason alone, PR practitioners should be familiar with code authoring tools.

A term that does not refer to a programming language but is used in the same sentence is **CGI** (Common Gateway Interface). It is the doorway that everyone enters to reach Web application programs. A computer passes a user's request through the CGI to a Web page application, such as an online mortgage calculator, and then sends data back through the CGI to pass on to the user. With CGI, one can write a program for computers with different operating systems, such as the Macintosh and the PC, and users of these computers can use the programs without worrying about whether they will work.

Java is a programming language built for use on the Internet. Java builds portable applications that can run on one computer or several at a time. Java is also used to build **applets,** the small programs that do something when added to a browser. For example, when your cursor crosses a word on a Web page and the word changes color, that is a Java applet in action. Sun Microsystems (http://www.sun.com/) introduced Java in 1995. (Microsoft Corporation competes with Sun by offering its own proprietary programming language called **ActiveX.**)

Whew! There we are—a penny tour of programming languages and authoring tools. PR practitioners will hear Web technicians use these terms constantly. Know the basic differences among key terms so that you won't get lost in conversation.

SEARCH ENGINE TECHNOLOGIES

No one knows the size of the World Wide Web. We know that it is more than a billion pages, but it gets larger every second. Content on the World Wide Web is flung everywhere on company computers, in news organizations, on university servers, on small home PCs, and more. The Internet knows the addresses of these locations, but not what resides at each address. Put another way, the post office knows the address of every householder in Tokyo, but not the books on the shelf of each Tokyo home. Web content is the book on the shelf. Search engines now look as well for audio, video, images—GIFs and JPEGs (see Image Technology)—and streaming media, such as online radio stations.

The most common search engine names are **AltaVista, AOL NetFind, Excite, Google, HotBot, Infoseek,** and **Lycos.** Yahoo! is not a search engine because it uses people to inspect and catalogue sites, whereas search engines use software to do their work. Yahoo! is called a **direc-tory**. Few search engines examine the entire Web. For the most part, they carry less than 30 percent of the Web. This means that two search engines can produce different results in response to the same search term. This is the reason that technicians developed a second type of search engine, a metasearch engine. A metasearch engine takes the keyword that you are searching and submits it to several search engines at once. It then combines results. The idea is that by searching several search engines at the same time, you get better results than by using just one. Popular metasearch engines include **Dogpile** (http://www.dogpile.com/), **Savvysearch** (http://www.search.com/), **Mamma** (http://www.mamma.com/), and **Metacrawler** (http://www.metacrawler.com/).

Search engine software, called a spider, visits sites, reads their pages, and creates entries in a search engine's index. Each search engine uses a different kind of spider, which creates further confusion. Some spiders stop at the first page, the home page. Some spiders crawl each page of a site and index everything. Because the Web is so large, spiders search many pages at once. Alta Vista's spider, for example, indexes three million pages a day, but even that is not enough to capture the entire Web.

The second part of a search engine, the index, is a giant directory, like a telephone book, that holds listings that a spider has found. And, just like a telephone book, some listings are always out of date because Web sites change constantly. This means that the spider must return, usually every thirty days, to look at a site again. This is important because when you use a search engine, you search its index and not the Web itself.

The third component of a search engine is software that sorts listings to find sites matching keywords you are searching for. Here too, every search engine is different. And, in fact, new solutions appear regularly to overcome the annoying habit of search engines returning 6,000 hits for a search term, which is virtually useless.

Every search engine indexes Web sites based on rules built into the engine. Most use the location and frequency of keywords on a Web page. Some look for hidden descriptions on the top of a Web page called Meta Tags, which come in two parts. One part is a description of a site in the form of a short sentence. The second part is a listing of keywords that describe the site. Still other search engines look at the number of links to a site to gauge its popularity. For example, if 500 Web sites link directly to your site, you would get a higher rating than a similar site with 50 Web sites linking to it. Meanwhile, other search engines rank sites by the ones that users click on when the search engine returns its results. Sites that are clicked on more often are ranked higher than sites that are not. Still other search engines enlist the aid of those using the engine to rank sites.

Search engine technology changes constantly. For example, some search engines like **Google** (http://www.google.com/) do a contextual search by looking at text around key terms. For example, the term "pool" can refer to a game, a swimming pool, a pond, and a financial technique. Searching for "pool" will return more than 4.3 million references on Google; searching "pool rules" returns 457,000 references on Google; searching for "pool game rules" returns 106,000 references, of which the third was a link to a site with rules for pool games such as snooker and billiards. Most search engines do not search by context and cannot narrow searches this quickly.

To learn about search engines in detail and to follow their progress in capturing Web content, try http://www.searchenginewatch.com. This site is devoted to examining search engines and their technologies.

What PR practitioners should understand about search engines is that they are fallible. Just because one search engine does not give you the results you are looking for, do not give up. Use another search engine, or better still, use a metasearch engine. The next chapter discusses search techniques that you can use on the Web.

SECURITY TECHNOLOGIES

Anyone who reads a newspaper or watches television news knows that the Web is not secure. **Hackers** delight in finding and exploiting holes in the Internet, mostly for fun but sometimes for profit. The term *hacker* is an unfortunate misnomer; "hacker" originally meant a programmer who found clever solutions to programming challenges. The term *cracker* described people who entered systems without authorization. This distinction has been largely lost in the general media.

Security breaches are of several kinds. There are: theft of services, theft of information, impairment of sites, and vandalism. A typical service theft is using the telephone without paying for it. A typical content theft is stealing credit card numbers or personal passwords. Site impairment includes assaulting a site with thousands of requests simultaneously so legitimate requests cannot get through. This is sometimes called a **ping storm** or **ping flood**. More recent versions of this have been called **denial of service** or **distributed denial of service** attacks. Vandalism includes changing the text on a Web page and leaving messages behind that are frequently off-color or activist related.

Security technologies are cat-and-mouse games with hackers. For each new technique a hacker comes up with, defenders build a block.

The game is never-ending, but some computers and systems are so poorly protected that well-known cracking techniques are enough to get into them.

There are many terms to describe programs that attack computers. You will see new ones regularly, but frequent terms include **virus**, **worm**, and **Trojan Horse**. There are variations on every technique. The place to find out about hacker activities is http://www.cert.org. This is the Computer Emergency Response Team that works twenty-four hours a day, seven days a week to monitor hacker attacks on the Internet.

The point to remember as a PR practitioner is that you need to take reasonable precautions online, just as you do when you walk across a street or drive a car. Part of the job of working online is learning basic safety. There are safety measures that you will hear frequently and you should recognize. One is a **firewall**. A firewall is a set of software programs that stop packets—that is, data—from entering a computer until the software determines that the packets are legitimate. Often firewall software is installed on a different computer, separated from other computers, to prevent incoming packets from reaching a network directly.

Public key infrastructure (PKI) is another term you will hear. This refers to a range of methods to secure data from prying eyes, including **digital certificates** that identify individuals and organizations by name, serial number, expiration dates, and a digital signature. Then, there is data encryption. Encrypted data is increasingly difficult to crack, but not impossible. To decipher encrypted data, you need a key or massive computer power. PKI uses two keys—one public and one private. Anyone can use a public key to encrypt a message, but the public key cannot decrypt the message. That is done only by the private key, which is never sent online and remains securely on one computer. One can send messages online without worrying about someone stealing and decoding them, unless that person has extraordinary computer power— and even then it can take weeks or months to break through the encryption. What this means is that messages are secure for practical purposes. Even governments cannot call regularly on the computer power necessary to decrypt every coded message.

Public relations professionals working on confidential matters, such as a merger or acquisition, sensitive personnel matters, or extremely proprietary company information, should understand how to encrypt and decrypt data online. Sending e-mail without encryption is an invitation to thieves, and even sending it encrypted does not guarantee that skilled thieves cannot get it—it just makes the task harder.

A final term that you will hear is **secure sockets layer (SSL)**. This is a method that manages secure transmission of messages online. An SSL is a program that fits between an application, such as a browser, and the software that sends data over the Internet. The program uses a method to pass data back and forth between the application and the Internet software that is called a **socket**. SSL is often used in e-commerce and in news services that distribute confidential information, such as PR Newswire or BusinessWire. If you have confidential releases that you are sending out to a newswire service, use an SSL method. The way to tell if a connection is secure is that you will get a warning message that you are entering a secure area. You will also get a warning message when you leave the secure area.

SHAREWARE, FREEWARE

Shareware is software that a developer gives away free to users on a trial basis, usually thirty days. If users like a program, they pay for it, and if they do not, the program deactivates itself after the time limit expires. **Freeware** is software that a developer gives to you for no charge, but the developer keeps the copyright, so other developers cannot use it in programming. **Public domain** software is available to anyone to use in any way. The most frequently mentioned public domain software is a computer operating system called **Linux**. **Vaporware** is software that does not exist or does not do what a manufacturer says it will do.

Do you really need to know all this? Probably not. But, if you are looking for a program to help you do a special task, try shareware and freeware sources first so that you do not have to spend a bundle of money buying a brand-name product that you might use just once. One of the best-known shareware sites is http://www.tucows.com.

SOUND CARD

Manufacturers today sell computers with **sound cards** pre-installed. That was not always the case. For most of the early history of the personal computer, there was no sound. Then, technologists figured out the way to place all the electronics for **digital signal processing** onto a card that plugged into a slot inside a computer. Sound cards turn bits (1s and 0s) into sound waves, or take sound waves from a microphone and turn them into bits. You cannot listen to CD-ROMs, DVDs, or online radio and telephone conversations on your PC without a sound card. Sound cards are improving rapidly, and music that once seemed tinny is now full-bodied and much like what you hear on a dedicated stereo radio receiver. The one point to remember about sound cards is that millions of computers still do not have them because the computers were built when sound cards were an extra expense. If you are planning a public relations event where you will send audio online, survey users first to make sure that they have sound cards. Otherwise, it is talking to the deaf.

Another point to remember is that two-way conversation online requires more than a sound card. You need a microphone and software to send sound data to the appropriate address. Few machines today are set up for two-way sound online, but it is growing.

STREAMING MEDIUM

A **streaming medium** enables online music, radio, and television. Before streaming media, you could download a sound file (often called a **WAV** file) into your computer and play it, but you could not listen to a live radio station, for example, because a radio station sends sound in a continuous flow. With streaming media, you can tune in thousands of radio stations worldwide over the Web and listen while you work. This, of course, extends messages that public relations sends by radio and television far beyond a traditional broadcast area.

Streaming media let you send and receive data from one computer to another in a continuous flow like water from a faucet. On the Internet, however, data does not flow in steady streams like a faucet. Data floods in bursts or trickles intermittently. Moreover, when pumping huge audio and video files through tiny electronic straws (see Broadband) that connect most computers to the Web, data backs up like water in a clogged sink.

Streaming media get around erratic data flows by placing an electronic storage "tank" at the computer getting the data. Data fill the storage tank to the point where a streaming application can work, then the tank releases data to the application like a faucet. You will notice, for example, that when you play a radio station or song online, the application does not start right away. That is because the tank is filling. Once the application starts playing, data continue to fill the tank erratically from the Internet, but as far as the application knows, it is getting a steady flow of sound or video packets from the storage tank.

The growth of streaming audio online has been extraordinary. Most of it relies on compressed audio (see Compression) because audio files are too big to deliver to most PCs, even with streaming media. Compressed audio is often called **MP3.** It is part of an audio/video compression technology called **MPEG** (Motion Picture Experts Group). MP3 refers to compression technology optimized for audio files. MP3 is the ultimate trash compactor. It crunches data bits. A typical compact disc (CD) sends data for processing into music at 1.4 million bits per second. With MP3, the same music can be processed at only 112,000 bits per second.

Streaming media require software players that allow one to raise and lower the sound, dial new TV or radio stations, choose a song, and do everything that you would do with a radio or TV, including presetting stations. One popular software player is **RealAudio**, a free player from RealNetworks (http://www.realaudio.com/). RealAudio plays FM-stereo quality sound and plugs into your Web browser. A competing player is called **Liquid Audio** (http://www.liquidaudio.com/). You download both of these players directly from the Internet.

To get an idea of the radio programs that you can listen to, go to http://www.radio.broadcast.com/. There are 400+ radio stations listed there in numerous formats, some of which exist only on the Web as **Web radio**. The cost of building a Web radio station is so small that it is a technique to consider for employee communications. One could build an in-house radio station that sends company news and programming to every company location, no matter where it is in the world.

We have spent most of our time discussing sound. It is time now to turn to streaming audio/video (AV). AV has had the same historical path as audio, but it has been slower in evolution. The reason for this is the size of AV files that must stream online. In the early days of personal computing, there was no way to view AV. Videoconferencing required special installations with dedicated machines, high-speed phone lines, and heavy compression to send anything at all that could be seen and heard at the other end. Even then, the picture looked distorted, lips flapped out of sequence with sound, and it was not always clear what you were looking at. Technologists invented ways to send AV files and play them locally using software players, such as **QuickTime**, a product from Apple Computer (http://www.apple.com/). A QuickTime file combines sound, text, animation, and video, but it plays only short sequences and is not useful for live television.

Among the earliest videoconferencing software on the Internet was **CU-SeeMe**, a product developed at Cornell University in 1992. It is actually closer to chat technology (see Chat). **Webcams** next entered online video. These are also called **cams**, **home cams**, or **live cams**. A Webcam feeds a video picture to the Internet that you can view on a PC. Webcam pictures, for the most part, are not streaming media or full-motion video. They are a sequence of video stills that change every few seconds or minutes. There are thousands of Webcam sites online. Go to http://www.discovery.com, which keeps a roster of Webcam sites, or Earthcam (http://www.earthcam.com/), a directory of Webcam sites. One publicity technique using Webcams is to place cameras where one can view another person. This has become a business—for example, serving parents who want to keep an eye on their children in day care centers. Such uses, however, have raised issues of privacy.

Streaming media today allow full-motion video. RealPlayer technology available from RealNetworks is set up for streaming, full-motion video, and sound. That said, video is still smeary, difficult to view, and small on the screen. While streaming audio is well developed, it is questionable from a PR perspective whether streaming video is as useful. One should consider carefully whether to provide online live audio or live audio/video from a press conference, for example. Streaming audio/video is not a tool to use indiscriminately.

TELEPHONE

Internet telephony is fast growing and provides advantages that public relations professionals should know about. Internet telephony is referred to as **VoIP** (Voice over Internet Protocol). It takes a sound wave from someone speaking, digitizes it, chops up the data bits, stuffs the bits into packets, and sends the packets over the Internet where bits are reassembled and then converted back to a sound wave (see Internet Technologies).

Early VoIP was a toy that was barely useful for business. It required a microphone, speaker, and sound card on each PC and software to make a phone call. Calls were poor in quality and often exhibited latency that was once characteristic of international phone calls. Latency is when you say something and there is a delay before the other person hears it. Latency frequently results in one party talking over another because humans are not programmed to wait several beats before speaking.

The second objection to VoIP was that it lacked the features that one expects in an office phone. These include the ability to forward calls, to use an intercom, to see the number and name of the person calling, to arrange conference calls, and more.

The only reason cited to use VoIP for business was cost savings, but here too, traditional cost savings from bypassing phone company tolls is going away as phone rates drop. In spite of these objections, VoIP has come into its own. Today, calling over the Internet can sound no different from calling on a regular telephone, and the Internet phone has all the features of a traditional office phone.

Several technical events led to practical VoIP.

- Telecommunications companies built high-speed nationwide Internet-based data networks that carry voice and data traffic quickly from point to point without lots of stops in between. This resolved sound quality and latency problems.

- Telephone equipment companies married the traditional office telephone system, called a private branch exchange (PBX), to VoIP and provided all the features on an Internet phone that one gets on a regular office phone.
- Organizations that use Internet-based phone systems realized the savings they can accrue from having one network rather than a computer network and a telephone network.

What PR practitioners will find with well-developed VoIP systems is that some irritants of modern office work are swept away. For example:

- An Internet telephone keeps its phone number no matter where it is on a network. A person moving from one office to another simply takes the phone and plugs it in. The phone system automatically routes calls to the new location. This is true whether one works in the same office building or moves to another office in another city. PR practitioners can look to the day when they get permanent phone numbers for the entire time they work for a company. The savings in revising phone directories and lists is large.
- An Internet telephone goes anywhere and remains on the local phone network. For example, a PR practitioner can work at home with an Internet phone plugged in and get calls made to the office extension. On the Internet, no one needs to know where you are.
- An Internet phone system creates a virtual office where fellow workers seem to sit next to each other. For example, one can talk to a colleague by intercom three states away. PR teams working in multiple offices can talk to each other as if on the same floor.
- Calls on Internet phone systems are local calls. There is no long distance number and there is one exchange number. One dials the extension number of another party. That person could be next door or across the continent.
- Incoming calls to automatic call distribution systems are routed to the next available person, no matter where that person is—at the office, at home, in a different office.
- Internet phone systems have voice mail, caller ID, call forwarding, and all other features that a typical office telephone has.

PR managers will find that Internet telephone systems will make it easier to coordinate more people and activities across offices. The downside of Internet telephony is the danger of one system. If an Internet phone system goes down, not only will phones be out but e-mail and other network traffic expire as well. One-system solutions require greater protection and caution. However, even with the extra expense of security, Internet phones should be less expensive to run than two systems.

TELNET

Telnet is not a term that you see much any more. However, the PR practitioner should be aware of it, in case there is an instance where it needs to be used. Telnet refers to software that lets you enter another person's computer across the Internet and to use that person's computer like your own. It is also called **terminal emulation**. Telnet is often used in multiuser dungeon (**MUD**) games discussed earlier. The PR practitioner is likely to encounter it when data residing in one computer must be made available to others without shipping it over the Internet—for example, a database with sensitive information. One can dial in, use the information, then depart. A Telnet session requires the person whose computer is accessed to give permission. This is usually a user ID and a password.

TILDE

Sometimes a Web address has the following strange character: ~. This is a tilde, and it has a special meaning. It signifies an individual user's Web site when that user stores the site on an Internet server provider's (ISP) computer. For example, the name of your ISP's Web site is smith, as in www.smith.com. The name of your Web site is myname. To get to your Web site, the address would be http://www. smith.com/~myname. This is actually a shortened version of the real address, which is http://www.smith.com/www/users/ myname. The tilde makes the job of remembering and entering an Internet address easier. There is no real need to know this, but it does answer why that strange character keeps showing up. If you want to win bets over drinks, the tilde has other names as well, including twiddle and squiggle.

WAP

This ridiculous sounding term has a serious meaning—Wireless Application Protocol. Public relations practitioners already use WAP. It refers to the standard way, or protocol, for letting wireless devices—cellular phones, radio transceivers, beepers, personal digital assistants, and the like—access the Internet. WAP is making the Internet and Web mobile and ubiquitous. Potential applications for such mobility are many, but practical use is a question. For one, screen size on most mobile devices is tiny. What one sees on a telephone screen cannot be what one sees on a computer terminal.

E-mail is an obvious use for wireless mobility. With WAP, one no longer needs to set up a laptop, plug into a wall, and download. Wireless laptops already receive data, but WAP makes the job easier. WAP is an obvious candidate for coordination over large spaces, such as outdoor concerts or fairs. One can e-mail precise instructions to many individuals at once that might be misunderstood when transmitted by voice. Public address system announcements can be sent just as easily by WAP. Documents and other downloadable files can be sent to the road warrior through the phone to a printer or a personal computer for storage.

You might hear other terms when WAP is discussed, and there is not much need to remember them, but here they are anyway:

- WAE: Wireless Application Environment
- WSL: Wireless Session Layer
- WTLS: Wireless Transport Layer Security
- WTP: Wireless Transport Layer

All wireless phone companies make WAP-enabled devices, and if you are looking for one, it will be prominently labeled on the box.

Another technology similar to WAP is Bluetooth (http://www. bluetooth.com/) a radio frequency connectivity technology that provides easy, quick, and reliable short-range connections between devices. Bluetooth gets rid of annoying cables in computing, an advance that will benefit any PR practitioner with a laptop. Bluetooth technology applies as well to phones, video cameras, home networking, and more.

WEB CONTENT MANAGEMENT

Web content management technologies respond to a growing challenge on the World Wide Web. Sites are huge. It is relatively easy to update content on a site with 50 or even 100 pages, but when sites reach 10,000 or 100,000 pages, they are beyond human scale. Thus, a class of technology is emerging to handle publishing, updating, and archiving of Web-site content. This is the equivalent of running an electronic library that also supervises the authors of the books deposited in the library. Web content management, for example, defines standards for writing and formatting content that goes on a Web site. Increasingly, PR professionals will run into Web content management and software tools for it. Major web content management tools include Vignette (www.vignette.com) Rhythmyx (www.percussion.com) and openshare (www.openshare.com).

WEB TECHNOLOGIES

We discuss **Web technologies** here to emphasize that they are one part of the Internet. The Internet was fully functional before the Web. PR practitioners who use Internet and Web in the same breath with the same meaning dismiss technologies that provide interactive communications for millions.

Web standards were first published in 1991. The first packet-switching network that was to become the Internet started working in 1969. Understanding Web technologies as a piece of the Internet is important to learning how to use the Internet to advantage.

What are Web technologies? It might not surprise you that even the ruling body, the World Wide Web Consortium (**W3C**), that administers all things Web has struggled with that question. The Web has grown and evolved furiously. In a document published by W3C in May 1999, the consortium defined Web concepts for the first time. (See http://www.w3.org/1999/05/WCA-Terms/.) We cite a few definitions here, but see the twelve-page document for a detailed list. W3C's basic Web technologies (called Primitive Elements) are

- **Uniform Resource Identifier (URI),** also known as URL: This is an address of a resource.
- **Resource:** This is anything that has an identity on the Web. It can be a Web page, an image, a service, a collection of resources.
- **Resource manifestation:** This is a version of a resource provided at a specific point in time and space. On the Web you have real-time information that shows up only when you enter a page, such as real-time stock quotes. The Web page changes based on live information provided, but underneath its basic design stays the same.
- **Link:** This is a relationship between two or more resources, such as Web pages.
- **Anchor:** This is the destination of a link. It can be a Web page, a spot inside a Web page or a manifestation within the Web page.
- **Client:** This is the Web browser, e-mail reader, or any other application that retrieves and/or renders resources, such as Web pages.
- **Server:** This is the computer or any other application that sends out resources upon request.
- **Proxy:** This is a computer or application that rests between a client and server and acts as both client and server. The client using the

proxy knows that it is present. A common proxy is a firewall used for security to prevent hackers from getting direct access to a network (see Security Technologies).

- **Gateway:** This is a computer acting as a server on behalf of another server to supply resources upon request. The client knows that the gateway is there but does not know that it is acting on behalf of another server. A typical example is a File Transfer Protocol (FTP) gateway that downloads files into another computer.
- **Message:** A communication between two network services on different hosts, such as e-mail.
- **Request:** A message that requests an action to be carried out within a specified resource, such as "send the Web page I asked for."
- **Response:** This is the message that answers the request, such as, "Here is the Web page you asked for."
- **User:** Anyone who uses a client, such as a browser or e-mail reader.
- **Publisher:** Anyone who publishes a resource, such as a Web page or Web site.

These are basic elements of Web technologies. Variations on basics become more elaborate by the day as technologists create applications.

Web terms that you will encounter most often are **domain name** and **URL** (Universal Resource Locator). These are synonymous. A domain name/URL is a word version of the numerical address that underlies all URLs. The Web uses numbers and not words to identify and find another computer (see Internet Technologies). Addressing computers match the word-based URL to the numerical address. The computer reads the following address—http://www.online-pr.com—as follows:

- http: This packet is going to an address that follows Hypertext Transfer Protocol (HTTP), a set of rules for sending and receiving data, text, sound, image, video, and other multimedia files.
- www: This packet's address is on the World Wide Web portion of the Internet. This is the third-level domain name.
- Online-pr is the specific domain name address of the computer where the pages for Online-pr.com reside. It is called a second-level domain name.
- .com is a top-level domain name that identifies the kind of organization that has this address. Here are the top-level domain names:

| Com | A commercial organization. |
| EDU | A four-year, degree-granting college or university. |

Org	A miscellaneous category; typically a not-for-profit organization
Mil	A U.S. military service.
Net	An organization that provides network connection devices.
Gov	A governmental organization.
Country Code	A top-level domain name followed by a two-letter code signifying a country. E.g., .uk = United Kingdom; .fr= France; .ie = Ireland; .ca = Canada. For a list of domain suffixes, see http://www.currents.net/resources/ dictionary/noframes/nf.domains.html

The organization that administers domain names for .com, .net, and .org is The Internet Corporation for Assigned Names and Numbers (ICANN). It is at http://www.icann.org, and it keeps a list of accredited registrars for domain names. The Internet Council of Registrars (CORE) maintains a shared registry system for the management of Internet Domain names for every country in the world. It is at http://www.core-nic.org/.

At a meeting in Nov. 2000, ICANN chose seven new top-level domain names, listed below. If you have not seen these already, you should encounter them soon.

aero	Air-transport industry
biz	Businesses
coop	Cooperatives
info	Unrestricted use
museum	Museums
name	For registration by individuals
pro	Accountants, lawyers, and physicians

For practical purposes, the PR practitioner need only remember that the Web is a part of online. It might be that the Web overtakes commercial services such as AOL. It has done so already for some commercial services, such as CompuServe and Prodigy. They have moved from separate entrances to reach their content to on-ramps leading directly to the Internet highway. It may also be that other uses of the Internet wither and are replaced by Web technologies. For example, electronic bulletin boards pre-existing the Web and called Usenet news groups are in decline as bulletin boards move to the Web; but Usenet newsgroups have not disappeared and might not for years.

However, until consolidation occurs, if it ever occurs, the PR practitioner should remember that online has many parts and that online public relations orchestrates those parts to communicate effectively.

Failure to orchestrate can cut one off from target audiences and prevent messages from getting through. This means that knowing how target audiences use online services remains an important part of online public relations. One cannot go to a directory, such as the Standard Rate and Data Service, or look up the ABC audit of readers and demographics that has long been a part of print publishing. Such services are developing, but they have a long way to go, and it is unlikely that they will ever be comprehensive. The Internet is too large.

Using Online Media in Public Relations

This chapter discusses ways that public relations practitioners can use online media to communicate effectively and build relationships. Because the Web is robust in transporting media of many kinds, communications techniques are nearly infinite. New ways of using online media emerge monthly, and this challenges practitioners whose job it is to produce results. Guidelines are few and still developing.

Testing should be a regular part of communicating through online media. What works well for one practitioner might not work for another. Plunging blindly into an online program wastes time and resources. Because little is known, there is potential gain from controlled experimentation. With some online uses, the cost is so small that the only consideration is whether a message reaches key individuals and informs rather than alienates. On the other hand, some emerging technologies, such as mass customization of marketing approaches to customers, require huge resources that are beyond most public relations budgets.

ACTIVISM

Activist Web sites include reasonable critics and carpers as well as hate sites for which there is little a public relations practitioner can do. Generally, any attempt to shut sites down has ended badly for organizations. Successful forays against activists have come when sites violate copyright, trademarks, or published proprietary information. But even in these instances, compliance has not always gone well. For example, the Associated Press learned this when it tried to stop misuse of an AP photo of a Cuban boy being forcibly returned to his father. Two online artists created a spoof using the AP photo and a sound track from a Budweiser beer commercial. When the AP issued a cease-and-desist letter, it was buried in phone calls and e-mails protesting its action. AP later admitted that it probably should not have acted as it did.

Sites such as Untied Airlines (http://www.untied.com/), a critical appraisal of United Airlines' customer service, have been around long enough and run professionally enough to become established in their own right. A site like ihatebillgates (www.ihatebillgates.com) is as much about fun as it is about criticism of Microsoft's founder. On the other hand, McSpotlight (www.mcspotlight.org) is a serious attempt to tar the reputation of McDonald's Corp. This page claims that it is part of a McINFORMATION NETWORK, a group of volunteers working from several countries and continents with the purpose of "compiling and disseminating factual, accurate, up-to-date information—and encouraging debate—about the workings, policies and practices of the McDonald's Corporation and all they stand for" (*Source:* Web page). This kind of activist hunts for new charges and should be watched. "Fish Abuse by Walmart" (www.petlibrary.com/goldfish/walmart.htm appears to be an example of a site that has little traction in its protest of treatment of goldfish at Wal-Mart Stores Inc.

The best way for a PR practitioner to begin to handle activist charges is ascertain whether they are true. Crisis management begins with facts. If charges have a factual base, the organization can make changes to resolve the issue. If charges are not true or are a matter of opinion, it is best to track activists' progress—or lack of it—without necessarily getting involved with them. If rumors become serious and begin to affect the organization, the organization needs to act as Procter & Gamble did (www.pg.com/rumor) to combat charges that its logo was a satanic symbol.

As a matter of practice, PR practitioners should search variations of their organizations' URLs to make sure that no activist (or porno operation) has established a copycat or stealth site close to it in spelling. This is a common trick that most organizations prevent by buying up .com, .org, and .net variations on their URLs or by suing organizations for misappropriation of trademarked names. Thus, for example, Procter & Gamble might buy the following URLs to keep them out of the hands of activists:

- pg.net
- pg.org
- p&g.com
- p&g.org
- p&g.net

It is interesting to note that at the time this book was written, Procter & Gamble owned none of these URL variations. One belonged to a company in Chicago, another was for sale, and the rest were available.

However, little prevents an activist from switching letters in a name ("United" to "Untied" or "pg" to "gp") and opening a site.

The way to find out who owns a Web site that is critical of an organization is to check a URL registry. Each site owner must register the site's URL with an official registrar. The registrar then makes the registration available on the Web through whois, better whois, and nslookup. You can find these at `http://www.arin.net/whois/arinwhois.html`, `http://rs.internic.net/whois.html`, `http://swhois.net/` and `http://dns411.com/`. For example, the owner of the Untied.com site that stalks United Airlines is listed as follows:

```
Registrant:
Untied Airlines UNTIED2-DOM
   523 Pine St. W #201
   Montreal, QC H2W 1S4
   CANADA
```

Domain Name: UNTIED.COM

Administrative Contact, Technical Contact, Zone Contact, Billing Contact:
   Cooperstock, Jeremy
   Untied Airlines
   523 Pine Ave. W. #201
   Montreal, QC H2W 1S4
   CANADA
   (514) 398-5992

Record last updated on 09-Apr-2000.
Record expires on 25-Apr-2001.
Record created on 24-Apr-1997.
Database last updated on 22-Sep-2000 13:38:31 EDT.

Domain servers in listed order:
NS1.COMPWEBTECH.COM 216.2.103.101
NS2.COMPWEBTECH.COM 216.2.103.102

There is a lot of information in this listing, but the most important for the PR practitioner is the name, address, and phone number of the owner.

Criticism and charges leveled at an organization in newsgroups are handled differently. This kind of activism is a serious problem for public companies, and it has nothing to do with the moral convictions of an activist. Stock manipulators post rumors and other false information in newsgroups and chat rooms frequented by traders in order to drive the price of stocks up and down. The manipulator profits by selling against the stock's trend. The technique was so common that the Securities and Exchange Commission (SEC) even charged a 15-year-old boy with such manipulation.

One way to find the sources of criticism and charges and to learn the extent of negative opinion is through content analysis. The PR practitioner records the sources of newsgroup postings and their frequency. If the same sources show up disproportionately, it is a group feeding on itself or an individual attempting to build a campaign. If comments are widespread from many sources, it indicates that charges have taken root among an online population.

A second way to analyze messages is to examine the charges. If charges are about a specific point, and the same point occurs over and over, the issue is focused and can be dealt with directly (Either the criticism is true or not.) If charges are multiple and none dominate discussion, criticism reflects general dissatisfaction with the organization that may or may not be of merit or worth combating. Successful companies always have activists who "pile on" in an attempt to cut them down to size or to force them to confront specific issues.

The worst mistake PR practitioners can make is to ignore what is happening online. Organizations that fail to monitor what is said about them open themselves to ugly surprises. Depending on the size and public recognition of an organization, practitioners should establish a monitoring program that tracks online activists monthly, weekly, or daily. Global organizations should maintain a database of criticisms that can be analyzed to see how issues are advancing or retreating.

ADVERTISING

Public relations practitioners use advertising in traditional media. They can use it online too. In traditional media, PR practitioners advertise to raise issues; to appeal directly to target audiences, such as shareholders during merger and acquisition battles; to respond to crises; and to communicate viewpoints in ways that publicity might not achieve. However, it is unclear how effective advertising is in online media for PR purposes. One challenge facing practitioners is that online advertising is not one thing, such as a banner ad on a Web page. Online advertising includes

- **E-mail**. Solicitations sent to individuals in bulk.
- **Banners:** These can be on the top of a Web page, at the side, or floating. They can be animated as well with moving images.

- **Animated ads:** Images appear, move about the screen, and disappear.
- **Superstitial ads:** Ads that pop up in boxes on the screen.
- **Interstitial ads** that sprinkle appeals through content, such as ads placed within the copy of e-mail newsletters and news columns.
- **Info-rich ads** that incorporate layers of information within them so users do not have to leave a site.
- **Web sites**: Sites dedicated to merchandising a movie, promoting a political candidate or products and services.

Online advertising has characteristics of broadcast (display) ads and direct marketing. By broadcast, we mean ads placed in a general medium, such as a newspaper, radio station, TV program, or magazine that do not precisely target individuals. By direct marketing, we mean ads targeted according to predetermined characteristics of individuals getting the ads.

Appearances are deceiving online. Advertising sent to one's individual e-mail address is often untargeted junk mail, called spam (see Spam). Banner advertising that looks like broadcast or display ads can be carefully targeted based on a specific user's interests or pattern of surfing. On the other hand, the opposite is true as well in both cases.

The key benefits of advertising are guaranteed reach, frequency, and message presentation. Publicity, by relying on persuading journalists and others to carry its messages, cannot guarantee place, time, content, or the eyeballs that will see a message. On the other hand, messages that a journalist verifies through objective, third-party reporting are more credible. The trade-off between guaranteed exposure and credibility does not change in online media. Whether or not PR practitioners use advertising online, they should remember that the credibility equation does not change.

Response to online advertising is low. Clicks on online banner ads are less than 1 percent and response to junk e-mail is probably less than that. This is why some companies spend so much time to animate ads and to make them interactive in order to attract more attention and interest. Other companies, such as **DoubleClick Inc.,** have spent much time, money, and technology to target advertising to individuals. DoubleClick's assumption is that individuals buy products based on their interests, but it is still unclear that knowing where a person goes online always translates to sales. On the other hand, what DoubleClick and companies like it are doing fits a direct marketing rule of thumb that success comes first from lists that one uses, second from offers made, and third, from copy and graphics. DoubleClick is an intelligent list builder, and what it does is important for PR practitioners to understand. Most effective publicity comes from knowing the right reporters to contact based on their interests. Reporters complain constantly that PR practitioners fail to do their homework before contacting a journalist.

Some believe that other direct mail rules of thumb apply as well to online advertising, such as

- Responsiveness: Individuals who interact with an organization are more likely to purchase its goods and services and believe its messages. Visiting a Web site is not enough. Registering on a Web site or signing up for a newsletter is a prerequisite. Buying a product or service online is automatic qualification.
- Recency: People who bought a product or service most recently are more likely to buy again in the near future. They are also more likely to believe the organization's messages.
- Frequency: The greater the number of times one buys from a source, the more likely the individual will buy again from that source.
- Monetary value: The more that person has spent with a source over a specified period of time, the more that a person is likely to continue spending.
- Desire and timing. People do not buy what they do not need.
- Trust: People buy from companies/individuals they know.
- Testing: Direct marketers test every offer until they find what works. For example, online coupons associated with banner ads boost click-through significantly.

What is a public relations practitioner to make of this? Online advertising is immature, and using it for public relations purposes is venturing into the unknown. There are examples to which one can point, but most come from political campaigning.

Presidential candidates have found that well-run Web sites are less expensive to run than direct mail or telemarketing campaigns, and Web sites reap more contributions and volunteers. They have learned also that visitors to candidate Web sites stay longer and get more involved than they can with a thirty-second TV ad. Finally, they have had success with direct outreach by e-mail to find volunteers and spur contributions. On the other hand, fancy political Web sites alone do not equal success. Web sites must convey immediacy and urgency, and they must blend with a broad range of communications that candidates use, especially face-to-face campaigning.

Integration with other media already is a rule of thumb for online advertising. Television ads and programs reference supporting Web sites. E-commerce Web sites buy ads on radio and TV and in print media to create awareness. Major advertisers sponsor both a television program and a Web site supporting that program. Hollywood has experimented with advertising Web site sweepstakes within TV programs.

It might seem ironic that online media competing against television for audiences find it necessary to use television to win audience attention, but it is not. Television is a better medium for reaching the most people in the least amount of time. Mass e-mailing does not reach the number of individuals that a Super Bowl ad can, and intrusion into one's e-mail box is resented more than commercial breaks during a football game.

Online, marketers are acting in a similar fashion. They break banner advertising into two groups—ads placed on a few large Super Bowl-like sites, such as AOL and Yahoo!, that reach millions of users, and ads placed on targeted vertical portals (**Vortals**) that link to users in specific areas such as sports, entertainment, or music.

Public relations practitioners should use online advertising carefully, testing each step as they go. It appears that the best use now for online ads would be in support of crises or urgent issues that would motivate individuals to get involved quickly, such as a major recall of a product. Practitioners should make sure to integrate online advertising and publicity with traditional media and to coordinate themes and promotions across media to extend reach and awareness.

Stay up-to-date on changes in online advertising. The field shifts so rapidly that techniques used today are less useful tomorrow. Burnout is frequent because everyone overuses a good technique immediately. Finally, as with all online communications, respect privacy. Companies such as DoubleClick have had to fend off criticism from privacy groups and regulators for collecting too much information on individuals. If someone wants to be left alone, leave that person alone. Unwarranted intrusion not only fails to build a relationship, but it increases animosity toward the thing promoted and the organization. Public relations is about relationships.

Some basic considerations for use of banner ads in public relations:

- Place banner ads at the top of a Web page for the greatest visibility.
- Add motion and/or interactivity to increase response.
- Include an offer, such as a giveaway, to increase response.
- If possible, use a service like DoubleClick that inserts ads into Web pages based on users' interests.

For e-mail advertising, the following guidelines are useful:

- Target e-mail advertising carefully, and do not send it unless one chooses to receive it (an **opt-in program**).

- Always let users choose not to receive e-mail ads and honor their requests (an **opt-out program**).
- Reserve e-mail ads for urgent reminders, special offers, time-dated information, and news.
- Use a subject header that captures attention.
- Get news up front in body text and keep text short with plenty of white space.
- Test, test, test everything.
- Place Web links in e-mail solicitations if you are directing individuals elsewhere.
- Personalize e-mail as much as possible by capturing addresses.
- Consider rich media. Some firms can send fully animated and multimedia commercials, such as movie trailers, in e-mails that garner more attention than text.

The subject of online advertising is large, and dozens of sites tell marketers what to do and provide information resources. Here are a few sites that public relations practitioners should know about:

- `http://www.doubleclick.net`: This company has led the way in developing technologies in support of targeted banner advertising. It provides in-depth information on its site about its programs and technologies.
- `www.channelseven.com` focuses on news and resources for online marketers.
- `http://adres.internet.com` is a resource site for online marketers.
- `http://digitalwork.com` provides do-it-yourself resources.
- `http://wilsonweb.com/webmarketing/` collects articles and studies about online advertising and marketing.

ALLIANCES

Online is a natural arena for alliances among organizations and interests. By banding together, they have a larger voice and greater penetration. Alliances are of several kinds. There is a basic step of **link swapping** (also called **reciprocal linking**) in which two or more sites carry links to each other's Web site. Link swapping makes travel through the Web easier for users. They do not have to look for similar sites because their links are on the home page of the site they are visiting. Link swapping differs from paying for links to be carried on a page.

Portal services such as Yahoo!, and many search engines and directories charge fees for links, and companies pay for placement of their links in order to drive traffic to their sites. These are called **affiliations**. See Clickz (http://www.clickz.com/) for in-depth discussions of how to do affiliation programs and consult resources like Revenews (http://www.revenews.com/) and Make Money Now (http://www.makemoneynow.com/).

Link placement works to get a directory or another Web site to carry a link that is of mutual interest. For example, some directories in niche industries strive to be as complete as possible and ask for links to relevant sites. Organizations place links, or even files, on Web sites that are grateful to have them. For example, a hand tool manufacturer might ask a woodworker's advice site to carry a link to the manufacturer's tool catalog as a convenience to woodworkers. The link expands the resources of the woodworker's advice site and gains greater exposure for the manufacturer's tools.

Partnerships are where two sites join to market together. For example, a running club and shoe company sponsor each other and share promotion programs. **Associate programs** are a form of marketing in which a Web site carries a banner ad for your site and the Web site owner is paid when someone comes from the owner's site to your site. For example, an individual's site carries a banner ad for a bookstore. When someone clicks on the banner to go to the bookstore, the site carrying the banner ad is paid a fee.

Public relations practitioners should investigate the possibilities of alliances as a matter of practice.

ALT TAG

An Alt Tag is a descriptive text line displayed in place of an image on a Web page. It tells you what the image is and it acts like a caption on a photo. Often when you first click onto a site, especially with a slow connection, you will see empty rectangles where images go and text that describes the images. It might look like this:

Library Books

Alt Tags are useful for two reasons: 1. They describe an image for a browser that cannot load it; 2. they describe larger images sufficiently so that one does not have to wait for them to appear. The Alt Tag is used inside another formatting tag written in Hypertext Formatting Language (HTML)—the <IMG> tag, which states that an image is to be used in this location. The format is <IMG SRC="url"ALT="text">. This phrase means get the image at the following address (URL) and the description of this image is "text."

PR practitioners should place Alt Tags on all large images. It is a courtesy to users to let them move at their own pace without waiting for an image to appear.

ANNOTATION

Web page annotation is the equivalent of placing Post-It Notes^{TM} on a Web page. It is an electronic means of adding comments or reminders or any number of things for which one might use a "yellow sticky." Web page annotations are stored in one's Web browser and related to a specific Web page. For public relations practitioners who use such reminders, annotation is a handy online tool. Generally, it makes sense to place annotations on pages that you visit frequently or pages that you are going to send to another person. For example, you can send a Web page with a news story about your company's product or service to another individual with an annotation right on the page. In addition, you can place "yellow stickies" with passwords or user IDs on Web pages that require them so that you do not have to root through your desk drawer for the secure place where you last saw them.

One annotation software package is from iMarkup Solutions, Inc.—http://www.Websticky.com/. Markup software can also be placed on a computer server that holds a Web site so that visitors can do markup themselves. There is yet another flavor of annotation software called uTOK (http://www.utok.com).

AUDIT

An audit examines target individuals, media, and messages. It determines the effectiveness of messages and media in communicating to an organization's employees, customers, shareholders, and other key individuals. An audit accepts that messages and media must overcome high barriers to have any chance of communicating effectively. The barriers include countermessages and media from competitors, influentials and critics and other noise that influences and/or distracts.

Audits start with message receivers and work backward through media to messages. The PR practitioner strives to understand the interests of employees, customers, shareholders, and other key individuals and the competition for their attention. This is done through a multitude of techniques such as direct observation, surveys, focus groups, online tracking, and more. After the practitioner distills the characteristics of key individuals, the audit moves to media.

A media audit considers all media reaching target individuals because every medium competes for attention. This is complex because of the number of media involved—for example, face-to-face, phone calls, TV, radio, newspapers, magazines, newsletters, e-mail, faxing, memos, pagers, surface mail, meetings, Intranet, Web page, and more. PR practitioners rank media preferences with the same techniques used to understand audience characteristics. The media audit teaches one flexibility and pragmatism. It is easy to be captive to a medium that one knows well, but if target users have no desire to use the medium, the public relations practitioner should adjust. Audits also teach one to experiment with media to find newer and better ways to communicate effectively.

For example, a company might reach employees through direct talks from supervisors, a print newsletter, e-mail, Intranet, and Web page. But a survey determines that employees favor only direct talks from supervisors. Moreover, the survey reveals that supervisors have failed to pass on information, that a printed newsletter is not reaching employees, that e-mail is bombarding employees and annoying them, that the Intranet is overloaded with useless content, and that the Web page is out of date. The media audit should surface these barriers and provide solutions for fixing them.

Other questions to investigate during the media audit are

- Information availability and access: Do users know in which medium the information is, whether on a Web site, Intranet, or elsewhere? How easy is it to retrieve information from the medium?
- Information inclusiveness and comprehensiveness: Does the medium put all information in one place about a topic and make it easily accessible? Does information cover every topic a user needs to know? If the information is on a Web page, is there a search engine, site map, table of contents, and navigation bar to help users find content quickly?
- Information ease of use: Does the medium present information clearly or does one have to hunt through text and/or scroll a lot?

- Information consistency in presentation: Does the medium present content in a way that users can understand that it is part of a whole?

Practitioners should be aware that media preferences change constantly and sometimes quickly. One cannot depend on a single-point media audit to determine how to communicate for years to come. It is best to incorporate measurement into every medium and to audit changes constantly.

The final step is the message itself. This is a matter of the relative value of the message against all other messages being sent to target individuals. Does the public relations message have a clear purpose, acceptability to users, and currency? If not, it should not be sent because it is useless noise. The message should be tailored to audience interests and to the most effective media for reaching each audience, whether online or not.

Organizational visions and objectives can be stated in an infinite number of ways. A message should state them in the most probable ways to gain attention and action from key individuals. Message receivers should understand quickly that it is in their best interests to accept and conform to the message. Because the message must do this against all other messages and noise, few messages or media can ever achieve this high standard. That is why practitioners integrate messages and media to pass over, through and under barriers in as many ways as affordable.

Here are some of the questions that PR practitioners should ask about messages:

- Message value: Is there a reason for anyone to return to the information in the message?
- Message credibility: Do credible testimony and resource material back up the message?
- Message excess: Is message presentation overloaded and in need of textual, visual, or other editing?
- Message integration: Does the message complement and supplement other media content?
- Message interactivity: Does the message solicit user action and response? Are there e-mail links for feedback if the message is online?
- Message tone: Is the message welcoming or forbidding, and is the tone appropriate for this group of individuals at this time?

The two forms that follow can be used for an audit. They are checklist reminders of the assessments that public relations practitioners should undertake when auditing.

Audit	Audience Analysis
Client	
Date	
Business Objective	
Communications Objective	
Feedback devices	
Success measures	

Effective communication starts with the message receiver. You want the message receiver to DO something as a result of your communication. This action might be increased awareness, greater knowledge of the message, more support for decision making, making a purchase, or requesting after-purchase service. To evaluate your communications, we need to know more about key person(s) to whom you are communicating.

Key Internal Audience	Check (if key)	Summary Description
Stockholders		
Board of directors		
Senior executives		
Senior managers		
Mid-level managers		
Line supervisors		
Staff		
Line workers		
Clerical workers		
Volunteers		
Specific divisions or departments		
Other		

Key External Audience	Check (if key)	Summary Description
Customers/consumers		
Potential customers/consumers		
Contributors		
Potential contributors		
Community organizations		
Activist special interest groups		
Political leaders—local, state, national, foreign		
Legislators—local, state, national, foreign		
Government agencies—local, state, national, foreign		
Industry associations		
Competitors		
Other		

For each key group of individuals, here are typical questions that you might ask, but DON'T get bogged down in the answers. Audits are action-oriented and NOT ends in themselves.

1. What are the demographic characteristics: ages, gender, marital status, education level, income level, race, ethnic background and psychographics, such as lifestyle, cultural values?
2. Is this group of individuals an ally or potential ally? What do we want them to do as the result of communications?

3. Is this group of individuals neutral but might be influenced? What do we want them to do as the result of communications?

4. Is this group of individuals an adversary or potential adversary? What do we want them to do as the result of communications? Who might join with adversaries?

5. What is (are) the self-interest(s) of the members of this target group of individuals concerning your organization?

6. Where is this group of individuals located? Geographic location, political boundary, Zip code, telephone area codes?

7. What members of this group of individuals exercise political/economic power or formal/informal leadership among the members of this group?

8. Who are the knowledgeable individuals—opinion leaders—who influence members of the public?

9. What persons are actively involved in this group's decision-making processes and what role do they play in decision-making?

10. Who are the competitors for this group's attention that can distract them from your organization's message?

11. How does this group of individuals think/feel about the organization?

12. How does this group behave? For example, involved, activist, passive, apathetic, go-along?

13. How would you describe the nature of their opinions about your organization? For example, rational, irrational, emotional?

14. How would you describe the intensity of their opinions? For example, slight, moderate, strong, zealous/fanatical?

15. How accurate is the organization's perception of this group's views?

16. How accurate is this group's perception of the organization's views?

17. How much of this group is online today and how is it online? Is it on a high-speed LAN, low-speed modem, a mixture of LAN and modem, partially online and partially offline?

18. What media reach this group of individuals?

Audit			Materials Checklist	
Client		Date		

An audit compares an organizations business, marketplace, customers, friends and enemies, competitors

Business Objective:

On-line Communications Objective:

Item Checklist	Check (if needed)	Request Date	Received Date	Source
Academic studies				
Annual/quarterly financial reports				
Audit reports				
Business plan				
Buyers/beneficiaries of products/services reports/interviews				
Complaint files				
Consultant reports				
E-mail traffic reports				
Employee focus group reports				

Employee opinion surveys				
Employee/internal communications (Ex: Interviews, employee annual reports, newsletters, bulletin board and electronic mail announcements, videos)				
Field reports				
Government reports				
Industry association reports				
Interviews with key internal persons				
Market research reports				
Marketing plan				
Members of concerned publics reports/interviews				
News media reports/clips				
Online marketing/use plan				
Professional society reports				
Public statements made by key leaders				
Published/unpublished histories				
Sales materials				
Shareholder surveys and focus groups				
Speeches delivered by senior management				
Stock market analyst reports				
Strategic plan				
Subject matter experts reports/interviews				
Vendors/suppliers reports/interviews				
Web logs and counts				
Other				

AVATAR

The previous chapter defined an avatar as a symbol or image that one makes up to identify oneself in a multi-user dungeon (**MUD**). Avatars also are used in chat rooms and other online environments where one can become what he or she wishes. From a public relations perspective, an avatar can be a useful tool to identify a company or organization, such as the company's logo, when responding in newsgroups and chatrooms, although they did not catch on when AOL first tried them. An avatar could be used in Intranet chat rooms, for example, to represent various departments, such as human relations, marketing, and accounting in anthropological ways that would make these departments seem less distant. Before using an avatar, experiment to find the right depiction of the organization, unit, or individual that it represents. (Note the illustration on the next page of Female avatars.)

BOOKMARK

A bookmark denotes two processes online. One kind of bookmark stores the address of a Web site in a browser so that one can go back to

it. The other kind of bookmark denotes a place inside a Web page to which one can jump quickly. It is a local link.

Microsoft's Internet Explorer browser changed the name of the browser bookmark to "**favorites**" and allows one to group them in various ways. However, Web promotions still request individuals to bookmark a site under the assumption that a person would be more likely to come back to it. However, this technique has limits. Most online users visit only a few sites frequently and most sites occasionally or rarely. To displace an individual's favorite site through bookmarking is unlikely unless a user has a perceived need for the new site because it complements or supercedes content in sites the individual already uses. Bookmarking alone is not sufficient to gain increased use of a site. It is more likely that the site will reside unused among other bookmarks and eventually be deleted. What bookmarking teaches the public relations practitioner is that content matters. If content is compelling, individuals will bookmark a site. Hence promotions should emphasize the usefulness of site content over pleas to bookmark.

Bookmarking has another, and more insidious, effect on organizations that use online media. Inevitably, one person's bookmarks are not another's. This leads to a routine visible in most offices. Individuals wander from desk to desk and inquire if someone has ever found a site that has (fill in here). It is better to develop and maintain **link sites**. These are Web pages that categorize Web sites by topics and provide links to them to find information. Link sites do not replace search engines. Rather they concentrate in areas that employees need for daily work. They are shortcuts that let one bypass searching and get immediately to information desired. Link sites, like bookmarks, are never exhaustive, and they require constant updating.

Bookmarking within a Web page is a tool that the public relations practitioner should use often. Essentially, this kind of bookmark is a local link that lets one travel through a page quickly by clicking on the link. The benefit of such bookmarking is that a Web page author can provide an outline or topic headers for a page at the top and users can click on these to go to relevant sections quickly. The key to bookmarking within a Web page is to summarize page content concisely and clearly enough so that a user is not confused about what he or she is looking for. A second key to bookmarking is to help the individual return to the top of the page or to get out of the page by placing hyperlinks in text near bookmarked areas that allow one to return or move on.

BROCHUREWARE

Brochureware describes a class of Web page that is a minimal use of online communication. Such a site also is called **Shovelware**. These are sites on which a brochure or text is loaded without consideration for ways that online media differ from printed matter. A brochureware site looks exactly like someone dumped a printed brochure onto the Web page. There are no links to other pages. There is usually long and boring copy, and the site's design might look good on a printed page but is less than satisfactory on a computer screen. Although brochureware sites are sometimes recommended for companies that want to place business cards on the Web, public relations practitioners should discourage attempts to build them when they are little more than reused copy. Brochureware betrays ignorance of differences between online and print media. Though this might not bother a business, it bothers users who have to wade through copy.

If a site is particularly small—say, five pages with minimal copy— brochureware can be acceptable, but then the public relations practitioner should ask whether a firm should have its own Web site or not. Many Web sites serve as directories to services, and a company with little to say about itself might be better off in an online directory.

There is another definition for brochureware—hyping vaporware— software that is supposed to exist but does not. In this case, an organization prints a brochure describing software that you cannot buy because it has not been built. This too is a practice that public relations practitioners should avoid.

CHAT

Chat was discussed in the previous chapter but is raised again here because of its importance to online public relations practitioners. We noted that chat has grown rapidly. We also noted that chat is an accepted tool for publicity, internal coordination, and customer contact. Celebrity chats promote movies, records, television shows, and other entertainment. Workers chat with colleagues and clients. Companies use chat to help customers on e-commerce Web sites.

Chat requires voluntary participation from two sides. One can opt out of chat simply by turning off chat software. This is not uncommon when one needs to concentrate and chat requests continue to pop up. Chat can be a time waster when one spends time chatting rather than taking care of business.

The first rule of chat is to know to whom you are writing in real time. Chat rooms, especially commercial chat rooms, allow one to use a **handle** or made-up name. Made-up names are disguises. The public relations practitioner should understand that it is difficult to know whether one is talking to a friend, enemy, competitor, hoaxer, concerned citizen, customer, or someone else when chatting with someone using a disguised name. When the practitioner does not know the identity of another chat participant, chatting should proceed carefully and the practitioner should edit remarks closely before posting them where they can be misconstrued or used against the organization or individual the practitioner represents. This, of course, slows down real-time chatting, which is why some chats use formatted and vetted answers. In fact, customer response organizations regularly cut and paste stock replies to hundreds of chat and e-mail questions. Such formatted answers lose some of the spontaneity of chat, but they are safer.

The public relations practitioner should ask what the purpose of chat is in a particular instance and why it should be used rather than another method, such as e-mail. Chat requires a presence that is costly in terms of staffing. Someone has to be there to answer when an individual requests a chat.

There are several chat forms to consider:

- Promotional uses of chat are well-defined and limited in scope. A person conducts one online chat at a specific time that is not repeated.

- E-commerce uses of chat are tied to an organization's customer service department, which is staffed for answering toll free telephone calls.
- Using chat for coordination is a hit-and-miss affair that depends on whether an individual on the other end of a chat request is available. Usually, it is best to coordinate such chats in advance of the time that the chat is to take place.

In other words, use chat carefully in a planned manner to achieve specific objectives. The key question to ask is what one gains from immediacy. In cases of urgency, chat is desirable—for example, user support. A frustrated user can get online to find out why a machine is not working, why software is crashing, or why a recipe failed when a dinner party is about to start. Chat at the point of decision-making also is useful. A person wants to buy a product but has questions that a customer representative can answer on the spot through a chat screen. In crises, chat can help answer questions quickly that might otherwise clog telephone lines. If the objective is to build relationships with individuals, chat is useful. It provides direct contact to a person and/or organization that otherwise might be difficult to reach. If this use of chat is intermittent, it should be clearly spelled out to potential chat users. It is frustrating to enter a chat room and find it empty.

Chat requires discipline to work well. It is not the same as a conversation in which one takes audible cues from another to determine when to speak and when to listen. Chat responses can spill over and disrupt one another. Chat is slower because one must type a response and this is dependent on an individual's typing ability, unless one has a question or response ready and simply hits the send key. The nature of chat is such that chat users frequently write in shorthand. Phrases are compressed into acronyms that save time and key strokes. Also, chat participants use **emoticons** to convey feelings. There are dozens of emoticons and **acronyms** and only the most skilled chat users would know them all. Public relations practitioners should understand key ones and know where to look up more mysterious terms and symbols. The following are emoticons and acronyms occur frequently:

Emoticon	Acronym
☺ = smile	**AFAIK** = As far as I know
;-) = smile with a wink	**B4N** = Bye for now
☹ = sad	**BG** = Big grin
:-o = I'm surprised	**BTA** = But then again
:-II = mad	**BTW** = By the way
:-D = Big grin	**CU** = See you
	EOM = End of message

EOT = end of thread (discussion)
FAQ = Frequently asked questions
IMHO = In my humble opinion
IOW = In other words
LOL = Laughing out loud

For a longer list of emoticons and acronyms, see http://www.whatis.techtarget.com. Some chat participants spell out words in parentheses to indicate emotions. A frequent spelling is (smile), and it indicates that one is making a joke. (Joking online is dangerous when context is missing. Individuals can take one seriously to the detriment of conversations and relationships.)

Further, as noted in the earlier chapter:

- Chat with more than one person needs a moderator. Otherwise, it becomes a confused series of partial messages.
- Chats with large groups do not work at all. When 5,000 people wait in a chat room to talk to a movie star, at best 10 will be able to submit a question. The rest watch.
- Large-scale chats require moderators to screen questions and sometimes, an adept typist to write responses. Because such chats are more promotional than conversational, replies can be largely prewritten.

CLIP ART

Many Web sites would be duller without clip art. Clip art comprises tens of thousands of images of every possible kind that one can electronically clip and plug into a Web page without getting permissions for copyrights or paying royalties.

Clip art is not new. Books of generic images have been available for use since before the invention of printing. The difference in online media is the overwhelming availability of imagery. One can download clip art directly from online sources or buy CD-ROMs with 10,000 images ready to use. Clip art includes stock photography, cartoons, architectural figures, symbols, stylized fonts, and more. Online, a variation of clip art is **Borrowed Art**. These are images that one borrows from another site as long as one does not violate copyright.

There are search engines that focus specifically on finding images. Try, for example, http://www.richmedia.lycos.com. There also are sites that specialize in storing tens of thousands of static and animated clip art images for downloading. Many of these images are for sale, but they are inexpensive to buy. Try http://www.clipart.com

to get an idea of what a clip-art site will carry. You will find that these sites have usage restrictions on their clip art. They will prohibit retrieval of their art from sites other than their own, reselling their art and other restrictions designed to keep another Web site from profiting from the art itself.

There are three points that public relations practitioners should consider when dealing with clip art:

1. It saves money.
2. It can provide images that help make the point that one is communicating.
3. Using clip art does not save time.

Much clip art is bad art. Putting it on a Web site would cheapen the look of the site rather than enhance it. The task is to find clip art that does not look like clip art and has not been overused, and this is not always easy to do. One might review hundreds of images to find a handful that can serve the intended purpose. It is easy to tire during the search and to settle on images that look good but do not make a point effectively. If one is pressed for time, it can be easier to have an artist create an image that makes a point precisely. Using this approach is better when one needs an image that is not common. Clip-art libraries carry popular images. It is easy to find fifty different drawings, illustrations, or photos of computers and more difficult to find a rendering of a carbon-based molecule.

COMICS AND CARTOONS

Online is a fertile ground for comic strips and cartoons— especially animated comic strips and cartoons. Public relations practitioners have long used comic strips and cartoons to communicate effectively, and the medium thrives as easily online as it does on paper. In fact, with animation, it is potentially better because electronic drawing tools are abundant and electronic animation relatively easy to achieve. Comics and cartoons now are little movies online. To get an idea of how sophisticated they are, visit Multipath Movies (http://www. brilliantdigital.com/) and view some of the episodic, animated cartoons there.

Comics and cartoons can be single panel, single strips, or serial strips just as they are in the print world or feature-length animations with sound and music. They can be original or republished material, such as Dilbert cartoons. They are all generally copyrighted, and one must seek permission to use them and must, of course, pay a royalty. There are

Web sites that specialize in creating cartoons to facilitate corporate communication, especially communication of complex messages through humor. Anything that can be said about cartoons in print applies to them online. Poorly drawn or lame cartoons are no better online than they are in print, and inappropriate or inexpert use of animation hinders the message that one is trying to communicate rather than enhances it. The public relations practitioner needs to apply the same judgment and creative use of cartooning online as off.

COPYRIGHT

Copyright is an inflammatory issue online. Those who believe that all information should be free are pitted against those who seek compensation for intellectual property. The complication in this long-standing argument is the ubiquity of digital bits and the ease with which they can be copied and transmitted. So far, copyright holders have defeated those who have borrowed music and other materials without permission, but the war is not over. There are countries that do not recognize copyright law. In those countries, borrowing continues. This is a major problem for intellectual-property holders because the Internet has no geographic or legal boundaries. On the Internet, one can reach a computer located in Antarctica just as easily as a computer located next to your desk. Further, technologies are rapidly developing that make borrowing of intellectual property easy, and difficult to stop. Gnutella is one of them. It is free software that allows users to share files. Gnutella does not have a single computer that is responsible for holding files and maintaining a connection to a network. Any user can connect to any other user running Gnutella. As a result, copyright holders have to track and sue hundreds of individuals who are sharing copyrighted files from their computers. This is expensive to do.

Because online carries multimedia easily, few media are safe from copyright violation. One can **pirate** text, music, imagery, video, and anything else that online media can carry. Schemes to prevent copying have largely been ineffective. Hackers find ways around schemes, and then publish these to the online world. Piracy is so widespread that there is a wink-wink attitude that prevails online. It is something like this, "Yes, we know about copyright and we honor the intent of copyright, but when we need something, we borrow it carefully."

Public relations practitioners sometimes adopt this attitude. It is not uncommon, for example, for public relations agencies and departments to get one copy of a newsletter then to reproduce it to avoid paying for more than one subscription. Because it is easier to copy anything online, publishers are legitimately fearful that content placed online will be ripped off. Some have given up trying to protect content and give material away free. Others continue to try to protect their materials through various methods, such as

1. Locking off materials to all but subscribers, such as the Wall Street Journal. For the most part, **subscription sites** have not been successful. Unless there is a compelling need for information, individuals do without it or find the data elsewhere—and online is so large that it is possible to find most data elsewhere. Secondly, hackers are adept at breaking through locked-off sites, so such sites tend to hold out the law-abiding individual but not chronic intruders.
2. Stamping a name on materials, such as images, that cannot be removed. This is an effective approach because if an image is copied, the name is copied along with it and moves with the image. Copyright violations become obvious. This is a technique that Corbis, a stock image library uses. See http://www.corbis.com.
3. Hunting down violators and suing them for violating copyright. The music industry designed a search engine to find Web sites holding copyrighted songs. The industry follows up any discovery with a cease-and-desist order if songs are offered without paying royalties to copyright holders.
4. Encoding materials: As we discussed earlier, encoding-decoding schemes are attacked constantly by hackers who find such schemes offensive or a challenge to break. To date, every encoding scheme has had a limited life span. Holders of copyright engage in a never-ending war to find new ways that hackers then try to defeat. There will be no end to this going forward.

Because public relations practitioners guard the reputations of organizations they represent, honoring copyright should never be a question. It is what one does to protect the name of an organization, even if the organization has been loose about copyright protection. Copyright is an issue where public relations practitioners need to remind those with whom they work of the need to get permission. Individuals at all levels from CEO to mail room personnel tend to forget.

CREDIBILITY

Online communication is less credible than face-to-face communication. Hence, PR practitioners work harder online to establish credibility.

Studies of journalists and others show that few trust an online message unless they know the source of the message and have independently determined the source's trustworthiness. Major hoaxes have victimized financial journalists and companies and have heightened this distrust. Studies of business negotiations have discovered that parties are less honest with each other and withhold more information when they write e-mail back and forth than when they converse face to face. The optimum use of online is to balance its indirect nature with direct face-to-face contact. Once a user knows you, working online is a convenience for both sides. This is one reason why merchants who have retail stores, or worked for many years to establish themselves as direct merchants, have an advantage. Consumers know who they are, or they can visit a physical location, talk to real people, and touch real merchandise. The simple rule is that one can never have too much credibility, even when the effort that one makes appears overdone. The credibility that the practitioner can build serves as a protection against errors and inaccuracies that creep into every communication, no matter how hard one tries to be factual.

To help establish credibility, PR practitioners should insist on placing as much information online as possible that reveals the background and authority of organizations and individuals. Do not stint on history, résumés, testimonials, or media clips. The more you provide, the easier it is for users to verify facts and to become open to a message. Placing links from your organization's Web site to outside sites is part of credibility enhancement. One helps users crosscheck information. Linking to a story about your organization on an established publication's Web page is particularly powerful.

Presentation is part of credibility as well, particularly when one is dealing with an active opposition. Dumping facts online in a jumbled and confused manner discourages individuals from finding what you have to say and damages credibility. Users want information in ways that they understand. Then, they want to evaluate it against other sources. You do not determine what is understandable: Readers do. This calls for usability testing (see Web Page Design).

Pure e-commerce retailers, particularly, have learned the value of brand credibility. They discovered that the bricks-and-mortar companies they were eager to push into oblivion did not go away easily. Customers trust names that they know and have had direct experience with more than names that they do not know. E-commerce exceptions, such as Amazon.com, established themselves early in segments that potential buyers could check quickly. Either you got the book you ordered or you did not, and the value of a book purchase was generally small. High-value and complex items, such as jewelry, art, and machinery, are still purchased primarily through relationship selling, although this may change over time as the credibility of pure online retailers is established.

In business-to-business selling with complex products and machines, customers want a real person on whom they can rely for getting answers. The Internet plays a support role. After a sale, the Internet has proven useful for delivering service twenty-four hours a day, seven days a week with little human intervention. It helps maintain and enhance credibility that was established during the sale.

For well-understood commodity products, such as sheet steel, screws, nails, and common hardware, online auctions have stormed the marketplace. Here prequalified vendors (their credibility is established before they are allowed to deal) interact with prequalified buyers. Cross-border e-commerce, particularly, requires a depth of credibility greater than that of a company's home country. Buyers fear the vagaries of laws they do not understand and of companies they do not know well. This is partially why multinational firms have localized Web sites in major countries in order to build credibility through local language and culture.

CRISIS COMMUNICATIONS

Online is a valuable tool in crises. Its virtue is immediacy and reach, but to date, Web pages have largely been used as repositories for information disseminated through TV, radio, and print. Online may achieve parity with other media as multimedia delivery grows and audio/video feeds become standard. Unfortunately, online has already reached parity in generating crises, especially in chat room attempts to boost or deflate a company's stock, attack management or otherwise upset an organization's ongoing operations.

Airlines, for example, have adapted their Web pages to handle accidents. They post releases, transcripts of news conferences, statements from company officials, and other messages to provide a steady flow of information. Notable instances of using airline Web pages for post-crash reporting include Alaska Airlines Flight 261 that plunged into the water off the coast of California early in 2000 and the Swissair flight that crashed near Newfoundland in September 1998. Alaska Air installed a link to a special section on its company Web site, "Flight 261 Special Report," where it reprinted all official communications, information from the National Transportation Safety Board, and an editorial from a Tacoma, Washington, newspaper. In the case of the Swissair flight, the company provided information and phone numbers in English, German, and French.

In another transportation-related incident, both Ford Motor Company and Bridgestone/Firestone placed prominent links on their home pages during a recall of 3.85 million Bridgestone/Firestone RADIAL ATX and RADIAL ATX II Tires and 2.7 million Wilderness AT Tires placed on Ford Explorer sports utility vehicles. This crisis was particularly difficult because Bridgestone/Firestone did not have the production or distribution capacity to handle the replacement of that many tires swiftly. Meanwhile, Ford Explorer owners were faced with driving vehicles whose tires could shred without warning and flip their SUVs.

The Ford and Bridgestone/Firestone home page links took users to pages of news and links that included recall information, press releases, statements from company officials, testimony before Congress, and other pertinent material. The Ford Motor site also cross-linked with the Bridgestone/Firestone recall Web page so that users did not have to look for that link. This recall was instructive in that it showed the limitations of media during crises. Bridgestone/Firestone did not handle the early steps of the recall well, and media interest skyrocketed with new charges being published and broadcast daily. The Web sites of the two companies were not a factor in handling this frenzy except as sources of official statements from both firms.

This raises a major point. Online does not replace other media and the many activities that occur in crisis communications. Online media complement, enhance, and integrate with other media, especially because many consumers may not have ready online access. Online provides another avenue for getting information out at a time when demand for answers is high. It does not do away with press conferences and press releases. It does not dispense with the need to deal with survivors directly face-to-face. It does not suffice to combat rumors and error in television, radio, print, and online.

As in all matters relating to crisis communications, information published online must be accurate and timely. It must also be easy to find. PR practitioners should claim highly visible space at the top of a company's home page to place links or news relating to a crisis. In a time of stress, users have less patience for poorly presented information. They want news NOW in a simple, direct, and credible presentation.

Web policy should reflect the immediacy of crises and the need for Webmasters and other Web-administrative personnel to drop what they are doing and to turn to the support of the organization. Policy also should stipulate lines of authority in a crisis so that there is no bickering among departments about who is going to post. Generally, PR practitioners should be in the lead in crises, but they might find this difficult to achieve if a legal department is involved with writing and editing of content.

Don Middleberg in his book, "Winning PR in the Wired World," provides five "must-do" steps for crises that are worth summarizing here because they emphasize the need for speed, accuracy, and credibility.

- Take preventive measures: create a contingency web site or a strategy for possible crisis situations.
- Establish relationships with key online news sites.
- Act online immediately.
- Be proactive in posting information so the online community does not hear the news elsewhere.
- Make a commitment to be honest and consistent throughout the site, cater to both the media and the public and offer as much information as possible, including toll-free phone numbers, up-dates, and online press center.

For crises that erupt in online sources such as in newsgroups or on Web pages, the response also should be integrated with use of other media. For example, a sensational charge against a company executive is leveled in newsgroups and on a Web page, from a seemingly credible source. The danger is that journalists in print, TV, and radio will pick up the charge and report it broadly. An allegation then becomes fact in the eyes of the public, and company executives lose credibility—any-thing they say is suspect. If the charge is false, PR practitioners should use online openly and vigorously to combat it, including publishing the facts online, engaging in newsgroup dialog, and responding to inquir-ies from reporters. By "openly" is meant that PR practitioners should never disguise their names or organizations, and they should be ready to sue those who do while bad-mouthing practitioners' organizations. If the charge is published in print or on radio and television, PR practitioners should respond rapidly in these media as well. If the case is debatable or worse, true, PR practitioners need to use a multimedia approach immediately as long as the company's board, CEO, or other senior executives act vigorously to rectify the situation.

The key to crisis communications is rapid response with facts that clarify the dimensions of the crisis before rumor and error take hold and the organization loses control of its destiny. Especially with remote crises such as a blowup of a chemical plant in a distant country, online provides a swift way of communicating, but the emphasis must be on getting facts first. There is not much that online can do to help this, if the people on the ground are not well trained to record events accu-rately and report them swiftly. Content is first, and distribution is second. However, with unfolding crises, it is easy to forget this, espe-cially when live TV news cameras are trained at a burning facility with toxic clouds boiling from it and reporters are chasing every rumor they hear.

CUSTOMER RELATIONSHIP MANAGEMENT

Customer relationship management (CRM) is an industry buzzword that applies to computer software and organizational processes that automate every contact an organization has with customers. The term is used loosely to cover everything from sales contact systems to customer databases and flow of products to customers from raw materials to delivered goods. CRM often starts with the first point of contact on a Web page and moves up to the warehouse where the product is picked and shipped, to the vendor for reorder of new product and from the vendor to suppliers needed to build the product. The depth to which customer involvement has moved directly impacts the communications that PR practitioners have with customers. One no longer talks to customers but interacts with them at many points before, during, and after a product purchase. The quality of the relationship has deepened and opportunities for reinforcing or harming the relationship become more abundant.

Dell Computer (http://www.dell.com/) built the first highly publicized example of an online customer relationship management system. The Dell Web site lets customers order preconfigured computer and service packages or design computers and services based on their needs. Dell then builds the computer and sends it to the customer and configures the services to go with it. Since then, CRM systems have progressed to deep involvement in customer support and service, including monitoring equipment such as electrical generation turbines on customer premises through the Web.

Traditional **call center**s performing inbound and outbound CRM and customer service contact have moved into online support and e-commerce as well. They use three techniques for customer contact and customer relationship management. The first is a pop-up chat screen on a Web site where customer service representatives (CSRs) answer questions with cut-and-paste answers. The second is telephony through the Web page where the customer clicks on a screen icon that automatically dials a call center. The customer talks through the PC's microphone and listens on the PC's speakers. The third is called page-pushing, in which a CSR can send to a customer a specific Web page while communicating with the customer. For example, the customer needs specific information to assemble a product, and the CSR sends the diagram page for how to assemble the product while chatting with the customer.

PR practitioners might not often use call center services, but they should be aware of what call centers are doing online, especially because CSRs are the first—and sometimes the most important—point of customer relationships.

CUSTOMIZATION

The ideal online experience is to deal with each individual uniquely. E-mail is sent to a journalist with content precisely matched to the journalist's interest. An e-commerce Web site presents just the goods and services that you are interested in. Your browser is set up just the way that you want it with just the content that you want to have on it.

There are many ways to achieve near customization, also called "mass customization" online. My Yahoo!, for example, is a Yahoo! screen that one can build in any way that one wishes. Cookies, the short pieces of code inserted into your computer, allow an online retailer to track pages that one goes to regularly and to send those pages quickly when that person comes to a site. This kind of customization has moved as well to suggesting allied products and services that one might like as well as alerting customers when a desired product has been received.

Mass customization requires huge computer and software resources that work in real-time, that is, in milliseconds to recognize a user, consult the user's profile, retrieve the user's preferred information, and to present this information to the user in the format that the user desires. When such customization is scaled for millions of users, a company's embedded investment in people and technology runs into millions of dollars. On the other hand, the relationship that a company can build with a customer has a greater profit potential and longer life than anonymous purchasing of products and services. It is as if each user has a personal shopper in a Web page who is looking out for his or her needs.

PR practitioners can learn from efforts to mass customize. Particularly when dealing with journalists, any technique that can help one isolate and identify a reporter's interests should be considered. Personal contact is still best, but it is not always possible when reporters receive hundreds of calls a day from PR practitioners who are selling story ideas. Media databases allow for extensive notation about reporters, and there are ways to track story ideas that have been presented and subsequent stories that have appeared. This kind of control, however, requires discipline and continuous maintenance. And, the benefits of tracking may not be evident immediately. However, over time, as one gets to know a journalist's likes and dislikes, story ideas can be tailored before making an approach. This avoids wasting a journalist's time, and it shows respect for the job that a journalist does. Moreover, it tends to result in a larger acceptance rate for story ideas.

Even on Web pages that do not use cookies, customization works by structuring presentation of content. If one sorts through the key audiences that one wishes to reach online, it is relatively easy to build an information profile for each and to design both e-mail and Web offerings that match those profiles. For example, a shareholder's page presents recent financial news about the company at the top of the page where a shareholder can read it at once. The page carries a ticker with the company's stock price as of the last few minutes. It provides direct access to shareholder services through a "click to talk" telephone link. It sets aside a secure section where shareholders can check on holdings.

A similar approach works for employee news. One can provide localized news by plant site or major office location as a part of general company news. One can click on a link to his or her locale and learn what has happened there in the last few days. Maintenance of localized content is more difficult and requires greater manpower, but if local plant sites have newsletters, newspapers, and magazines, the same people who produced the content for these can maintain their section of a Web site. This approach has serendipitous benefits as well in that it can serve as a source of news to the local plant community and media.

The important point about customization is to get rid of the notion of "mass media." Online is the realm of individualized and interactive media. PR practitioners trained in traditional media sometimes have difficulty adjusting their thinking online. They want big stories on sites with large circulation when it might be much more important to reach just a few key individuals who can affect outcomes. Online is closer to direct marketing.

CYBRARIAN

A cybrarian is a librarian and information resource professional who specializes in online research. PR practitioners in large organizations may deal already with online researchers who are magicians in finding facts that would take others hours to surface, if ever. There are thousands of cybrarians now, many of whom do contract research in specific topic areas. PR practitioners might find such contract research useful. As always, know with whom you are dealing before contracting with one.

DATABASE

A database is a way to store information so that one can get it back again in the same way that one stored it, or in new combinations. Database software falls into three broad types—the **flat file**, the **relational database**, and **keyword/phrase searching**. A flat file is like a Rolodex that you keep on your desktop. It files data according to a single characteristic, such as last names. All other information on a Rolodex card can only be retrieved after one has found the card under a person's last name. A relational database breaks down information on the file card and stores it so that it can be retrieved independently. For example, one can ask for names by last name, by first name, by towns in which one lives, by phone numbers, by street addresses, and so on. Keyword searching uses software that sorts bulk text by word or phrase. It is a high-speed filter that matches content and kicks out only those items that equal the keyword or phrase.

Databases are ubiquitous online, and public relations practitioners use them regularly without necessarily noticing their presence. Any online **repository** of information should have an information-finding tool to make it easier on users to get data they need. The question to ask is, "What type of database should be used in a given instance?" The answer is to learn what users are searching for and how they wish to view search results. For most Web sites, simple keyword/phrase search software is enough. For sites with enormous amounts of data, such as e-commerce sites with hundreds of products, each with options, a relational database is essential. For defined bodies of information, such as a dictionary or glossary, a flat file works well. A public relations practitioner might use all three kinds of databases in a Web site.

Each type of database requires careful determination of what to classify and how to classify it. A database is useless if it classifies data that few need or look for. **Classification** is not easy. It is a discipline that requires understanding of content and users. When building a database, the public relations practitioner should work with database specialists to avoid time-wasting mistakes.

Another term the public relations practitioner will hear is **data mining**. Data mining is a technique of manipulating huge databases to find trends and behaviors that would otherwise be missed. For example, one can isolate purchasing behaviors of discrete groups of individuals through data mining by linking census bureau records to Zip codes to store register slips and demographics. When used well, data mining can provide valuable clues to public relations practitioners in how to present messages effectively. It provides insight into users that the users themselves might not be aware of. One must be careful when data mining, because it is easy to be criticized for violating privacy. Here again, public relations practitioners need to use ethical judgment to determine how far to go.

DIGITAL PRESS KIT

PR practitioners have moved into distribution of releases, photos, sound files, and even video clips digitally. It is faster and easier to do than the old way of printing and mailing releases and photos on paper. Digital press kits have become something of a misnomer in the process. They are confused with online press rooms, and each resembles the other. Thus, for example, a movie studio posts digital press kits for its films, which consist of one page of hyperlinks to releases, stills, and production notes of each of its forthcoming films. A ski lodge's digital press kit comprises releases it has issued for the year. A major electronics company builds digital press kits for its products that include fact sheets, releases, and biographies of spokespersons. A student group in a NASA project provides a digital press kit that includes team member profiles, releases, and design presentations. Strictly speaking, a digital press kit is a package of materials sent to reporters by e-mail, or in the case of CD-ROMs, by traditional mail. It is not worth quibbling over definitions, however. Both have the same end of getting information into the hands of journalists and others. One is a push method—sending it to the reporter. The other is a pull method—placing it where a reporter can find it conveniently.

Reporters do not like digital press kits pushed onto them, especially if the press kits contain large photo files and other presentations that clog e-mail boxes and computer hard disks. Many especially do not like digital press kits in the form of CD-ROM disks that they have to load into their computers. As a general rule, do not send a digital press kit unless a reporter asks for it. When you first contact a reporter, keep a story idea simple and clear. If the reporter wants more information, then ask the journalist if he or she would like a digital press kit. It is better overall to leave the digital press kit online on a Web page and to provide a reporter with an active hyperlink to it by e-mail. That way, the reporter can click on the link and be taken to all the information that he or she could ask for without cluttering an e-mail box. Whatever you do, do not annoy a reporter.

DISINTERMEDIATION

Disintermediation applies to vast changes that online media are bringing to publishing. What it means is getting rid of the middleman standing between users and sources of information. For PR practitioners, it is getting rid of the **gatekeeper,** the editor and journalist between news sources and readers. In the editor's and journalist's view, it is getting rid of public relations practitioners who stand between journalists and sources. For activists and others, it is a chance to publish fact, opinion, and testimony that would otherwise be difficult to get heard.

Online, anyone can publish. There is no need to funnel content through someone to publish for you. This has profound effects. One can build a Web page where millions can view it anytime day or night. One can speak out in a newsgroup or pop off in a chat room to get heard. Online reinforces the need to adhere to basic principles of public relations and relationships. Both are built on trust and credibility. A consumer of information trusts an information source because the information checks out against other facts, testimony, and subsequent events. At any point where facts, testimony, and events cease to agree, credibility is damaged.

Online has as much or more misinformation as fact. Because anyone can publish, there is a welter of opinion, conflicting testimony, fantasy, and lies existing side by side. Bad information can overshadow good information, especially when bad information appeals to base instincts of human behavior. For that reason, the role of the gatekeeper will not disappear online. Gatekeepers check facts, testimony, and events that most users do not have time or inclination to do. Further, they discard irrelevant data and focus users on the meaning of facts, testimony, and events within the context of users' daily activities.

Disintermediation gives public relations practitioners flexibility that they did not have before, but it confers greater risk. For example, if a practitioner is afraid of what a reporter might write or say, one can record the journalist's interview and publish it online in its entirety so that users can see for themselves what has been left out of the final story. On the other hand, reporters can use e-mail to bypass public relations practitioners. Moreover, unhappy employees, or former employees, can just as easily reach out to reporters by e-mail, build their own Web sites to state their cases or go to newsgroups to complain.

Where gatekeepers, activists, and others are harmful is when they let personal opinions, biases, and performance interfere. That is, they decide what a story will be before publishing it, or they are too lazy to find out the facts before writing. (This is a common but rarely justified complaint of organizations that believe a reporter has victimized them.) Here is where public relations practitioners have power to respond by presenting a full body of facts, preferably before a story is ever written. However, it is better to cultivate an environment of trust in advance of publishing. No one wins tit-for-tat. Lack of trust poisons the environment.

A clear advantage of disintermediation to public relations practitioners is that it gives them a place to publish good information that otherwise is difficult to distribute. It might have been too expensive to mail fact papers, product brochures, financial information, and other organizational literature to vast audiences in the past, but with the Web, all this material has a place where millions can see it for nominal cost.

Increasingly, gatekeepers themselves rely on this information. Reporters visit company Web sites before they call executives. It is a quick way to brief themselves on what a company says it is doing, even though the reporters might not believe much of it. This places responsibility on public relations practitioners to make sure that information online is good, and here is where practitioners fail when they let Web sites get out of date or contain errors. Site maintenance is not just a nice thing to do: It is essential. An organization's reputation is affected when it is sloppy in how it speaks about itself. Even when a public relations practitioner does not have direct control over an organization's Web site, it is the practitioner's job as the guardian of an organization's relationships with key publics and gatekeepers to point out errors and to get them fixed.

DOMAIN NAME

The domain name of a Web site is an important marketing tool. A Web site name should be short and memorable: Short because it is quick to type in when one wants to find you, and memorable because there are millions of Web site names and you want something that people will remember easily. Unfortunately, choosing a domain name is not as simple as it used to be.

Before 1999, one company, Network Solutions, Inc., under contract to the U.S. government handled all domain name **registration** for .com, .net, and .org addresses. In 1999, the U.S. government got out of the domain name business and turned administration over to the Internet Corporation for Assigned Names and Numbers (ICANN: http://www.icann.org). **ICANN** walked into a hornet's nest of disagreement over the future of more than 6 million names already taken and the millions more to be assigned through eighty companies spread around the globe. The importance of domain names and ICANN's activities are so great that there is an organization dedicated to keeping its eyes on ICANN activities—ICANN Watch (http://www.icannwatch.org), and there are protest groups opposed to ICANN activities, such as The Domain Name Rights Coalition (DNRC) at http://www.domain-name.org/. If you are interested in tracking these issues, try Yahoo!'s full coverage page (http://fullcoverage.yahoo.com/Full_Coverage/Tech/Domain_Names_and_Registration/).

Some domain name issues are of critical importance to PR practitioners. One is over trademark protection. Cybersquatters had registered names of well-known brands and corporations and were offering to sell these for inflated prices. The organizations consider this trademark infringement, and the U.S. government agreed in an anti-cybersquatting act that opens domain name holders to heavy fines for taking trademarked names.

Ideally, the PR practitioner wants a short, branded domain name for a Web site that reflects an organization's name and the content of the site. If the Web site is for Acme Company, the practitioner would like to register Acme.com. But with more than 6 million domain names registered, that might not be possible. Someone—a legitimate organization—may have taken Acme.com (and, in fact, did in 1998). And if Acme.com is not a trademarked brand like Coca-Cola, there may be no recourse to getting it by law.

How does one find out what names have been taken? Go to **Better-Whois.com** (http://betterwhois.com/) and ask. For example, if you wanted to find out if online-pr.com was taken, you enter that name into the search engine. Better Whois.com then checks the name in the databases of all active domain registrars. It then tells you that the name is taken and by whom, when it was taken, and when the records for the name were last updated.

If you are fortunate, you might find the name you want on the first try, but chances are that you will have to try again. This is why you should have several variations on names ready to register. Acme.com might become Acmeco.com or Acmecorp.com or Acme.net. (Believe it or not, these names are taken.) You might have to give up the primary name Acme and describe the contents of the site. For example, if Acme is an office cleaning company, you might try cleandesk.com (taken) or dusters.com (taken as well) or pinneat.com (at last!). Finding a good name for a Web site tests your creativity.

Once you have found your name, consider whether you should register it in all top-level domains—for example, pinneat.com, pinneat.net, and pinneat.org. This blocks a competitor, activist, or other individual seeking to do you harm from aping your domain name. For example, e-mail hijacking is one of the dirty tricks that can be pulled on an organization that does not guard its name closely. By purchasing a look-alike name with only a few differences between the real name and look-alike, the hijacker waits for people to make mistakes in how they address e-mail. The difference between .org and .com can send one to a new site. The classic case is whitehouse.com—a porno site that apes whitehouse.gov—the Web site for the home of the president.

If your organization is a global company, also consider whether you should register it using a **top-level country domain name**—pinneat.fr (France), pinneat.uk (United Kingdom), pinneat.jp (Japan). It is surprising how many corporations forget to do this and subsequently lose a desired name in a country where they do business. By the way, sites that use a different top-level extension can be sent to the main .com site through a process called redirecting or bridging. Anyone who clicks on pinneat.fr is sent automatically to pinneat.com. To find out if a name is taken with a country code extension, you need to use a lookup service that checks country code databases. Try **Smart Whois** (http:// swhois.net/).

Registering a name is not as difficult as finding one in the first place. There are several registration services worldwide. For a list of ICANN-accredited registrars, go to InterNIC (www.internic.net) or ICANN (http://icann.org). Both will explain to you what is required for registration. For a database of country code top-level domain names, go to the Internet Assigned Numbers Authority (**IANA**) (http:// www.iana.org/cctlf.html) where you can find both the country code and the authority that administers it.

Initial name registrations last two years: Existing registrations can be renewed a year at a time. Registrars can offer one-year registrations up to ten years at a time. If one is not careful about renewal, the name will go back into the pool of available names. A registration service will provide ample opportunity for renewal, but it will work from data it has. If you change your e-mail or physical addresses, make sure that the registration service knows where you have gone. Finally, registrars set their own prices for name registration, so it pays to shop.

E-COMMERCE

Much has been and will be written about business transactions on line. Pure e-commerce businesses, such as Amazon.com, the online merchant, use public relations and publicity to support their growth. **Clicks and mortar** businesses—that is, traditional businesses moving online while keeping store-based retailing—also use public relations and publicity. In addition, Business to Business (BtoB) e-commerce and Business to Business to Consumer (BtoBtoC) use public relations and publicity to gain awareness for their offerings.

E-commerce provides public relations practitioners with a large potential for work. But, it is important to remain clear-eyed about what the work is. Much PR work is not online. It uses traditional media. Established e-commerce businesses have moved more public relations work to online, but they do not dismiss traditional media.

What has happened online in leading edge e-commerce businesses is instructive. A site like Amazon.com uses a broad range of public relations/publicity techniques to build relationships with customers. Amazon's online communications arsenal includes

- Sampling of music tracks.
- Self-authored and published articles about authors and works.
- Editorial reviews taken from its own and outside editors.
- Customer reviews published on the same page where a book or album is offered.
- Customer rankings: The level of popularity of a book, album or other item for sale in purchase circles affiliated with Amazon.
- Sales rankings: Books ranked by number of sales through Amazon.com.
- Listings of other works by an author or artist.
- Authors' interviews.
- Authors' bios.
- E-mail to let one spread word-of-mouth testimony about a book or album to another individual.

Some of this is republished content taken directly from press kits supplied by record companies and book publishers. Other information has been generated by Amazon.com or by Amazon.com's customers and visitors and adds to the aura of an online retailer with a close understanding of its merchandise and customers' preferences. All the information is part of the mass customization that Amazon.com uses on its Web site. Computers behind the Web page analyze what an individual has looked at or purchased before from the site and present similar content when the person returns. Amazon.com assumes that one's surfing and purchase patterns indicate one's interests, and for regular users of the site, this is likely to be true. Amazon.com understands the need to tailor information to individual interests and receptivity rather than rely on mass communication.

The need for building individual relationships with customers and other key audiences is just as intense in business-to-business e-commerce, especially where complex products and services are involved. Public relations practitioners willing to learn the inside of business-to-business products and services and to build credibility within their own organizations can provide valuable service to engineers, scientists, manufacturers, and others who know how to build things but not how to build relationships.

E-commerce is a compelling reason for public relations practitioners to learn online media well.

E-MAIL

We discussed the technology of e-mail in chapter 2. Here we deal with using e-mail to communicate effectively.

First to the anatomy of an e-mail:

Header Information	TO: jhorton@marstonpr.com **FROM:** jhorton@marstonpr.com **Subject:** X-raying E-mail **Cc:** **Bcc:**
Body	Stay tuned! We'll tell you how to use e-mail effectively
Signature Block	* * * * * * * * * * * * James L. Horton Senior Director Robert Marston And Associates, Inc 485 Madison Ave New York, NY 10022 Phone: 212-371-2200 Fax: 212-755-4598 E-mail: jhorton@marstonpr.com Web: http://www.online-pr.com * * * * * * * * * * * *

E-mail has three parts: **header**, **body**, and **signature block**. The public relations practitioner should use each well. The first part of the header, *TO:*, would seem to be simple. Either you get the address of the individual right, or your e-mail is kicked back. Actually, the address is one of the more difficult parts of e-mail. It is not always easy to identify the right person to send e-mail to, and indiscriminate mass mailing is disrespectful and annoying. Most employees, shareholders, especially institutional shareholders, and reporters have e-mail. Millions of consumers have e-mail.

E-mail list management is not a trivial subject. It is difficult to do and is just as critical as it is with direct mail. PR practitioners should outsource the drudgery of e-mail list maintenance but not the responsibility for getting names and addresses right. Lists are never completely accurate. They are more or less accurate. The practitioner sets the standard for accuracy based on the maintenance resources at hand and the list itself. For example, an e-mail list of 50 key institutional shareholders might approach 100 percent accuracy, whereas an e-mail list of 50,000 users of the company's product might never reach an accuracy level greater than 90 percent without huge resources committed to updating. As a practical matter it is better to keep centralized media lists and address books where all can look up addresses from a single location that is updated constantly. The time wasted in finding missing e-mail addresses or correcting addresses from one person's address book to the next is significant.

Practitioners cannot always know who a precise contact should be, especially a reporter, but at least they can find a contact who is close to where one needs to be. For example, there should never be an instance of e-mailing information about the latest Central Office telephone switch to a fashion editor at a newspaper. Unfortunately, building e-mail lists is not easy. There are few sources from which one can purchase accurate lists to start. List creation takes time and money.

Consider, for example, journalists' e-mail addresses. Some e-zines and news sites print reporters' e-mail addresses next to the reporters' names, but not all. On other sites, one can click on a reporter's name and write the individual directly, but not every site does this. Commercial media lists provide journalists' e-mail addresses along with phone number and mailing addresses, but they are neither complete nor wholly accurate. With more accurate (but not greatly accurate) mailing lists, such as *MediaMap*, one can identify reporters' beats and interests along with their e-mail addresses, but *MediaMap* has holes in its database where information is sparse or in error. Frustrated PR practitioners might consider spamming (see Spam) reporters—that is, sending out e-mail indiscriminately— but spamming is inexcusable laziness.

The *FROM:* line identifies the message sender. It is placed automatically on any message sent by an e-mail program. It is possible to disguise the *FROM:* line, called **spoofing**, but do not do it. Recipients tend to throw out mail from senders they don't recognize or that looks like a junk mail address. In addition, disguising the *FROM:* line is a breach of trust with the receiver who has a right to know who you are.

The **SUBJECT LINE** of an e-mail is important. It is the headline that entices a message recipient to open and read an e-mail rather than dump it along with fifty other pieces of junk mail received that day. Subject lines should tell a story quickly and invitingly and be clear enough that when they are archived, they can be found again. Boring or obscure subject lines invite readers to move along. Long subject lines risk being cut off in transmission. Pushy or sales-driven subject lines get thrown into the trash along with unopened e-mail.

Think of subject lines the same way that newspaper or TV editors think of headlines. They tell a story in a concise way—enough to let readers know the importance of content below the headline. Avoid making subject lines misleading. A subject line that promises one thing and body copy that says another are annoying and reduce credibility.

Junk mail houses often abuse subject lines, and some of their abuse fits under the heading of "stupid e-mail tricks." You do not want the reputation of a junk mail house.

CC: and *bcc:* lines are important because of what they show and do not show. A *cc:* line shows everyone else to whom a message was sent. A *bcc:* (blind carbon copy) line does not show who else got the information. (Some e-mail systems have *bcc:* but do not show it in a header). When sending the same e-mail to a group, you have the same choice that you have with a paper memo: Let others see who has received the memo or not. When dealing with workgroups, it is important for everyone to know who else has gotten the e-mail because that helps coordination. When dealing with individuals, such as a group of reporters, send it as a blind carbon copy. This kind of e-mail is about personalization. You are writing each e-mail recipient individually. When the recipient can read the names of the forty-five other individuals to whom you have mailed, personalization is lost. One common technique is to e-mail oneself and bcc: everyone else. This means each person gets an e-mail that carries only your name and the individual to whom it was sent as a blind carbon copy. The individual might guess that he or she is not alone in getting the e-mail, but they will not know who else is getting it.

Effective e-mail **body copy** is short. It makes a point quickly and cogently and gives a call to action in a few sentences. If a topic is too long to handle in a short e-mail, provide a means for a recipient to access more information quickly. Place a Web page address, spelled out fully as in http://www.online-pr.com), within the text for the user to click or attach a text file for the user to open. One rule of thumb for effective e-mail body copy is to keep it one screen in length. The recipient should not have to scroll down the screen to read, especially if you are trying to get the recipient to do something. There are other points to remember about effective body copy:

- Sequential selling: E-mail is a step-by-step sale. The first e-mail gets someone to reply. The second e-mail provides requested information. The length of the second e-mail is at the request of the recipient who may ask for lots of information or ask you to keep messages short. Third and fourth e-mails continue the dialog and build information and credibility until a decision is made.
- Grammar and spelling: For some reason, e-mail brings out the worst in writers. Body copy often contains grammatical and spelling errors. Sometimes this is due to the haste in which one writes, but there is little excuse for it. Use a spell checker, and if your e-mail program does not have one, edit e-mails carefully.

- Capital letters: By now, you should know that using ALL CAPITAL LETTERS IS E-MAIL'S VERSION OF SHOUTING AT MESSAGE RECIPIENTS. Do not do it unless you intend to shout.
- Emotions: Avoid emotional writing, such as joking and anger. It is easily misinterpreted. Check e-mail to make sure it does not convey unintended feeling. Unless you know an individual well at the other end of an e-mail and that individual knows you well, stick with neutral presentations of fact.
- Formatting: Most e-mail goes out as plain text without formatting. Some e-mail systems allow for word processing and hypertext with full formatting, but there is no guarantee that formatting will survive online or that a recipient's e-mail system can handle the formatting. Until you know how a recipient gets e-mail, stick with plain text and no formatting.
- Attached files: Be careful about files appended to body copy. They can be corrupted in transmission. The safest file is plain text without formatting and the next safest is the Rich Text File (see Rich Text File). One annoying habit of some e-mail systems is corrupting attached files forwarded through the Internet. In instances such as this, transfer the text of the file into the message body then send it. When dealing with journalists, do not append files as a general rule and get permission before sending an executable file—that is a software program that does something. Many newsroom systems are fearful of appended text files because they contain viruses, and they disallow executable files because they are the source of rogue programs.
- Video e-mail: Companies are developing e-mail into multimedia. For example, video e-mail is an attachment to plain-text e-mail. It has been used to send movie trailers to interested fans or video messages from a CEO or even copies of a company's TV advertising. The company that pioneered this technique is Mind Arrow (http://www.ecommercial.com)
- Interactive e-mail: Technologies now provide ways to deliver content through e-mail that establishes interactive links with other individuals, particularly instant chat rooms.

The final section of e-mail is the signature block. A signature block is the way for people to identify you and get back to you, if they wish. The signature block provides information about you that body copy does not. It identifies your company, where you are from, and alternate means of contacting you. Most e-mail programs automatically store and place a signature block at the end of a message. Some do not. Even if your e-mail program does not provide a signature block, write one out each time anyway.

An obscure signature block is suspect. One asks who this person is or what the person is trying to hide. At least one author (O'Keefe, *Publicity on the Internet*) does not recommend appending a signature block on a first e-mail contact with a reporter because the reporter will use the reply function to get back. However, with oceans of e-mail flooding reporters' electronic in-boxes, including a signature block each time is a way to enhance credibility.

Even though signature blocks are plain text, creative e-mailers have developed elaborate presentations around them, including quotations from authors, ASCII art made with typewriter characters and much more. Avoid doing this. It is a waste of space and time, and an elaborate signature block that looks great on your computer might look like hash on another's screen.

One final point about e-mail. If someone replies and asks you to remove them from your mailing list, do so at once. It is disrespectful to continue contacting those who do not want your e-mail, and it angers them. Should you ever have a reason to go to them in the future, a prior record of abusive e-mailing will not help your case.

We discussed **autorespond** messaging in chapter 2, but we raise the topic again because it is a useful tool, if used carefully. Automatic e-mail responses allow public relations practitioners to send frequently repeated information by e-mail without costly human intervention. There are many uses for autoresponse systems—for example,

- E-mailing event invitations to large groups. As people RSVP, an autoresponder sends back confirmations and directions (e.g., RSVP to party@company.com).
- Customer service answers to frequently asked questions (e.g., for cleaning instructions, e-mail to cleaning@company.com).
- Directions for activating an account or another process (e.g., for directions, e-mail to directions@company.com).
- Promotions where one is giving out information, such as recipes or consumer advice (e.g., for recipes, e-mail to recipes@company.com).
- Company advice and observations about current events (e.g., for latest company worldview, e-mail to companyviews@company.com).
- Product information and spec sheets for journalists and others (e.g., for product sheets, e-mail to productsheets@company.com).

Autoresponders handle thousands of personalized messages a day, and they work with Web pages as well. One important feature of autoresponders is that they capture e-mail addresses. This lets the public relations practitioner build a database of interested individuals.

The way to determine if a PR department should have an autoresponder is by examining information flow from the department on a daily, weekly, and monthly basis. Information that goes out a dozen times a day, 50 or 60 times a week, or 150 to 200 times a month can be sent more easily through an autoresponder, and the practitioner should consider reconfiguring work flow to take advantage of one.

The final use of e-mail that we will discuss briefly here is **listserv**. This is a software program that automatically distributes e-mail to addresses on a list. There are tens of thousands of listservs. For example, the word "marketing" in an online database (http://www.liszt.com) produced more than 180 separate listservs from all over the world on marketing topics. Generally, a group with a desire to track news, opinions, and events that might not be reported regularly will establish a listserv. Listservs usually have a moderator who determines what a listserv will redistribute. The moderator looks at submissions from members of the list and chooses those to send out. Listservs can be public or private. Public listservs carry information of general use; private listservs concentrate in information that has little value outside of the group that gets it. One gets on and off a listserv by subscribing and unsubscribing to it through e-mail. A database like Liszt provides explicit instructions for how to do this for each list that you might wish to subscribe to.

The public relations practitioner should consider using listserv in circumstances requiring an ongoing flow of information to large groups of interested individuals. For example, if one is coordinating a campaign to pass a law, a listserv is useful to let interested parties stay up with the progress, or lack of it, of proposed legislation. If one is tracking opinions expressed in the media on an issue of importance, a listserv can distribute article references quickly. On the other side of the issue, the public relations practitioner should check existing listservs to determine if an organization and its products and services are topics of discussion. Particularly with activist groups, it is well to understand what they are reading.

E-MAIL NEWSLETTERS

There are tens of thousands of e-mail newsletters of varying quality focusing on a myriad of issues. One Web site alone offers more than 100 newsletters on specific Internet topics.

An e-mail newsletter is a way to build relationships with individuals who have an interest in an issue or an organization and its products and services. But, e-mail newsletters are difficult to do well. They require careful reporting, editing, and presentation. Unfortunately, newsletters have a reputation of being a poor man's marketing tool. Online, they seem so inexpensive to create that the temptation is to jump in. It is only later that one finds how difficult it is to sustain a flow of good news, to manage mailing lists, and to get writing done on deadline in order to maintain frequency.

Do not start an e-mail newsletter without a clear idea of what intended recipients want for news, what a newsletter will report, and the resources needed to generate an interesting and relevant newsletter with enough frequency to build an audience. Newsletters are often abused as a communications medium, especially in print, and targeted readers often throw them out unread.

Most e-mail newsletters do not look like a typical newsletter because they come in plain text with little formatting. One cannot depend on fancy design to offset mediocre or uninformative writing. You can code newsletters in HTML (see chapter 2) to make them look just like a Web page or printed matter, but if a recipient's e-mail package cannot read HTML, the newsletter will show with coding inserted around text. It is nearly impossible to read. Some editors provide a newsletter in both formats—plain text and HTML. If the recipient cannot read one, the other suffices. Another approach is to use the Adobe Acrobat file format. This allows elegant presentation, but it also requires a recipient to download the Adobe Acrobat Reader software to open the file. If you use this method, be sure to provide a direct link to Adobe where recipients can get the software. Internal e-mail newsletters on the same e-mail system can use all the features of a word processor like Microsoft Word, depending on the e-mail system in use.

One effective presentation format for plain-text e-mail newsletters is to place all headlines at the top of the newsletter. That way a reader can determine quickly what he or she might wish to read and its approximate location by its order in a serial ranking. A second approach is to keep articles short. Some e-mail newsletters report in little more than a paragraph with a hyperlink to a Web page that holds the longer story. Although this requires the user to take an extra step, it is easier for readers to get a sense of the news.

Few readers finish a long plain-text e-mail newsletter. One rule of thumb is to keep an e-mail newsletter to two or three screens of text set at 65 to 70 character width (to prevent line breaks) with plenty of air space around each story, and each story clearly set off with lines or asterisks. A writer will find that there is little room for discussing topics at length. A good way to think of copy in a plain-text e-mail newsletter is to compare it to wire service copy for radio. Each wire service radio story is a short but complete synopsis of a news story that a radio announcer can intone in seconds.

With formatted newsletters, length is still a consideration. Because of the resolution of computer monitors, most readers will print a newsletter to read it on paper rather than scan it on screen. This means that multicolored formatting can be reduced to black and white, and the need for clear, cogent, and brief writing is not diminished. Further, you will need to check your color combinations to make sure that they will resolve in black and white and that text does not blur into backgrounds.

It is wise to include your signature block at the end of each newsletter so that readers have a way of contacting you. Many good stories come from readers themselves. And, always give the option to subscribe and unsubscribe to an e-mail newsletter. Provide the option to unsubscribe at the end of each newsletter that you send. It does little good to build an e-mail list of names that have no relevance to actual readership.

Newsletter mail list management is a major consideration. If one is maintaining a list of fewer than 200 names, it is possible to edit it manually. Soon after that, it is time to automate the process so that one does not waste more time maintaining lists than reporting and writing. One method is to use the same automatic subscription software that listservs use (see listserv). Another method is to assign mailing list management to a service. Some of these services are free, and some charge nominal monthly fees. For large mailing list applications with thousands of names, there are services that provide sophisticated database technologies. Look at eGroups (http://www.groups.yahoo.com) and SparkList (http://sparklist.com) to get an idea of how these services work. Large newsletter providers including iEntry (http://www.ientry.com/) and Briefme (http://www.briefme.com/) also are worth examining, and Liszt (http://www.liszt.com/) has a directory of thousands of online newsletters.

Many sites on the Web discuss e-mail newsletters. Try http://www.wilsonweb.com and http://www.promotionworld.com for more information.

EXTRANET

An Extranet is an Intranet (see Intranet) partially opened or joined to an outside organization's network. Extranets tie organizations, vendors, and customers together in cooperative business relationships that are forging new ways of doing business. See the Intranet listing and scan the information that Intranets carry. Vendors will want to know product specifications, for example; dealers the status of available company products and services; and customers the warranties and service conditions on their products. Before the Extranet, getting this information required calling the company, asking a company salesperson, or otherwise waiting for information to arrive by mail. With an Extranet, a user goes directly to the information, but an Extranet does more than cut out steps. It reduces the total cost of administration required for maintaining and delivering information through one-source publishing. Previously, data was republished for different audiences with an attendant increase in cost and error from rekeying.

The public relations practitioner is unlikely to be involved in establishing an operations-oriented Extranet, but the practitioner should be aware of an Extranet's existence. An Extranet can be used to publish relevant news to Extranet users. This might be key personnel changes that vendors, distributors, and dealers need to know. It can be new product or service introductions. It can be news related to a company crisis to give external audiences the facts they need to maintain confidence in an organization's ability to survive and succeed.

Treat an Extranet as a potentially valuable news medium for the organization. This may require coordination with Extranet administrators. The same online sources that discuss Intranets also focus on Extranets.

EYE CANDY

This loosely used term refers to graphical elements in Web pages, and it raises an important issue. Eye candy means both artsy and aesthetic graphics that support a Web page message and unnecessary decoration that distracts from the message. (A third use on pornography sites refers to beautiful men and women.) The essential meaning of eye candy is to delight the eye through visual appeal. Unfortunately, it is a common failing among designers to strive for striking visual effects to the point of submerging the message of a Web page. This is no different in print design where PR practitioners have fallen far too often for the allure of eye candy over content. In fact, some awards contests for public relations materials place too much emphasis on design over communication.

Web designers who place too much focus on eye candy can make the same mistakes that print designers make. These are nonsensical errors like placing dark type over dark backgrounds, using a typeface so small that it is nearly unreadable, laying text over busy backgrounds that interfere with legibility, or choosing fonts that cause a reader's eyes to ache in a short time.

The job of the public relations practitioner is to maintain balance between eye candy and content, and that is not always easy to do. Designers can assert a proprietary right over the look of a page and try to insulate themselves from "meddling." Award-winning designers particularly might believe that it is their job to find visual elements that grab and hold attention graphically. It takes patience and persistence to rein in this kind of personality without frustrating creativity. One way to handle eye candy is to define clearly what a page is supposed to do before it is designed and to insist on clarity of purpose throughout designing.

Web pages do not have to be dull or have the same look. They can be exotic or simple depending on the message one wishes to send. The only rule is that graphic elements remain subordinate to the larger purpose of the page and do not become an end unto themselves. The rule is the same for animated graphics. Because the Web can animate virtually anything, there is a tendency among Web designers to overuse animated graphics without a clear purpose for doing so. Animation adds complexity. It should be a natural outgrowth of the message the page is sending and not a gratuitous stick-on. Alas, on many pages, animation adds little to meaning.

FICTION

Fiction of all kinds and genres continues to find a place online, and PR practitioners should not discount it as a creative means of gaining awareness for a message. Fictional techniques are excellent for sending messages that might otherwise be ignored, such as the need for awareness about and prevention of AIDS or the dangers of taking recreational drugs. Unpleasant facts can be dressed in more appealing presentation. Fiction also can be used to discuss issues, such as creating a scenario that demonstrates the outcome of a policy.

Early in the history of online, authors created fiction for it. It often involved puzzles and challenges in fictional formats. The earliest online games were text-based and involved quests that required readers to figure out what to do and where to go. When games became visual, the text-based approach faded.

Many fictional techniques have been tried, some new and some old, and more will be invented. There are soap operas that include photos of characters and their diaries. There are serialized stories with episodes, much like a Dickens novel. There are stories with accompanying graphics, much like children's books. Some fiction is hypertext that allows readers to choose the unfolding of a story based on decisions readers take about characters and events. Some fiction is open-ended and allows various authors to add to a story over time. Famous authors like Stephen King have written for online, and there are dozens of classic novels reprinted online in full text.

Using online fiction should be done carefully. One should know that a target audience appreciates reading online or is willing to download fiction for reading later. One should choose a popular style that a target audience is likely to appreciate.

FILTERS

Filters are software technologies that prevent publishing of content. They block access through preset and user-entered criteria. Filters also direct e-mail to appropriate persons for response in customer response systems. There are many kinds of filters and they are used everywhere online.

E-mail filters are sometimes called **bozo filters** in a derogatory reference to individuals whose e-mail one does not want to receive. Bozo filters automatically screen e-mail by the name of the sender or sender's e-mail address. It is one way to reduce spam (see Spam) and to get rid of online hecklers or flamers. Internet and Web-based filters have several names, including porno filters and kid filters. Firms such as Surfwatch (http://www1.surfwatch.com/) and Web Sense (http://www.websense.com/) sell or provide filters that search for and block words referring to objectionable content.

There are several points about filters that public relations practitioners should know, because filters are not a panacea. For one, use of a filter should be automatic in organizations where

- Objectionable content can create a problem among staff.
- Staff waste time because of porno and other site surfing.
- There are large volumes of e-mail that need to be directed to specialists for response.

Second, filters are stupid by nature and cannot distinguish between acceptable use of a word and use that refers to objectionable content. If you were to look up the "sex life of a tsetse fly," a porno filter might block the content as objectionable. In cases such as this, you must go to the Webmaster and have the Webmaster remove the site exclusion from the filter database. Third, smart pornographers and others counter filters by using innocuous names to identify e-mail, Web sites, and contents. Unless a Web site has been logged into the software, it will pass the filter. Fourth, filters can block e-mail that you want because the e-mail uses prohibited terms.

There are two concerns about allowing unfiltered content into an organization—reputation and legality. Disclosure that hate speech and objectionable sexual and other content is readily available on an organization's computers could harm the organization's reputation. Second, it could generate lawsuits from employees and others who are offended by such material. What is on an organization's computers is a responsibility of the organization.

FREE SPEECH

Many countries do not accept that speech is free. For these countries, the Internet is a problem because, for the most part, there is little control on what is said on the Internet. Commercial online services, such as AOL and CompuServe, can control what is transmitted, but the Internet is often beyond the reach of law.

Some countries have attempted to control the Internet by denying it to their citizenry or by shutting down objectionable Web sites and arresting those who e-mail proscribed content. But other than a complete prohibition, there is no real way to block a free flow of information. The Internet has no boundaries and does not recognize geography or political institutions. Chinese dissidents can e-mail as easily from the United States as they can from within China. A Web site in Farsi can just as easily be located in France as Iran.

Governments are trying to control speech, such as child pornography, but they have said that they are limited in what they can do. The U.S. federal government and Federal Bureau of Investigation, for example, have both said that they cannot police the Web effectively, especially to stop hackers, even though they have dramatically increased online enforcement budgets. An individual can live in a country without reciprocal legal agreements with another and publish harmful materials—for example, companies' and governments' intimate secrets. Junk mailers, hard-core pornographers, and hackers all show an ability to survive online and to speak freely, even when legal authorities go after them.

A further barrier to controlling Internet speech is that it is relatively easy to stay anonymous. One can use an anonymous remailer to get rid of a name and address. This is a computer to which you send e-mail. The computer strips the address from the e-mail then forwards it to the intended recipient. One can **spoof** an address—that is, create a false address and cloak the header of a message to make it difficult for anyone to know where the message came from. On the Web, one can use a service like The Anonymizer (http://www.anonymizer.com), which blinds the Web site that you are visiting and prevents it from knowing who is accessing its pages. There are proposals to expand Internet addressing to the point where each device is allowed one address and one address only. This would get rid of faking addresses, but it would not get rid of anonymous remailing.

That said, it is harder within legal jurisdictions for individuals to attack companies without legal repercussions. For example, companies vigorously protect trademarks. Lucent Technologies, the telephone equipment manufacturer, once sued a porn site for using the address Lucentsucks.com. The Securities and Exchange Commission (SEC) has cracked down on persons who spread rumors to inflate or depress the price of stocks. The Department of Justice has targeted hackers who disrupt service or vandalize Web sites. Law enforcement departments nationwide have gone undercover to find and apprehend purveyors of child pornography. The Internet itself has long had a version of rough justice when an individual gets out of control, such as launching **denial of service** attacks against the person's computer. These attacks bombard a computer with requests until it can no longer function. Self-styled "hactivists" have threatened to unleash these attacks against companies they do not like.

It is unlikely that a time will come soon when speech on the Internet hews to rules of civility. Public relations practitioners can never assume that an organization's reputation is safe from libelous material and **hate speech**. But, on the other hand, the practitioner has plenty of online space and ways to defend the organization too. They should not fear online, but they should respect its power and understand how to handle it. To begin, they should understand that there are always **flamers**—people who vent—and chances are, **flamers** will rage against a practitioner's organization at some point. The key is to distinguish good flaming from bad.

Sometimes there is good reason for online users to "pop off." When an organization or individual has performed a bonehead act or botched customer service or otherwise made a mess of things, a scream can have therapeutic effect and alert an organization or individual of a need to apologize and/or reform. Public relations practitioners should be on the alert for this kind of flame. It provides valuable insight into the workings of individuals and organizations. Thousands of sites criticize companies and their products and services. Go to Yahoo! and look at its section on consumer opinion (http://dir.yahoo.com/business_and_economy/shopping_and_services/consumer_advocacy_and_information/. There are also sites that specialize in listing gripes for unhappy consumers.

Through **online monitoring**, practitioners can find and fix problems before accusations spread and involve others. Any large organization should be regularly monitoring what is said about it online by checking Web sites where its name and/or products appear, by reading newsgroups and watching chat rooms. The practitioner can also proactively **troll** among online newsgroups to lure them into telling what they feel. Trolling is like fishing in that its baited statements seek to provoke reasonable response, but one has to know how to troll just like one needs to learn how to fish.

Some individuals arecompulsive haters who attack everything and everyone. They appear to be sated only when at their most vile. Usually, the PR practitioner can ignore haters. More temperate newsgroup or chatroom members recognize them for what they are and ignore them or tell them to pipe down. (This never works, of course). They will also **flamebait** this kind of individual by making outrageous statements that entices the person to vent. (Of course, the hater flamebaits and trolls as well to gather supporters for the latest cause.) Sometimes, in an effort to control or stop a **flame war,** balanced members will praise an attacked organization or person and point to good features in ways that one would not expect in the normal course of relationships with key publics.

Perhaps the most difficult individuals are ones who seem reasonable but attack in ways that malicious intentions are concealed. They can gather supporters quickly to their causes. Rumor-mongers can harm an organization by passing on unverified information as if it were true. Procter & Gamble, for example, fights assertions that it is allied with devil worshippers. This scurrilous rumor came from a misreading of the company's "man in the moon" logo. In such cases, public relations practitioners and lawyers must stop speech causing direct harm through tracing sources and suing them, unless they are clever enough to hide and/or counter assertions with facts. Tracing requires technical experts, but countering assertions with facts uses longstanding public relations techniques.

One must take care in **self-defense** never to overstate a case, because others online are likely to find the flaws in arguments and exploit them. The public relations practitioner should remain calm and open. Responding to a flame in kind does not help the reputation of an individual or organization the practitioner is tasked to guard. The practitioner, if possible, should move an online debate offline by meeting with critics directly. This has two benefits:

- Misunderstandings online can be resolved more quickly face-to-face.
- If one can meet directly with a critic, the critic might stop broadcasting objections to online audiences.

For the most part, the ability to speak freely online helps organizations and individuals. The damage wrought by a few should not be allowed to overwhelm the advantages of open and broad communication. Organizations such as the **Electronic Frontier Foundation** (http://www.eff.org/) provide a valuable resource for free speech issues.

As noted earlier, free speech stops where organizations have control over computer and communications equipment that they own. This has been challenged but not successfully because organizations are also liable for the speech that passes through their networks. However such control has its limits. Where organizations are too rigorous or sensitive about what is said online, they can create serious morale problems. Many companies are aggressive about enforcing discipline, and one study revealed that more than 60 percent of 224 companies surveyed had disciplined workers for abusing the Internet.

Public relations practitioners should consider a **use policy** a standard part of organizational online access. A use policy states clearly what is acceptable and not online and provides an organization the authority to act on misbehavior. A use policy, normally prepared by legal staff, should at least include statements that

- Uphold laws and regulations prohibiting transmission of copyrighted material, threats, obscene material, and trade secrets.
- Prohibit placement of unlawful information, files and images on a company or client system.
- Bar the altering of files or programs on a company/client system without permission.
- Forbid use of viruses or other software that can damage a network and the information on it.
- Forbid use of a company network for nonbusiness purposes that can clog the network, such as online trading, music downloading, and private business.
- Uphold the right of a company to access and disclosure of individual e-mail.

Organizations have a right, and in some cases a duty, to stop e-mail internally that might be acceptable elsewhere, such as X-rated jokes and use of derogatory ethnic terms. Well-known corporations, such as *The New York Times*, have dismissed individuals who forgot restrictions on free speech when using an organization's networks. Some companies now use software that records every keystroke of an employee's computer, even errors, corrections, and revisions. This software is justified on the basis that a company has the right to know what its employees are doing.

GAMES AND CONTESTS

Because online is interactive, it is an ideal venue for games and contests. There are thousands of games and contests available and they are popular. One estimate is that 38 percent of all online users play games of some kind. Contests are so prevalent that one search engine, iwon.com (http://www.iwon.com/) gives away cash prizes daily in order to build traffic. Public relations practitioners should not ignore the power of games and contests to help spread an organization's messages and to support its reputation. But, like anything else, it is difficult to produce a good game or contest, and it is best left to professionals to do so.

When considering use of a game or contest, first look at the kinds of games and contests that target individuals play and the level of involvement they require. One way to do that is to search on "contests and promotions" in a search engine that looks for exact phrases or to visit a site like Contest.com (http://contest.com/) that describes itself as a portal for contests and for contest developers. You can also search sites like 100 Top Game Sites (http://www.100topgamesites .com/) or Searchwho (http://games.searchwho.com/), which has a special section devoted to games. You will find thousands of games and contests offered through the Web. You might find that you cannot compete online against what is out there already.

Next, before developing games, look at what is available to buy. There are many shareware sites that sell low-cost games from simple versions of Solitaire to multiuser dungeon shootouts. There are free games as well that one can download and use without worrying about copyright. Reviewing what is available opens one's eyes to how difficult it is to produce a game that individuals will play for a long time.

If a game is intended to be the central tool for message transmission, the practitioner should prepare to spend a lot of money and time developing a game or series of games that can engage individuals for extended periods. This is a risky endeavor. Commercial game developers rarely have runaway hits. Individuals tire of games easily and move on. If a game supplements the message and media that an organization is using, then modifying a shareware or free game might be the most cost-effective approach.

Few sites offer prepackaged contests for purchase. These are generally custom-developed for organizations by promotion agencies that know how to build and administer contests. Because there are thousands of contests, one should not expect a great return from one without a unique or rich prize.

Games and contests waste space online if they are not used. They become fillers of no great importance or consequence. The practitioner should measure the use of game and contests regularly and be prepared to change them or take them down if they are left idle.

HOAX

Online is fertile territory for practical jokes, especially jokes that play on fears, sympathy, or greed of participants. Among the more common pranks are e-mails alerting recipients to a powerful new virus that will wipe your hard drive clean, crash your network, and declaw your cat. No matter how preposterous such e-mails are, someone always takes them seriously. PR practitioners are frequent victims along with everyone else.

Hoaxes would be funny if everyone understood them for what they are. Unfortunately, many do not and they can create serious problems for nonprofit organizations and commercial businesses alike. The American Cancer Society and Make-A-Wish Foundation have been victimized time and again by chain letters that purport to be fundraising efforts or contain sob stories of little children who have one final wish before they die. One of the more absurd hoaxes was a crude e-mail drawing of "Tickle Me Elmo" with accompanying text that claimed that The American Cancer Society would donate three cents to cancer research for every person that passed on the picture. The Society was disturbed enough to open a page on its Web site to combat hoaxes, and it provided links to sites that track hoaxes for those who want to find out what is real and what is not. A listing of just a few hoaxes provides an idea of the things that get passed around:

- Sympathy chain letters. Send an e-mail to a sick person.
- Computer virus alerts.
- AIDS alerts: You can catch it in the following ways.
- Secret food recipes of major corporations.
- Organ theft alerts: Guard your kidney!
- Evil companies allied with Satan.
- Evil products allied with Satan.
- Paranoia about government activities.

The PR practitioner can do everyone a favor by stopping such hoaxes when they get loose in an organization. There are several ways to do it. One is by pointing out the absurdities, if absurdities are evident. Another is by contacting the organization named in the hoax to find out if the organization is aware of what is being said and how you should respond. A third is by going to one of several sites that track hoaxes to check on suspicious e-mails. Among these is Urban Legends (http://www.urbanlegends.com), which traces myths that get started anywhere, not just online. Another is Kumite.com (http://kumite.com), a site run by a security expert who has a hobby of tracking hoaxes. A third is a site for nonprofits that lists hoaxes by name and discusses them. It is Don't Spread that Hoax! (http://nonprofit.net/hoax/hoax.html). Finally, there is HoaxKill, a site run by a software company called Oxcart Software (http://hoaxkill.com).

Although it is tempting to test the gullibility of the human race through creating and distributing a hoax, do not do it.

INFORMATION RETRIEVAL

This is a huge topic, as large as the billions of pages of information available on the Internet and commercial services. There is no central-ized index online that works perfectly. Everyone is faced with the same challenge—finding information, failing to find information, or feeling uncertain that he or she has found it all. Using one search engine or catalogue (see chapter 2) is never enough to cover what the Internet holds and, anyway, search results can be useless—50,000 hits and not one of them is what one needs, but then, who would know because no one has time to look at them all?

Public relations practitioners deal in information to persuade indi-viduals to support organizations and individuals. They are, as some would say, concept salespersons peddling ideas based on facts and persuasion. Hence, PR practitioners need to be skilled online informa-tion finders.

As a general rule, commercial services are better indexed than the Internet. They are smaller, and they have disciplined ways of filing information. A service like CompuServe (http://www.compuserve.com) provides its own internal search engine and has its own research center. The Internet, on the other hand, is a vast warehouse filled with files from floor to ceiling. Users consult some files constantly. Other files, few ever look at. But, relying on frequently accessed files only is short-sighted when one is looking for hard-to-find facts.

The public relations practitioner should use a **search process** when trying to find information. This series of steps helps one narrow searches to likely resources. The process is not unlike library searching where one learns to find information tucked into books on miles of shelves, but it is quicker.

The first step of online searching is to ask about the availability of information sought. One can answer even simple questions in different ways, whereas searching for complex information requires a process. Try, for example, "Who was the 10th president of the U.S.?" An **online directory** like **Yahoo!** (http://www.yahoo.com) is one place to start to find an encyclopedia or U.S. history Web site. Yahoo! looks for the best pages to place in its directory. It does not intend to be a comprehensive record of Web sites. Asking for U.S. presidents on Yahoo!, one finds two sites that identify Whig John Tyler (1841–1845) as the tenth president. Another and faster way to approach this simple question is to use a search engine that allows natural language queries. **Ask Jeeves** (http://www.ask.com) lets you type a question then gives you an answer. The Ask Jeeves answer was better than Yahoo!'s directory because it provided a package of information that included a picture of John Tyler and a bio.

The second step of online searching is to use at least **two sources** to verify information that you find. This is no different from a journalist's multisource rule for reporting stories. The Web is filled with opinion, error and misinformation. Look for independent sources to verify facts and check the credibility of sources themselves. Even with simple questions such as the tenth president of the United States, check two sources because the amount of information one can find will differ and may prove useful. One rule of thumb is to see if a site has a section that tells who owns and operates it. Sites that do not have an "about us" are suspect. There is a lack of openness that casts doubt on content. Sites belonging to activists or others who strongly advocate a point of view need to be carefully checked. Look at http://www.virtualchase.com/quality/index.html or http://www.milton.mse.jhu.edu/research/education/practical.html for checklists to evaluate information.

With complex information, there is a greater variance of fact and opinion. For example, both Yahoo! and Ask Jeeves might not provide an immediate answer if one wants information about an event or policy that occurred during John Tyler's term of office, such as the Log Cabin bill. In fact, both services came up blank on this request. This is where the third step—a search process—enters.

The third step in searching is to use **phrase searching** and a **metasearch engine**. Phrase searching uses a search engine that can look for a set of words in exact order. Single **word searching**, unless a word is unusual or precise in its reference, invariably brings up thousands of useless hits. Most search engines use **Boolean search** techniques (named after English mathematician George Boole) to enhance word searching. Boolean searches connect or exclude words—for example, log AND cabin AND bill NOT home. Boolean searching is harder to use for most PR practitioners, whereas phrase searching captures what one is looking for more quickly.

Metasearch engines (see chapter 2) are search engines of search engines that send a request to several search engines at once. Phrase searching a metasearch engine casts a broader net, but not all metasearch engines allow phrase searching and not all metasearch engines search the right search engines.

Asking for "log cabin bill" on the metasearch engine **Metacrawler** (http://www.metacrawler.com), for example, quickly surfaced two references to John Tyler's administration. The same phrase search on a metasearch search engine called **Profusion** (http://www.profusion.com) raised six references on the first page.

If phrase searching and a metasearch engine fail to find the information that one is looking for, then the fourth step—brute force—comes into play. The brute force method is a last chance at finding a specific phrase without resorting to indirect methods. Here one chooses a large search engine, such as **AlltheWeb.com** (http://www.alltheweb.com), and performs a phrase search. AlltheWeb.com, for example, produced six accurate hits on "log cabin bill" instantly in less time than the metasearch engines. The problem with brute force is that even with phrase searching it digs up a lot of junk. Many engines will provide a relevance rating that provide a statistical calculation of how close a particular site might be to what one is looking for, but these are not always accurate. One way to handle brute force searching is to plow through references until it is clear that the engine is getting farther off the mark. Frequently, this happens within the first 100 results.

If brute force fails, the fifth step relies on one's creativity and intuition to find relevant information indirectly. It is surfing with intent. This approach often fails but can produce information that has not been well-indexed or has been listed under different terms—a frequent occurrence. Go to sites that appear to be close to the information that you need and look for terms close to the information that you want. Search on these terms. Also, check links from these sites to other sites. These might send you to frequently asked questions (FAQs) that describe the data that you are looking for or to a **link site**, a collection of links focused on a topic. Link sites can save time because someone has done the hard work of finding obscure information. If after searching affiliated sites, FAQs, and link sites, you still have not found the information, then it is possible that the information is not available or has been locked off.

Other types of search engines can help in the fifth step. Among these are **concept search engines** such as Google (http://www.google.com/) that look at words surrounding a key term. Sometimes these will produce better results than phrase searching alone. Then, there are search engines that rank sites by how often users access them. These are good for general information, but not for hard-to-find information that is not often accessed. Finally, there are **expert sites** that let one consult a live person who might provide the answer or refer you to where the answer is located. Expert sites depend on the "experts" staffing them, and many are not experts but individuals with a better-than-average knowledge of topic areas that one is investigating. Use an expert site carefully. Answers from experts might be wrong.

What we have discussed so far is searching for specific facts and content online. Other types of searches do not use these methods. These include

- **News searches**
- **Multimedia searches**
- **Reference and resource searches**

News searching and monitoring have their own well-established methods online. Sophisticated news search engines will use keyword, concept, fuzzy, Boolean, and statistical filtering. However, they restrict searching to news sites. Most news search engines download news to folders by topics that the user sets up. For example, one can set up a folder for the XYZ company name and other folders for XYZ's thirty product names. When these names show up in news streams, the news search engine stores the reference and/or story in its database then downloads them to the appropriate folder.

There are two key points that a public relations practitioner should check about a news searching site—the sources it searches and filters offered. Most news sites do not search all news sources, and, as a result, they can miss stories that show up in odd publications or little known e-zines—magazines that exist only online. Practitioners should check the sources covered by a news search engine before trusting it, and a good news searching/monitoring site like eWatch (http://www.ewatch.com) will list them.

Filters are another matter. Even the best filters can dump lots of trash into news monitoring folders, and as was mentioned, if keywords or concepts are not used in a news story, a filter will not pick up the story. A defense against filters missing stories is to place a lot of keywords and concepts into the search filter, but the downside of this tactic is that the amount of inappropriate news collection goes up. Determining how to search a topic is art and craft. One needs to try several combinations of keywords and concepts to find an optimum mix. But even then, it is possible to miss important stories because they are tangential enough to keywords and concepts that they slip by.

Some news monitoring sites provide statistics that can be useful. For example, if the name of a new product is the keyword, one can track the progress of publicity about the product through the number of mentions daily. Software graphs the mentions to provide a quick measurement of progress over a period of time. However, such graphs can be deceptive because they might not reflect true news trends. If one is serious about news monitoring, a service such as **CARMA** (http://www.carma.com) should be considered. CARMA provides sophisticated in-depth news analysis. Similar analytics can be built in-house using a database like Microsoft Access, but the PR practitioner should not attempt a do-it-yourself approach without a grounding in database theory and practice.

Another class of news retrieval is the **aggregation site**. This class of Web site collects headlines and stories from multiple news sources and places them on one page for quick reference. The public relations practitioner who wants a quick update on news can use an aggregation site. There are many aggregation sites by general news and industry topics. Two typical ones are http://dailynews.yahoo.com for general news and http://www.newslinx.com for Internet news. The downside to aggregation sites is that they are selective in the news they carry based on the news sites they cover. It is always best to visit at least two news aggregation sites to make sure that one has not missed an important story.

Multimedia search engines look for picture, sound, movie, and streaming media files, such as online radio stations. These are a subset of text search engines. With rapid growth of multimedia and expanding bandwidth, multimedia searching is increasing. One common use of multimedia searches is to find music available for downloading or listening. Public relations practitioners can also use multimedia searching as a quick way to identify visual and audio resources—for example, finding background music for an event, images for a slide presentation, or film clips for a video. Remember that much, if not most, of this material will be copyrighted, so one needs to get permission to use it, but it is still quicker than older methods of searching catalogues, consulting brokers, and plowing through thick directories.

Reference and resource searches find information in established works, such as encyclopedias, classic literature, online books, online dictionaries, and other sources that one would find at the reference desk of a library. Reference works are abundant online and several sections of the author's site (http://www.online-pr.com) list them. For example, there are more than thirty dictionary, thesaurus and other word-definition Web sites. One Web site alone (http://yourdictionary2.com) is a compendium of dictionaries for 100 languages.

The amount of published information available free online to the PR practitioner is astonishing. There are generalized directories, such as the CIA World Fact Book; specialized directories, such as an encyclopedia of symbols; full encyclopedias, including Encyclopedia Britannica; calendars, mapping sites, phone books, people finders, weather and time sites, Zip code directories, and reference desks. There is little reason for a practitioner to go to a library and even less reason for a practitioner to feel that basic information he or she needs is nowhere to be found.

Finally, there are specialized search engines and catalogues for specific areas of the Internet. Newsgroup search engines and listserv catalogues are two of these.

A newsgroup search engine stores most, if not all, bulletin board messages and conversations that occur on Usenet newsgroups. A frequently used search engine for newsgroups is **Deja.com**, now a part of Google (http://www.groups.google.com/). Usenet newsgroups pre-date the Web, and there are tens of thousands of them discussing tens of thousands of topics. PR practitioners search them to find out what is being said about an organization and its products and services. Large organizations usually find themselves a topic of conversation, and much of it will be unsubstantiated opinion. The importance of such talk is that it can tip off PR practitioners to issues and opportunities.

For example, a large consumer electronics company tracked critics and supporters through newsgroup monitoring. The company discovered that its electronic camera users were fanatically faithful, whereas its upper-end television owners were frequently unhappy with the quality of sets they purchased, the service they received, and attention they got from the company. The company also learned that audiophiles bubbled about breakthroughs that it made in digital sound recording.

The difficulty with newsgroups is that some are migrating to Web sites, depending on the topic. For example, the electronics company found that two of its most important sites for monitoring were bulletin boards associated with online consumer electronics magazines. Unfortunately, these sites are not indexed by a specialized newsgroup search engine, so users find them in different ways. Another source of opinion has surfaced as well that is part newsgroup and part discussion, but is not part of a newsgroup search engine. These are product/service review sites. Companies like Amazon.com (http://www.amazon.com) publishes user comments about books and products offered for sale. These reviews can flatter or devastate, and they have power because they are placed at the point of purchase. Similar Web sites, such as **Epinions** (http://www.epinions.com) allow anyone to appoint himself or herself a reviewer of any product or service. The credibility of these sites varies, but they should be checked.

A **listserv catalogue** carries notations on listservs used on the Internet. As was explained earlier, a listserv automatically e-mails materials to individuals on a list. Liszt (http://www.liszt.com), which calls itself a mailing list directory, carries more than 90,000 mailing lists. A listserv catalogue will not tell you much about the level of discussion within a listserv. It can only point you in a general direction. Unfortunately, tracking a listserv still requires signing up for the list and monitoring.

Two attributes help the PR practitioner when retrieving information on the Internet. The first is persistence, and the second is process. It is unlikely that the Internet will ever achieve the organization of a well-catalogued library. But, search engines and catalogues on the Internet are refined continuously. The practitioner who keeps abreast of these advances will find that information retrieval is easier than it used to be. One final note: Practitioners should use judgment about searching. One can search forever and get nothing done. Finding information is a first step to action. If the information is not there, one may still have to act. Much of life and management is ambiguous.

INTRANET

An Intranet is the most important online employee communications medium. Intranets use Internet protocol and processes on networks that may or may not tie to the Internet. These include Hypertext Transfer Protocol, Hypertext Markup Language, File Transfer Protocol, Internet e-mail standards, and Internet Protocol addressing systems (all discussed in chapter 2).

Intranet technology delivers low-cost multimedia to computers of every kind, no matter the computer's operating system. It provides cross-organizational communication using low-cost and global standards. Intranets speed delivery and presentation of data, text, sound, visuals, and video in ways that were never available before. They have a potential for building user-based learning organizations that join functions in the pursuit of an objective.

Before (and after) Intranets, organizations ran multiple computer systems that were incompatible and rarely universal. Accounting had one system, R & D another, marketing and manufacturing still others. Organizations could overlay e-mail on these systems, but it too was part of yet another system standing on its own.

What can an Intranet carry?

- Company directories and maps (if multilocation)

- Employee handbooks
- Benefits information and processing
- Resource materials
- Training (learning on demand)
- Sales and marketing information
- Company information—stock prices, earnings, sales, history
- Products and services plus specifications for them
- Company news—recent releases, internal information
- Link libraries
- Organization diagrams
- Office locations worldwide
- Internal marketing promotions
- Divisional information
- Departmental budgets
- Suggestion boxes
- Discussion groups
- Links to external Web sites
- Links to Extranets
- Videoconferencing
- Technical support
- Administrative support
- Software and tool downloads
- Demonstrations
- Order processing
- More, much more

An Intranet is an internal Web site (sometimes called a **personal portal**) that can be as complex as the organization that constructs it and as useful as an organization decides to make it. An Intranet is organic. It develops as an organization learns to use it to

- Unite individuals in the organization behind common issues
- Transform the organization to handle constant change.
- Increase productivity.
- Provide competitive advantage.
- Tap intellectual property held in the minds of employees.
- Create wealth.

An Intranet can come in several guises. It can be a source of published information. It can provide forms and scripts for limited employee interaction, such as registering for a training course. It can provide full interactivity with all employees talking and listening to one another, and it can become a part of an organization's core operations with integrated applications for information sharing and processing.

One department does not build an Intranet. They are too important for that. Teams design an Intranet around business goals, and public relations professionals will be members of teams. Each department providing content to and using an Intranet will have representation on an Intranet team. These include organizations such as human resources, corporate communications, marketing/sales, and customer/vendor relations. The tugging and hauling among team members and politics among departments can be overwhelming, especially matters of sharing information, relying on information created by others, forming employee teams harnessed to the Intranet, and keeping an Intranet a viable tool over time.

The simplest Intranet is a basic page and online presence. There is not much to it and probably not much use of it either. A more complex Intranet places organizational information on the internal Web page. This gets into issues of what to publish, the accuracy of information and maintenance. The next level is the collaboration Intranet that seeks to reduce time to market through enhancing team organization across an organization. This requires teams to coordinate openly and honestly. If teams have not coordinated before the Intranet, they will not coordinate after. It takes reformation. Finally, there is the Intranet that becomes part of company workflow, such as order routing and processing. The difficulty of this step is that it must connect to existing systems and work alongside or replace them. The real challenge is to get individuals to depend on the Intranet and to learn new ways of working that are simpler and more effective so that the organization can change embedded management processes.

Intranets shift the flow of information in organizations. They flatten access to information by making it available to all at the same time. There are fewer and, in some cases no management filters on data. This means that employees must learn to interpret information for themselves and to act without waiting for management to direct. This, of course, requires management's approval, and that might be difficult to get. With a fully developed Intranet, a company makes use of intelligence at every level rather than mid and top levels directing information and actions to the bottom.

Building an Intranet has several steps:

- Executive approval and funding
- Design
- Legal and policy considerations
- Information storage
- Development
- Maintenance and Security

Public relations practitioners may be involved in every one of these steps. In order to get executives to approve an Intranet or to enhance an existing Intranet, the practitioner can help assemble evidence needed to make a case persuasively. In site design and creation, the first step is to understand the audience. The public relations practitioner is trained to learn a target audience's ability to understand concepts, its technological skill, its demographic and linguistic differences, its desire for quick information, and need for feedback. The practitioner can be an audience advocate through design, content creation, and installation of interactive elements.

Policy particularly is where the practitioner can provide value.

- Content policies define what goes on an Intranet. A PR practitioner's goal is to remind all parties of the role of information in preserving and building relationships with employees. The Intranet team deals with current or archival information and, beneath these two categories, general information tailored to a job or to a person, such as remaining vacation days for the current year.
- Design policies determine the look and feel of an Intranet. The PR practitioner should push for a consistent look and feel across the Intranet along with universal authoring standards for how content is created and placed on it. An Intranet like the World Wide Web can be a disorganized dump of useful and useless data that confuses all and requires too much effort to use.
- Administrative policies determine who owns the parts of the Intranet and is responsible for their operation. The PR practitioner should opt for roles in employee communication and organizational news transmission. The practitioner also should fight for clear, concise language written and edited in proper Internet style that has the minimum of jargon and is understandable to the majority of the readers.
- Legal policies on the use of logos, proprietary information, trademarks, copyrights, and permissions also should concern the PR practitioner.
- Security policies are not the province of the PR practitioner other than making certain that they are followed in corporate communications departments. Viruses are everywhere, and an Intranet can spread them quickly.
- Usage policies determine what an organization tolerates with respect to Intranet usage as well as who pays for Intranet maintenance. The PR practitioner should push for policies that keep Intranets as tools and not playthings.
- Funding policies can be incendiary, and relate to whether an Intranet is centralized or decentralized. If centralized, all divisions pay into a fund, but the danger is that divisions may believe that the Intranet is not serving their unique needs. If funding is decen-

tralized, then each division will ask for power to develop its part of the Intranet in its own way. This can compromise the look, feel, and integrity of the Intranet. Either way may require continuous negotiation to preserve the business objective of the Intranet and employee involvement in it. Because an Intranet is easy to establish, an unhappy department can build its own guerrilla operation in a short time.

There are many mistakes that Intranet teams can make when building and maintaining an Intranet. Some are more common than others. They include

- Failing to gain and keep support from management and employees. This is why some call for centralized administration of an Intranet with decentralized infrastructure under the control of each division.
- A poor action plan for building it.
- Setting goals that cannot be achieved.
- Failing to focus on users.
- Ignorance of technology required. An Intranet development team might not be able to put in essential features because it does not know how to do it.
- Forgetting to make an Intranet interactive.
- Stuffing the Intranet with poorly edited and poorly structured content.
- Failing to meet deadlines.
- Failing to stay up with new technology and to apply it when appropriate.
- Failing to keep the Intranet maintained, fresh in feel, and useful.

Intranets ultimately pull users to them because they have the information that a user needs to do a job better, faster, and less expensively. If they do not do that or they cease doing that, users leave.

Intranets are huge topics of discussion beyond the scope of this text. Several books on building and maintaining Intranets are available through a source like Amazon.com. The PR practitioner assisting in the development of an Intranet would be well advised to read at least two of them. For online resources about Intranets, try The Complete Intranet Resource (http://intrack.com/intranet).

INVESTOR RELATIONS

Online has changed the way that investor relations practitioners communicate. Today, financial data is ubiquitous, beginning with the information that companies report to the Securities and Exchange Commission (SEC). It is available on the SEC Web site and other sites that make the SEC's EDGAR database easier to use. For example, see http://www.freeedgar.com/, http://www.www.10kwizard.com/, and http://www.sec.gov/. Secondly, general financial information is abundant online from Yahoo!'s financial information site to online news media such as TheStreet.com (http://www.thestreet.com/), CBS Marketwatch (http://cbs.marketwatch.com/), the Wall Street Journal online (http://interactive.wsj.com/), and news-wire databases that carry every release a company has issued through the newswire (see http://www.prnewswire.com/ and http://www.businesswire.com/). Third, there are dozens of sites that provide stock and mutual fund data, charts and graphs, access to analyst reports, economic data, corporate information and other financial data. (See the author's Web site, www.online.pr.com, for examples.) Fourth, the SEC's Regulation FD on fair disclosure has radically changed the way that investor relations practitioners communicate. The SEC rule restricts undisclosed conversations with stock analysts and institutional shareholders that guided these groups in advance of the marketplace as a whole. Essentially, the SEC stated that what is disclosed to one person should be disclosed to all at the same time, and the Web is useful to do that. Business Wire (http://www.businesswire.com/), for example, eliminated the fifteen-minute delay that it once imposed on posting press releases to its online database so that financial newswires could report first. Fifth, corporate Web sites have proven to be good repositories of financial information about companies and industries. Virtually every public company has a shareholder information section that contains its financial news releases, annual report, recent analyst calls, latest stock quotes, and other data. Sixth, the rise of online broadcasting services has made live news dissemination easier. Services such as Best Calls (http://www.bestcalls.com/) track investor conference call schedules and the calls themselves so that investors can listen in. Seventh, the rise of online trading services, such as Schwab (http://www.schwab.com/) and CSFB direct (http://www.csfbdirect.com/), and investor newsroom and chat sites, such as Silicon Investor (http://www.siliconinvestor.com/) and Elite Trader (http://www.elitetrader.com/), have allowed millions of investors to trade and discuss stocks without calling their brokers.

The net result of all these changes is that millions of investors via the Web have the same access to financial data as Wall Street insiders. The downside of this, however, is that rumors and lies have risen online as well. Companies have been plagued by bogus press releases run online, which caused dramatic stock drops; by stock touts in chat rooms and newsgroups making outrageous claims; and by direct attacks on company executives from unhappy shareholders. The investor relations practitioner today is as much a company defender as company promoter.

JOB HUNTING

PR practitioners know the benefits of online for finding jobs, and overall, it is easier today to find listings through the Web. On the other hand, the Web is not a complete resource, and practitioners should not abandon use of traditional methods such as looking at want ads and direct mail to potential employers.

Job hunting online consists of four broad categories: General job sources, public relations associations, public relations search firms, and company Web sites. For the most part, job listings are for middle- and lower-management positions. Senior managers are still found largely by executive recruiting firms or through direct contact.

There are dozens of general job listing sites on the We, including such broad national sites as Monster.com (http://www.monster.com/), Careerbuilder (http://www.careerbuilder.com/), and Vault.com (http://vault.com/) and local or state sites. News groups also carry listings such as misc.jobs.offered and biz.jobs.offered. You may find, however, that PR jobs do not often appear in newsgroups. Overall, job listing sites vary in quality from excellent to poor. One should never check just one site, and practitioners should avoid sites that make one pay to search listings or to post a résumé. On the other hand, practitioners looking to hire talent should expect to pay to list job openings.

Public relations associations, such as the Public Relations Society of America (PRSA) (http://www.prsa.org/) and International Association of Business Communicators (IABC) (http://www.iabc.com/homepage.htm) also carry job listings, but they are by no means complete.

Some public relations search firms are represented on the Web, but others are not. Moreover, the quality of PR search firm Web sites varies from useful to unusable. Practitioners should not depend on search firm Web pages, and they are better used as sources for names and phone numbers of search consultants. For a listing of names, phone numbers, and Web sites of PR search firms, use an online directory such as O'Dwyer's PR Services Directory (http://www.odwyerpr.com/) or Online Public Relations (http://www.online-pr.com/).

Company Web sites are frequent sources of job listings, but in this case, one should know the companies in which one is interested or the search can be long and fruitless. Often, listings will concentrate on specialties not in public relations. On the other hand, large public relations agencies, such as Burson-Marsteller (http://www.bm.com/) and Fleishman Hillard (http://www.fleishman.com/), carry career sections that practitioners should check. For listings of PR firms use a directory such as Impulse (http://www.webcom.com/impulse/) or O'Dwyer's Directory of PR Firms (http://www.odwyerpr.com/).

Finally, there are tips and techniques for online job hunting that practitioners can employ on their own. For example:

- Post a digital version of your résumé with examples of past work experience on your home page if you have your own Web site.
- Place the word "résumé" in the Web site address to increase your chances of pickup.
- Place links to Web sites of present and former employers, colleges, professional associations, and publications on your digital résumé.
- Create a simpler version of your resume to send to a recruiter or employer and let them know that a longer version is available online.
- Read the privacy policies of online job boards to prevent unwanted eyes from viewing your résumé.
- Use niche job boards in your field to post your resume.

There are a series of tricks to find resumes on the Web that might be of use to job hunters who want to know who they might be working with. They include

- Flipping: Find résumés or conference rosters to a company that might yield biographies, e-mail addresses, and other details. Use a search engine, such as AltaVista. Use "link:" or "linkdomain:" (Hotbot) to search for links to a certain company's Web site. Type "link: (name of company)" and "title" and title:résumé (e.g., Link:IBM and "public relations" and title:résumé).
- X-raying: Identify employees by going to those places on a company's Web site that are not accessible from the home page. Type "host:" or "url:" before a company's name with the key words (e.g., host:lucent.com and "public relations").
- Peeling: Find staff directories or contact lists embedded in web addresses. Look at long addresses and systematically cut them back until you reach words like "résumés" or "people" or "attendees" to see if name lists show up.
- Anchor Search: Web pages have words called "anchors" that describe the page and that can be a giveaway. Type anchor:"view résumés" and "title" (e.g.: anchor:"view résumés" and "public relations").

- Harvesting: Look at documents, résumés, and home pages for keywords, links, references, and locations that can assist further searches.
- Peer searches: Use a metasearch engine to find people with similar qualifications. Have the metasearch engine search on key information such as a company's e-mail address or name and see if it turns up staff rosters.

MEASUREMENT

Measurement is a challenge to public relations practitioners and advertisers who want to know if campaigns on Web sites are working.

FAST (Future of Advertising Stakeholders: http://www.fastinfo.org) is a nonprofit group of companies that has joined together to make Web-based advertising "comparable in quality and nature to those employed for other commercial media. . . . That is to encourage the development of accurate, unbiased, precise, reliable and actionable estimates of consumers' opportunities to see ads and other online media content" (FAST Web site).

FAST defines three types of online advertising measurement and a set of principles that are also of use to PR practitioners baffled by measurement questions. The FAST principles do not solve measurement problems, but they provide a way to think about them. FAST principles also do not account for interaction with Web advertising or Web content but only viewing of it. This is a significant omission because when a user clicks on an ad (called a *click-through*), the user reveals an interest in the ad's message that viewing alone does not. Arguments over whether to measure viewing or click-through have sparked sharp disagreement because far more people view ads than click on them. Further, click-through is a direct marketing and not a display advertising measurement, a point of contention between two industries with different economics and goals. Display advertisers believe that they should get credit for the awareness of a product or service that a display ad creates. Direct marketers get credit only for responses to advertising that they create. Ideally, measurement includes both viewing and click-through, and most major sites are using such a combined approach.

According to FAST, what one measures online are "media audiences, their size, market-relevant characteristics and media-relevant behaviors" (FAST Web site). What one looks for are measures that are at least as good as traditional media, moving to measures that are more accurate and detailed than traditional media measures.

FAST defines measurements as

- **Site-centric**, focused on Web site server log entries.
- **Ad-centric**, focused on ad server log entries.
- **User-centric**, focused on the person using online media.

Since these definitions were constructed, another has been added focusing on **browser-based measurement.** This technology downloads a tiny software program, or applet, inside an ad sent to the browser on a user's computer. The applet sends back real-time data on where an ad is running and how the user interacts with it.

For the most part, the PR practitioner will be concerned with site-centric and user-centric measurement, but the "objective is to count or estimate the number of occasions when a person has the opportunity to see an element of online media content –advertising or editorial" (FAST Web site).

User-centric systems use panels, similar to TV rating panels, to determine media and marketing characteristics of site users. Services such as Nielsen/Net Ratings (http://www.nielsen-netratings.com/) and Media Metrix (http://www.mediametrix.com/) offer these panels, and they are expensive—too expensive for many PR practitioners. Panels are not precise even when statistically accurate, and they have been controversial. For example, Nielsen television ratings can tell how many households watched a TV program and the broad demographics of these households, but it cannot tell if you watched the program and your demographics. Theoretically, with huge online user panels (and online panels can measure in the millions), one could define how large sites are viewed by user, by page, and by demographics, but this will not work easily with smaller sites. Moreover, the statistical validity of online panels is still in question.

Both site- and ad-centric measurements count the delivery of ad and editorial exposures through analyzing logs on the computer server where a Web site is kept. But, they do it in slightly different ways. With site-centric measurement, each time a user requests the server to send a Web page, the server stores the address of the user's computer and the address of the Web page. A site-centric measurement can track a page request back to a specific IP address number—that is, your computer or the organization where your computer resides— but it cannot tell much about you. Further, site-centric log analysis remains in the control of a Web site owner, who has an incentive to boost traffic counts, and not an impartial third party, such as an audit firm.

Ad-centric measurement, on the other hand, uses server-log analysis from companies that place ads on networks of Web sites, such as DoubleClick (http://www.doubleclick.com/). The benefit of this kind of measurement is that it counts consistently the ads sent to a Web site and to a user. However, these systems can have difficulty identifying precise demographics of users accessing a site, although they can maintain through use of cookies a close record of what a person views. FAST also sees a conflict of interest with these companies because they have an incentive to claim a larger number of viewers than existed. FAST says that both site- and ad-centric measurements require impartial auditing. Two firms that offer such impartial auditing are ABC Interactive (http://www.abcinteractiveaudits.com/) and BPA International (http://www.bpai.com/).

For PR practitioners, getting page-level detail of a site's traffic, even though it is logged, is not easy. There are no PR-based reports yet of how many visitors saw a specific Web page where, for example, a story about a company has appeared. (However, it is reasonable to assume that someday a service will make page-based measurement available for PR.) Ideally, what PR practitioners might like is a combined report that includes the count of individuals who saw the page and of those who interacted in some way with the story through writing to the reporter, discussing it in a newsgroup, or sending the story to another. All these levels of interaction exist on Web news sites, but they are not universal nor are they measured. Such a combined report would be a huge leap forward over traditional media measurement, even though server log analysis is not precisely accurate because organizations can use a single Internet (IP) address for many employees.

So what is a PR practitioner to do until the future arrives? Stay with the crude measurements of clip appearances and total site traffic that can be documented. Regrettably, web clipping reveals only that a news story appeared, but not how many read it. This is not much different than what practitioners do today when they use circulation figures of magazines and newspapers.

META TAGS

Meta tags are optional description lines placed at the beginning of a Web page to identify it to search engines and to help search engines classify the page in their databases. These tags are invisible to Web page visitors unless the visitors look at the page in HTML formatting code, also called source code. Most search engines log Meta tags in their databases but not all. Go to **Search Engine Watch** (http://www.searchenginewatch.com/) to find a listing of search engines that read Meta tags and those that do not.

As a practical matter, PR practitioners should use Meta tags, even though they are of limited value in getting a better site ranking from search engines. Tags are of two kinds:

- **Keywords** describe the content of a site.
- **Content description**, a sentence, summarizes what the site is about.

Often search engines print the content description of a Meta tag in a short listing when they deliver results to users. This short description provides an opportunity to describe the site and to invite users to come to it. It is a promotional tool. Keyword descriptors heighten the chances of your site coming up when a person uses that descriptor while searching. The challenge with keywords is the numerous ways in which a person can ask for content that is on your site. This makes for long keyword sections in Meta tags, in order to cover possibilities. Here is an example of Meta content description and keywords.

```
<meta name="description" content="Online Public Relations
is dedicated to helping you deliver better, faster, and
less-expensive online PR.">
<meta name="keywords" content="PR, online PR, Online pub-
lic relations, marketing PR, promotion, publicity, On-line
PR, public relations online">
```

One thing to avoid is repeating the same keyword over and over to trick a search engine into giving a site a better ranking. Search engines stop such deception through automatic limitations on repetition. Here are some other tricks that search engines ignore as well:

- Invisible text: An early and oft-used trick was to repeat a keyword on a home page with text matched to the color of the background. Search engines caught onto this quickly.
- Tiny text: This attempts to do the same thing as invisible text, but it uses tiny script. It does not work either.
- Page redirects: These are pages that automatically send you to another page in a short period of time. Some search engines do not like these.
- Multiple page submissions: Some people submit their pages several times on the same day. Search engines do not like that.

Some recommend that Meta tags be placed on every page of a Web page, and others do not. Placing Meta tags on each page allows one to tailor tags to the page, and it enhances the opportunity for search engine pickup. This is good advice, but for large sites, it generates extra work.

A final use of Meta tags is to tell search engines when not to index a site. There are reasons that one might not want the contents of a page placed in a database where it is generally available. There are times too when one does not want a site indexed at all. These are semiprivate sites for individuals who know where the site is and know how to find it, but are not really open to the population at large. For example, one is a site that is intended solely for the use of an organization's employees. In this case one can use the following phrase:

```
<META NAME="Robots" CONTENT="Noindex">
```

Unfortunately, not all search engine robots respect that tag. They go ahead and scan a site anyway.

One final note about Meta tags is of concern to PR practitioners. Competitors and others can hijack tags and descriptors. The author discovered an instance of this when searching the name of a specialized consulting company. Each time the company's name came up in a search engine, the competitor's name came up below it. A search of the competitor's site showed that it had placed the name of the specialized consulting company in its own Meta tag keyword index. The consulting company was not amused, and there have been lawsuits over such chicanery.

MULTIMEDIA PUBLISHING

Online is ideal for publishing data, text, sound, video, and images. The challenge is learning how to publish multiple media well. The best implementations integrate multimedia into a package. Each part of the package supports the message one is delivering. To see how this works, visit a multimedia news page, such as **MSNBC** (http://www. msnbc.com/). On a typical MSNBC page, you will find

- The headline and lead of a story in large type. The rest of the story does not show unless you click on a text link for "complete story." News skimmers can either scan and go on or click to go in depth.
- A live quote from a stock ticker for the company discussed.
- Links to recent financial reports about the company.
- Links to the *Wall Street Journal* Interactive edition with more news.
- Video and audio news reports about the story.
- Pictures related to the story.
- Links to previous stories on the topic.
- A link to a bulletin board to discuss the story.
- A minisurvey asking readers to rate the story.

Here in one neatly formatted and easy-to-use page is everything that one might wish to know about a topic. The editors use multimedia to deliver news from all possible angles. This is multimedia publishing at its best, but it is not flashy nor are there animated graphics whirling in the foreground

PR practitioners have already learned a great deal from this approach to multimedia. Corporate Web pages regularly publish text news about an event and any video or audio that went with it. For example, an appearance by the CEO in a financial forum is placed on the site as a video file along with the text of the CEO's remarks. Video and audio recordings of the annual shareholders' meeting are kept on a site along with a four-color presentation of the company's annual report and product brochures. Video and audio on topics of interest to users also find their way to appropriate sections. In some cases, video and audio links are provided to major events such as trade shows.

Analyst teleconference calls are opened live to listeners and archived on sites for future reference. Slide programs that go with the calls are placed there as well. A ticker gives the company's current stock price. "Click to talk" phone links and chat screens also have found their way to sites. One can click a phone symbol on the screen then talk through a computer's microphone to a service center or write requests through a chat window.

Such multimedia technology is not for amateurs. It requires expert technologists to install and implement. PR practitioners should get help from the start, but they should know how to structure and deliver multimedia information to users in order to guide technologists.

NEWS DISTRIBUTION SERVICES

News distribution services, such as **BusinessWire, PR Newswire,** and **Internet Wire**, thrive online. They have global reach today for a fraction of the cost of distribution wires they maintain. Secondly, they can deliver more media than with their wire services. Further, major online services are indexed in online databases and are searchable by stock symbols, keywords, and phrases. A partial listing of databases that carry PR Newswire includes

- Altavista
- America Online
- Bloomberg
- Bridge
- CompuServe
- Dialog
- Dow Jones news/Retrieval
- Excite
- Lexis-Nexis

- Lycos
- Microsoft communities
- NewsEdge
- Quicken
- Reuters
- Yahoo!
- Ziff-Davis Interactive

All these advantages benefit PR practitioners who use online news service distribution. In addition, online news distribution services do more than send out press releases. They service and archive video, audio, photos, press releases, slide shows, trade show news and calendars, news by industry, expert sources, and more. They provide streaming video and audio news. They will handle a company's investor relations site and create a site that looks like and is linked to an organization's Web site but is managed by the newswire. News distribution sources, such as **ProfNet** (http://www.profnet. com/), provide a flow of press queries to PR practitioners and experts to reporters.

There is one other advantage to PR practitioners of online news distribution services. The practitioner can see quickly the services that reach countries other than North America. For example, **Xpress Press** sends news to journalists in thirty-six countries (http://www. xpresspress.com/) while **Pressline**, a German service, reprints releases online on its Web site (http://www.pressline.com). The PR practitioner can experiment with different services to see if coverage from one country to the next is better. For practitioners working in global companies, online can save a lot of time in distribution of news to far-flung offices and plants.

One other point about online news distribution is worth noting. Internet start-up companies understood early on how online had changed wire service distribution. They issued dozens of press releases about themselves, many of which were hardly news, in order to generate "buzz" through online databases that the companies knew that both investors and financial analysts check. Although this technique has earned a bad name, companies still do it because they know that more information is better than no information when competing for venture capital dollars. Responsible PR practitioners have argued against the practice with little success.

NEWS PUBLISHING

Online is an abundant source of published news, if not the most influential. Today, most news ends up online either in real time or stored in archives. The well-known brand names of traditional news—*The New York Times, Washington Post, Wall Street Journal, Financial Times,* CNN, BBC, and so on—are online and bring their credibility with them. Furthermore, most of them are breaking news on their online sites before the news appears in print or on TV. Pure online publishing operations, such as Salon (http://www.salon.com/), Slate (http://slate.msn.com/), or Slashdot (http://www.slashdot.org/), have special interest appeal and less overall credibility, although their stories have occasionally beaten reporters in traditional publications. Online news publishing cannot be ignored because it is a prime news source.

There are two rules of thumb about online news publishing: Good or bad news spreads quickly online, and local news is not local. Once a story is published anywhere online, it is available globally.

News sources include

- **Enterprise news:** News stories generated and published first online.
- **Republished news**: Most news online is still published elsewhere and placed online at the same time or after appearing in another medium. For example, the contents of Business Week or Fortune show online shortly after subscribers receive copies.
- **Wire service news**: Wire services have transitioned to online delivery of news. Reuters leads in providing news to Web sites, but Associated Press is not far behind. AP started supplying news to commercial providers such as CompuServe well before the World Wide Web was invented. Many Web sites place Reuters and/or AP wire feeds directly onto their sites with little or no reformatting. Wire services such as Dow Jones, Bloomberg, and BridgeNews also are online.
- **Local news**: Most local newspapers, television, and radio stations have their own Web sites with locally generated news. These sites vary in quality and inclusiveness. Some sites are easy to use, and some are baffling.
- **Multimedia news**: Online invented integrated news reporting for readers and/or viewers. Multimedia news places text, audio, video, graphic, archival, and other information under a single headline. This provides an in-depth briefing on a topic from a single source. MSNBC is a leader in this development.
- **News aggregators**: These sites place text feeds from several sources into a single combined Web page display. Yahoo! has a large news aggregation site, for example. News aggregation tends to differ from multimedia news because it is not as tightly integrated.
- **News broadcasters**: Broadcast news services today exist online as well. This form of news uses streaming media (see chapter 2) to

provide a report that looks like any news broadcast one would hear on radio or see on local or national television.

- **News distribution services**: These are the traditional paid services such as PR Newswire or BusinessWire. There are many news distribution services on the Web, some of which exist only on the Web. (See **News Distribution Services**.)
- **Personalized news**: Major news organizations offer users personalized news. One enters a Zip or postal code, for example, and local news, weather, sports, television listings, and more are automatically fed to the reader. Typically, this news is taken from existing news streams and is not locally generated. One still has to go to the local news source for locally reported stories.
- **News indices and search sites**: Because there are so many news sources online, there are online indices and catalogues of news Web sites. These attempt to index in one place newspapers, magazines, and other news sources worldwide. American Journalism Review's AJR Newslink, for example, is a comprehensive site with 20,000 links to newspapers, magazines, and broadcasting sources—http://ajr.newslink.org. Editor & Publisher has a similar site (http://www.mediainfo.com/) and Publist (http://www.publist.com/) indexes 150,000 publications.
- **World news**: Several Web sites attempt to synthesize local news from across the globe into a single, well-edited package. Some of these packages republish news stories, and some are links to newspapers and broadcasters by country. A UK organization called Megastories is one example of an organization pursuing this approach—http://www.megastories.com.
- **Ezine/Webzine news**: These are news sources created for and published only online. Unfortunately, they are poorly indexed and often hard to find. And, they go in and out of existence quickly. Many do not provide news at all but entertainment in the form of short stories, poems, comics, and novels. Others provide commentary on politics, computers, the Internet, and a variety of other issues. E-zines are developing as a viable independent source of online news and are becoming more important as time passes.

With all these online news sources, is online a prime place for generating news stories? That is, should a PR practitioner approach online news media first with a story and traditional media later? The answer is, "It depends." Traditional media maintain credibility, if not the reach that online media have. Traditional media also have more journalists working for them than do online media, although this is changing. (Look at http://www.onlinenewsassociation.org/ and http://www.netpress.org/ for associations of online journalists.)

Even news publishers who report on online companies and activities, such as Industry Standard or Wired, are still published on paper, and their reporters work for the print edition as much or more than the online edition. However, some of their reporting never appears in the print editions but exists only online. In fact, more news media are building dedicated online staffs whose work appears online first.

Where publishers have assembled staffs of purely online journalists, one must ask whether the readership of this particular online effort is as great or as far-reaching as a print version. If it is, approaching an online journalist first might be the best thing to do. Depending on the topic, approaching online journalists first might be as effective as going to traditional media. Technology topics, for example, are covered in-depth online and have enormous readership. Medical topics are another area in which readership online is high. PR practitioners need to investigate each subject area in which they work to determine what to do.

Traditional print, television, and radio media will not go away soon, if ever. They have advantages that online does not have. It is still easier to pop a newspaper or magazine into a brief case and take it with you. It is easier to listen to the radio in a car, and television on a TV set is better than TV feeds on the Internet. Wireless appliances will not change that convenience right away, if ever. The notion that individuals will read newspapers off portable screens as they sip their coffee in the morning is a dream. The technology is not there, although should it reach the point where it is functional, traditional news organizations will save hundreds of millions annually in press, ink and news distribution costs.

We dealt with writing effective e-mails (see E-mail), but it is important to emphasize that brevity and newsworthiness are important when dealing with journalists. A typical journalist will get several dozen phone calls or voice mails a day, several dozen e-mails, several dozen mailed press releases, and several dozen faxes. The journalist can rarely look at them all. In fact, it is likely that a journalist will delete an e-mail from an unknown individual rather than read it. PR practitioners need to place even more emphasis on bringing the right information each time to a reporter and avoid wasting a reporter's time. It also means that practitioners should work hard to personalize approaches to reporters via e-mail, even in the subject line.

NEWSGROUPS

Newsgroups are **online bulletin boards**. They come in several forms—commercial bulletin boards on services such as CompuServe and AOL, Internet newsgroups that use Network News Transfer Protocol, and Web page bulletin boards. There are tens of thousands of online bulletin boards, and they are useful public relations tools for PR practitioners who use them carefully. On the other hand, online bulletin boards can be a source of ill will and flaming against practitioners who bungle their presence and appear to be selling rather than discussing a topic.

Newsgroup bulletin boards

- Place information before target audiences that want to know about it.
- Identify friends and enemies of an organization on the basis of who responds to a posting.
- Build lists of customers and friends through providing giveaways that prompt participants to give you their e-mail addresses.
- Enhance sales of a product or service.
- Gain understanding for an issue or position.

Proper use of newsgroups for publicity requires care. The practitioner's first step is to find a newsgroup that makes sense for the product or service being publicized or issue being discussed. This is not easy. On CompuServe and AOL, bulletin boards are called forums. CompuServe has, for example, 33 computer forums and 26 business forums, including the venerable PR & Marketing forum (PRSIG). On the Internet, there are more than 50,000 newsgroup bulletin boards in many languages divided broadly into:

- Alt: Alternative. An anything-goes category.
- Rec: Recreation. Discussion about arts, games, hobbies, and the like.
- Comp: Computers. Discussions about hardware, software, languages, operating systems.
- Soc: Society. Discussions about social issues and cultures.
- Misc: Miscellaneous. Discussions of just about anything that does not fit in the other categories.
- Sci: Science. Pure and applied science discussions.
- News: News about the Usenet news network and software.
- Biz: Business. Discussions about business, products, and services.
- K12. K through 12 education discussions.
- Humanities. Discussions about literature and fine arts.
- Talk: Talk. Discussions and debates about current issues.
- Regional: Discussions specifically about a country or U.S. state.

On all newsgroup bulletin boards whether commercial, Web, or Internet-based, the quality and importance of discussions vary enormously. Some newsgroups are barely alive. Others are crowded with interested users learning from each other. Some are venues of flamers who shriek at one another for no apparent purpose. Some are hate sites. Still others are a succession of come-ons and advertisements. It takes hard work and careful sifting to find bulletin boards that are right for a particular product or service, and some PR practitioners question whether it is worth the effort. The answer to that is that "it depends." Until the practitioner has searched what is available, there is no way of knowing whether a newsgroup bulletin board exists that is right for messages a practitioner is sending.

Finding appropriate newsgroup bulletin boards is a multi-step process.

- Step 1: Establish a preliminary list of newsgroup bulletin boards that seem appropriate.
  - ➢ Check commercial services. Scan AOL and CompuServe to see whether they have bulletin boards that match the product and service that you are publicizing. Both have search engines. Try several keywords related to your product, service or issue to see what comes up.
  - ➢ Check the Internet. Use a search engine like Deja.com, now a part of Google (http://www.groups.google.com/) to identify newsgroup boards that might seem appropriate.
  - ➢ Check Web sites: Because there is no organized way to find Web site bulletin boards, the practitioner might have to visit industry Web sites and check for active boards. Some are now more active than Internet newsgroups and commercial service forums.
- Step 2: Investigate the preliminary list.
  - ➢ Check to see how often messages are posted on a board. If a board has only one or two messages posted a day, it is not worth your time.
  - ➢ Check the tenor of postings, or **threads,** by reading thirty or forty consecutive messages without responding. This is called **lurking.**
  - ➢ Search messages for specific references to your marketplace, product, service, or issue and to see if participants tolerate postings. If your product, service, or issue is mostly discussed in a rational (not inflammatory) manner, the board is appropriate.
  - ➢ Check the bulletin board's Frequently Asked Questions section to see if there are rules about posting.
  - ➢ Find out who the moderator is, if there is one, and write for permission to place material on the bulletin board. If you can make friends with a moderator, it can go a long way to getting material on regularly. A moderated site is better than one that is not because the moderator focuses discussion and keeps it on track.
- Step 3: Define a final list of appropriate newsgroup bulletin boards. Investigation should reduce the number of boards to a handful. The handful, however, will reach the target audience.

- Step 4: Determine whether the online audience is big or influential enough to merit your attention. Recheck the threads on your final list to see how many different participants show up and the kinds of individuals who post. For example, newsgroups comprised of professionals from an industry you are trying to reach are valuable. Newsgroups with broad participation also are desirable. Groups with a cabal of unidentifiable participants might not be worth the effort.

One firm that publicizes pop music stars online uses a four-step publicity procedure with its target audiences. It monitors Web-based bulletin boards to find out what teens are saying about a pop artist. It then supplies information either formally or casually about the pop star and his/her album. It next focuses on the pop star's newest album to support sales. Lastly, it moves to older audiences to see whether it can broaden the base for the singer and album.

If you decide to post news on all sites you have identified, you are **cross-posting**. Be careful about cross-posting. Posting to too many sites is junk mail, and bulletin board participants will flame you. It is better to select three or four of the most appropriate sites and openly post to them. For example, in your announcement, list where you are posting in the subject header. This tells everyone what you have done and spares the nasty discovery of multiple cross-posts.

Posting on bulletin boards can be done in several ways. There are **announcements**, press releases, and disguised postings. Announcements follow the same basic procedure as e-mail (see E-mail). There is a subject line, header, and message body. The header contains information that one needs to contact you, so there is no need for a signature block (although one can add it.) The subject line is important because forums list messages by subject lines, and newsgroup readers often determine what they will read based on subject lines. The body of the message should be kept short and creative. If there is more than a short message can handle, provide a link that one can go to. Some recommend that you give something away in the body of the announcement because it promotes response.

Here is a sample announcement:

Subject Line	Trade Stocks for a Penny
Header	From: James Horton Organization: Robert Marston And Associates, Inc. Date: March 19, 2000 Newsgroups: misc.invest.stocks, www.siliconinvestor.com, www.elitetrader.com

Body	XYZ today announced that it has reduced its commission per stock trade to a penny per share with a minimum trade of one dollar ($1.00).
	XYZ said its new commission fee structure applies to all stocks on the New York Stock Exchange, NASDAQ, American Stock Exchange and ECNs. Accessing XYZ's service requires use of its free software. To download XYZ's software and for more information on the new commission fee schedule, click on:
	http://www.xyz.com/news
	For a free brochure on XYZ and its proprietary trading service, contact jhorton@marstonpr.com. Put "XYZ brochure" in the subject line and we will send you an Adobe Acrobat file of the brochure that you can print locally.

News release posting should be done with care. The author uses a prefatory statement that announces that the release is posted as a matter of record only. Posting such as this should be done strictly for information purposes and should be targeted precisely to the group that can use the information. It would be better to post a short announcement and a link to the release rather than the entire release, but if the release is brief, it can pass muster.

Disguised postings should be done with extreme caution, and there is a question whether PR practitioners should engage in anonymity. Active solicitation under a guise is unethical. However, some firms use postings to raise awareness without soliciting. One does it through carefully placed questions, such as "Has anyone heard about. . . ?" or, "Has anyone seen. . . ?" This is the same **trolling** discussed in e-mail. It attempts to start discussion that raises awareness. It takes skill to do such posting well without falling over the line to solicitation. And, if newsgroup participants figure out that the poster is a PR practitioner, the results could be disastrous.

There is much variation from bulletin board to bulletin board on what is acceptable, on how to post, on permissions required, and on sensitivities of participants. There is no space here to discuss variations, and rules change constantly anyway. The PR practitioner learns largely by trial and error. One constant is key. At some point you will make someone unhappy and you will get flamed or reported for spamming (see `news.admin.net-abuse.sightings`). If you are flamed or someone lodges a spamming charge against you, do not flame back, but defend yourself calmly. In your defense, point to what you have done to make sure that you tailored news to the appropriate newsgroup. Do not be afraid to engage an unhappy soul by e-mail, as long as conversation is reasonable. Sometimes you can come to an accommodation that helps everyone. As long as you proceed cautiously, posting on bulletin boards can be an effective public relations tool.

ONLINE LEARNING

From the beginning of online, it has been considered a venue for training and instruction. There are hundreds of colleges and universities around the world offering accredited (and unaccredited) online courses and degree programs. There are dozens of MBA programs offered alone. PR practitioners have many opportunities to use online learning in order to enhance skills or to impart training.

Unfortunately, teaching online is not easy to do and many instructors and trainers do not understand how to use the medium well. Course notes, readings, and exams are thrown onto Web pages without consideration for students who must plow through them. As a result, students often get frustrated and drop out.

Better implementations of online instruction are beyond the capabilities of most colleges and universities and corporate training departments. Several companies have arisen to provide the infrastructure needed to offer courses effectively. These are firms such as Ecollege (`http://www.ecollege.com/`), CognitiveArts (`http://www.cognitivearts.com/`), and Unext (`http://www.unext.com/`). They provide online all the services that a student would have on a campus from the registrar through the student union, library, and classroom. They overlay extensive software needed for instruction and help desks for students. The idea is that students online should not be disadvantaged because they cannot come to a campus.

Course creation and teaching require careful implementation. In fact, courses are developed specifically or reinvented for online. PR practitioners considering online learning should investigate programs carefully before entering one. Try **Petersons.com** (`http://www.petersons.com/`) to get an idea of the broad range of courses and online degree programs available.

PORTALS

Portals are doors to the Web. They offer an array of services, such as news sources, e-mail, personalization, shopping, and searching in one place so that users will choose the site as an entrance point to the

Internet. Portals are the closest "mass media" application on the Web. They want floods of visitors to entice advertisers to pay high rates. The largest portal is AOL, which did not start as a portal but as a commercial online service that migrated to the Web. The next largest is Yahoo!, which also did not start as a portal but as a directory of Web sites.

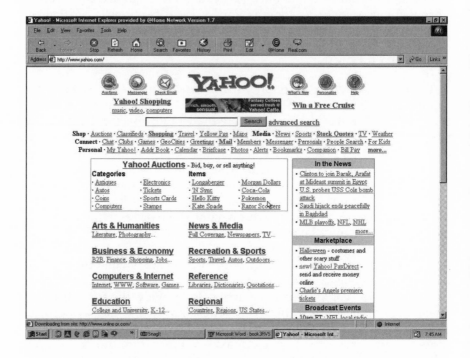

The term portal is used loosely. A vertical portal (**Vortal**) focuses on a niche such as art. A **personal portal** is designed to be an individualized doorway to items that a person needs and/or wants. This is also called personalization. "My Yahoo!" is a page on the Yahoo! site that one can customize for the kinds of information that he or she is looking for.

Because portals try to capture the largest number of users, their compact presentation is more textual than visual. PR practitioners can learn from this. Yahoo!, for example, places more than twelve distinct sections on one page in a carefully arranged, easy-to-read text format. **AltaVista** is similarly crammed with information, although it chooses to spread its page size more than Yahoo! What these sites acknowledge is that when content is king, it is more important to direct individuals to it than to look pretty with abundant graphics.

Practitioners who design news portals for journalists or personal portals for employees should examine the design of large portals closely. The key is to use the fewest clicks possible to reach information, and this is never easy to do. Many solutions have been developed to facilitate compaction of information into small spaces, but none is ideal. For example, MSNBC (http://www.msnbc.com) uses multiple drop-down menus that list all major news stories in a box that appears next to major topics such as news, sports, and health. The menu boxes are dynamic and change as the news changes. This kind of solution places tiers of information on a page by user interest. Other attempts to link information into easy-to-find spaces use graphical and three-dimensional approaches, such as a picture of a desk where each item links to information beneath or a 3-D aerial view of a city.

A portal's challenge, whether internal or external, is to present and link information in a way that facilitates rather than hinders access. This requires intimate knowledge of users and user behaviors. Within an organization, for example, a salesperson wants categories of information that differ from those of the accountant and the accountant's needs differ from those of an engineer in R & D. General categories of information might apply to all, but they may or may not be accessed all that much. To illustrate, a company phone directory might have high traffic, but a general description of company activities, products, and services might get an occasional visit.

The practical question is how to place these things in a portal so that multiple users with changing demands do not have to search. Complicating the issue is that studies of human physiology and brain function show clearly that less is more. For example, engineers learned that hundreds of switches in a typical airplane cockpit hindered rather than enhanced pilot functioning, especially in a crisis. Portals struggle with the same issue.

Portals tangle as well with the constraints of technology in attempting to condense information. What works well with one browser might not work well with another unless the portal uses the most basic coding that all browsers are standardized to handle. Secondly, portals must accommodate the slowest connection to the Web as well as the fastest. The slowest connection, however, dictates what a portal can do. Public relations practitioners, on the other hand, might not be constrained by these limits when dealing with a closed environment, such as an Intranet. If a company's users all have high-speed lines, consistent machines, and one standard browser, the practitioner can be much more flexible in designing a portal for information presentation.

PRESSROOM

The online pressroom makes organizational news available in a compact and easy-to-use place. Many organizations use pressrooms where journalists can download releases, photos, and other artwork, such as logos. Some pressrooms are locked off, and some are open to all. As a general rule, reporters do not like passwords any more than you do, so it is better to keep pressrooms open. Some pressrooms require that reporters register so that the company knows who is using its information. Reporters do not like this either, but they will do it if the content they are looking for is readily available.

Pressrooms carry a broad range of organizational and product/services fact sheets and background material in text and PDF format. (They are portals for journalists.) Logical organization of materials is a necessity. Reporters are not going to spend time searching for information.

Here are typical categories:

- Releases: current and archival and international, if a global company
- Media coverage: reprints or links to news stories
- Customer profiles and case studies
- Corporate profiles: company fact sheets, management bios, management photos, corporate history
- Contact information for PR staff and key personnel for offices, plants and worldwide locations
- Major job changes
- Industry news
- Calendar of corporate and industry events
- Speakers' presentations
- Recognition and awards
- White papers
- Product catalogs, specs, and R & D information
- Background and public information on legal issues and crises
- A photo library in three resolutions and download sizes (TIFF, GIF, and JPEG)
- Investor relations: quarterly and annual releases, financial graphs and stock quotes
- Important statistics that define the company's progress and industry trends
- A search engine and/or site map to help reporters find information
- An e-mail alert service when news is added to the site (although this is not desirable if news is added daily, because the e-mails will harass journalists)
- Forms for ordering video and/or stills

A pressroom should follow a two-click rule. A reporter should not have to click more than twice to find materials. *Above all, a pressroom must stay up-to-date.* The instant that a release goes out to the media, it should appear in the pressroom. The instant a fact sheet has changed, the revision should appear in the pressroom. Constant maintenance may require coordination with a Webmaster, or it can be done through a direct link to a service like PR Newswire that manages the process for you.

Generally, pressrooms the author has examined are cleanly designed and easy to view. Navigation and categories of information are clearly marked, and news is segmented by financial, product, and personnel with the most recent information placed first.

PRIVACY

Privacy is a flash point online. The public relations practitioner, concerned with building relationships between individuals and organizations, should respect privacy as a matter of course. But, one person's privacy is not another's and what one is willing to tell about himself varies from what others are willing to have known. A position that nothing should be known about anyone online is as unreasonable as the position that one can collect whatever is out there or can be detected through use of multiple linked databases.

TRUSTe.org (http://www.truste.org), a nonprofit organization that advocates online privacy, started with two assumptions:

1. Users have a right to informed consent.
2. No single privacy principle is adequate for all situations.

A one-size-fits-all privacy policy will not work on the Internet. In recognition of this, the Federal Trade Commission issued a law that forbids collection of personal information from children under the age of 13 without verified parental consent. The European Union separately issued rules for privacy that required negotiation with the U.S. Department of Commerce to ensure that European citizens could keep their personal information protected in the United States. Other privacy initiatives exist as well, including the **Online Privacy Alliance** (http://www.privacyalliance.org), a coalition of companies responding to privacy concerns.

An AT&T lab study (http://www.research.att.com/projects/privacystudy/) defined key points about privacy that PR practitioners should know:

- Some types of data are more sensitive than other types. An individual might tell you about his or her preferences for news and shopping, but be reluctant to provide credit card or social security numbers.

- Information shared with other companies is more sensitive. Individuals want to know how data about them will be used by companies other than the company that first gathered it.
- Users do not like automatic data transfer from a browser that includes information about them.
- Users do not like unsolicited communications.
- Users are uncertain about cookies. They do not mind using cookies for the original intent—providing customized service—but they are less happy about the use of cookies for advertising.

The best privacy policy a PR practitioner can follow is to avoid collecting information on anyone unless you have to do so. When you have to collect information for e-commerce or other purposes, write and implement a privacy policy that you fully disclose and that provides individuals with a choice to opt out. Make sure that any data that you collect is accurate, complete, timely, and secure.

TRUSTe's policy is worth noting. To earn the TRUSTe seal on a Web site, a Web site must notify each user:

1. What personally identifiable information is collected through the Web site.
2. Who is collecting the data.
3. How the information is used.
4. With whom the organization is sharing the information.
5. The kind of security procedures that the organization has put in place to protect against loss, misuse, or alteration of information.
6. How users can correct inaccuracies in the information.

Policy recommendations from the Online Privacy Alliance are essentially the same. The Alliance adds criteria for privacy seal programs that identify sites following good privacy policies, and it calls for a program that consults businesses, academics, and consumer and advocacy organizations in formulating policies. The Alliance wants a consistent and predictable way to implement privacy procedures that it is also independent.

Privacy issues will not go away. PR practitioners should remain alert to new assaults on privacy and be ready to respond appropriately. In addition, practitioners should expect more laws on privacy issues with stiffer penalties for failing to abide by privacy rules.

PR practitioners already have had to confront errors in enforcing privacy policies to the harm of the organizations involved. Companies sold data that they said they would not sell or a software error released data that was supposed to be private. Practitioners should treat instances such as this in the same way that they would respond to a crisis. A fundamental loss of confidence in an organization can cost its business or its influence. Provide customers and others a full accounting of what happened and what is being done about it. Organizations that hide after such breaches of trust will suffer when users stay away.

PUBLIC AFFAIRS

Online has influenced public affairs. One can find more information today online than any other way except the traditional methods of walking halls and dialing phones. Unfortunately, what one finds is often not enough. For example, bills under consideration in Congress still are not online, nor are the working versions of them. Content is scattered, and unless one knows exactly where a government program is lodged, it might take hours to find data, even with the use of search engines, such as Firstgov (http://www.firstgov.gov/) and Gov-bot (http://www.cs.umass.edu/govbot/). On the other hand, online has made it is easier for public affairs specialists to cover a broader range of topics remotely.

Political news is readily available through sites such as All Politics (http://www.cnn.com/ALLPOLITICS/) jointly run by Cable News Network and Time, Inc., On Politics (http://www.washingtonpost.com/wp-dyn/politics/) run by the Washington Post, and Yahoo!'s political news page (http://politics.yahoo.com/).

The White House, Congress, and government agencies are more accessible since their debut online. Sites such as Thomas (http://thomas.loc.gov/) and Congress.org (http://www.congress.org/) contain in-depth resources and links to information about the legislative branch. C-Span (http://www.c-span.org/) covers a broad range of activities in Washington through its Web site. Hearingroom.com (http://www.hearingroom.com/), a subscription service, carries every word from every hearing, including real-time text transcription with linked audio, searchable text, and written testimony.

Every major Federal Government agency and most states and municipalities have an online presence. Federal government agencies can be found through the Fed World site (http://www.fedworld.gov/) run by the Department of Commerce, and publications such as "The Hill" (http://thehill.findlaw.com/) offer comprehensive directories.

Political activism is well-represented online too, and Web sites such as Grassroots (http://www.grassroots.com/) and Speak Out (http://www.speakout.com/) target those who want to make their voices heard.

Outside of the United States, there are thousands of politically based sites by country and party. Some of these can be found through directories such as International Affairs Resources (http://www.etown.edu/vl/) and Political Resources on the Net (http://www.politicalresources.net/).

Campaigning has changed with the advent of online. At the national, state, and local levels, parties and candidates have learned to use e-mail well to promote candidates and to offset allegations from opposing camps. For example, the Democrats have built war rooms that work twenty-four hours a day during the presidential campaign to analyze issues and to fire off e-mails to more than a thousand reporters that either support their own candidate or rebut Republican claims.

Candidates' Web sites have proven useful for fund raising and for getting out their messages in detail in ways that they cannot achieve through traditional media. Meanwhile, reference sources show who is donating money to the candidates and how much they are donating, such as the Campaign Finance Information Center (http://www.campaignfinance.org/) and the Federal Election Commission (http://www.fec.gov/). Other reference sources look at issues, such as the League of Women Voters (http://www.lwv.org/) and Project Vote Smart (http://www.vote-smart.org/).

Online has changed the way that public affairs specialists go about their business, and in coming years, it will have a profound effect on the discipline.

PUBLIC RELATIONS RESOURCES

There are dozens of public relations resources online today, and practitioners should use them to do their work better, faster, and less expensively. The author's Web site (www.online-pr.com) lists more than 250 public relations and marketing resources, and the site is by no means complete. Every communications association, both domestically and internationally, has a presence online such as the Public Relations Society of America (http://www.prsa.org), International Association of Business Communicators (http://www.iabc.com/), National Investor Relations Institute (http://www.niri.org/), and Institute of Public Relations for the United Kingdom (http://www.ipr.org.uk/).

All public relations newsletters and magazines are represented online, such as PR Week (http://www.prweekus.com/), O'Dwyer's (http://www.odwyerpr.com/), and Ragan newsletters (http://www.ragan.com/). News media directories and distribution services are online, such as MediaMap (http://www.mediamap.com/), Bacon's (http://www.bacons.com/), and Press Access (http://www.pressaccess.com/Media/index.htm). Public relations and marketing directories and guides are online, such as PRplace (http://www.prplace.com/), CyberPulse's listing of PR agencies (http://www.webcom.com/impulse/), and PRSA's listing of silver Anvil winners (http://www.silveranvil.org/). Speakers' bureaus are online, and measurement services. Clipping services are on line and public relations vendors are online either with their own Web sites or in directories such as the O'Dwyer PR Services database (http://www.odwyerpr.com/) and Corporate Communications Studies (http://www.corpcomstudies.com/).

Public relations practitioners today should have a better understanding of what is available to them than in the past when it was not as easy to find information. On the other hand, there are still huge data gaps, and content is often scattered. Sometimes, looking for specific information can be frustrating and take far too much time.

PUSH AND PULL THEORIES

Push and pull theories of online communication are based on technology. One theory is that information should be sent (pushed) to individuals whether they have asked for it or not. Mass e-mailing is pushing, or broadcasting data. Pull theory is that individuals should get only the information they ask for. Pull theory is based on the fact that Web pages do not send information without a user initially requesting it.

For PR practitioners, the practical use of pushed or pulled data is one of audience preference. As a general rule, start with pull theory by creating and delivering content that users want. Move to push theory. When users want the information, ask them to give you blanket permission to provide it without having to request content each time. For example, ask users to let you e-mail information to them or to customize what they will see on a Web page.

Online is user-driven, and where rights of message-receivers are ignored, relationships become testy and can be broken. As a matter of practical online public relations policy, respect the individual and work hard to earn the individual's trust. This is the way it has always been, even before online media, because a person did not have to pick up a particular newspaper or magazine or tune into a TV or radio program.

RESEARCH

Organizations increasingly use online for primary research—focus groups, opinion polls, and surveys. For example, one gets a pop-up minisurvey on an e-commerce site. The survey will ask questions such as whether the shopping experience was pleasant and if not, why not.

Primary research online has limitations when one is trying to derive a statistically random sample that can be used to describe a larger population. In fact, it is hard to do, and even professional research firms are uncertain when they have achieved sample sizes that are sufficiently random to approximate a universe. Secondly, when one wants to get a direct feel for what target audiences are saying that includes watching their expressions and listening to how they speak, online is not the tool to use.

There are advantages of surveying online, however, that companies have recognized. When one is searching for a niche population, online can find them. When one is looking for large numbers of somewhat random responses, online is less expensive. When one needs speed in response, online is faster. Unfortunately, online also is a source of bogus, ill-advised, and poorly administered surveys. This happens because organizations ask questions without proper attention to survey mechanics.

There are many online research companies. Most are firms that performed traditional focus group, telephone, and mail research before getting into online. Companies include well-known names like Harris Interactive (http://www.harrisinteractive.com), NFO Interactive (http://www.yoursurvey.com), and The NPD Group (http://www.npd.com/). Harris Interactive boasts of a survey panel that exceeds five million online users who have agreed to participate in its polls. This panel was derived largely through a strategic relationship with Excite@Home, an Internet portal. From this panel, Harris has identified purchasing niches including information technology, telecommunications, office equipment, and small business owners. NFO Interactive and The NPD Group lure respondents through providing cash incentives for becoming members.

Here are some of the online research services that these companies offer:

- Survey panels

- Focus groups
- Custom and multiclient research
- Customer relationship services
- Audience measurement
- Chats with site visitors
- Competitive site analysis
- Online purchase tracking
- Online usage analysis
- Rapid response polls
- Visitor profiling
- Web site evaluation
- E-commerce reporting
- Attitude and opinion polls
- Focus groups
- Mystery shopping

Professional research firms are careful with customer information they collect because they know that if they violate privacy, they will be out of business. They are careful as well to keep surveys short (five to fifteen minutes in length) and easy to fill out, in order to enhance response.

Online surveys in general should be

- Brief.
- Easy to complete and pre-tested for usability.
- Administered with an incentive to motivate completion.
- Carefully written to prevent bias.
- Precise.

PR practitioners should use online survey research with the same care that they use traditional survey techniques. Surveying is garbage-in-garbage-out. A poorly designed survey yields poor results.

RICH TEXT FILE

A Rich Text File (**rtf**) is more a technology than a means of publishing information, but it is inserted here because of what it allows PR practitioners to do. Microsoft developed specifications for Rich Text Files in the early 1990s when it was confronted with incompatibilities among word processors that existed then. Users could not transfer formatted documents between word processors because each word processor worked differently. Rather, the document had to be stripped of all formatting and sent as a plain text ASCII file. This was inconvenient,

annoying, and a waste of time. The Rich Text File standard and specifications allowed files to retain most formatting and to move from one
word processor to another. Microsoft performed this trick by adding
formatting commands to plain text that every word processing and
operating system subsequently recognized. This was and is a break-
through. Today, it is still safer to send documents attached to e-mail in
Rich Text File than in word processor formatting. Sometimes the Internet will do strange things to wordprocessed documents. Practitioners
who have laboriously reformatted plain text (ASCII) documents know
how much time a Rich Text File saves. The fact that Rich Text File
documents move easily among different operating systems, including
the IBM PC and Apple Macintosh, is even more beneficial. As a practical
matter, PR practitioners should send documents by Rich Text File first
unless they are certain of the word processing software used at the other
end of an e-mail. In particularly difficult environments, documents
should still be sent the old-fashioned way in plain text, but this happens
less often.

SCREEN SAVERS

Screen savers, the still and animated images that pop up on your
personal computer when you are not using it, are not an online medium.
We include them here because they are frequent online promotional
giveaways and are easily downloadable. Sites offer screen savers the
way firms offer T shirts. They can be useful in getting a message across
if done with creativity. Screen savers can support tourism, for example,
by distributing images of a locale being promoted. Sports leagues use
them, such as the National Basketball Association, to promote teams
and players. Auto manufacturers use them to display the latest models.
Museums use them to promote collections and zoos to feature their
animals.

The number of still and animated screen savers is unknown, but it
certainly runs into tens of thousands. The PR practitioner who is thinking about offering a promotional screen saver online should try for
something immediately appealing and likely to reside for awhile on an
individual's personal computer. It is not easy to find such images or
animations.

SKIN

A skin is a graphic overlay on a software program that changes its
appearance. Skins are especially popular on music sites where the
screen picture of the amplifier or radio that plays music is modified

with weird, zany, and funny overlays. PR practitioners should consider offering a skin as a promotional item in the same way that one would offer a screen saver. Before doing this, however, look at some of the thousands of available skins in databases already. They will give you an idea of how outrageous one can get, especially for the youth market. Look at Searchwho.com (`http://mp3.searchwho.com/`) for sites that carry skins.

SPAM

Spam is junk e-mail or newsgroup postings sent indiscriminately. It is a dirty word online, and you do not want to be accused of spamming. The derivation of the word "spam" is wrapped in computer mythology and references to the British comedy group, Monty Python. The problem with spam is that it is intrusive and fails to respect the privacy of the user to whom it is directed. One does not build good relationships by burying others in junk mail. A second problem with spam is that it uses up space on the Internet that could be devoted to carrying messages people want. An official memo on spam and its harm, published by The Internet Society (June 1999), describes what happens when one sends out unsolicited mail to a mailing list or newsgroup.

> It frequently generates more hate mail to the list or group or apparent sender by people who do not realize the true source of the message. If the mailing contains suggestions for removing your name from a mailing list, 10s to 100s of people will respond to the list with "remove" messages meant for the originator. So, the original message (spam) creates more unwanted mail (spam spam spam spam), which generates more unwanted mail (spam spam spam spam spam spam and spam).

What irks Internet users is that they pay for junk e-mail that they do not want but get anyway. The reason is that users pay for Internet connectivity over which spam travels. Even more outrageous is that spam-filled e-mail boxes are difficult to plow through for messages that one wants; and finally, the sheer volume of spam causes e-mail systems to sag and fail.

There are two challenges that PR practitioners have:

1. How not to spam and still get messages out.
2. How to avoid being spammed.

There is no clear definition of spam. One person's spam is another's desired message. However, practitioners trained in media contact know that you should carefully research target audiences before contacting them to make sure they are indeed targets and open to a message, and you should respect their wishes about getting mail from you. If they do not want it, stop mailing.

The key to e-mail is a Golden Rule: E-mail to others as you would have them e-mail to you. Junk mailers do not research and do not respect anyone. They exploit the low cost of e-mail on the assumption that even with returns of a fraction of a percent, profits will exceed the cost of sending mass e-mails. PR practitioners should avoid this thinking and resist clients or organizations that endorse this business model. PR practitioners also should resist excuses used with spamming to ameliorate bad behavior. These are apologies within the message for sending a mass e-mail—phrases such as "this will be the only message that you receive," or invitations to get your name off a mailing list. Perhaps the most obnoxious behavior of spamming is to promise to remove a name from a mailing list and failing to do so. Among junk mailers, invitations to remove oneself from a list are often fraudulent, and attempts to unsubscribe generate more spam because you verify your e-mail address by sending an unsubscribe message.

Stopping spam is another question. It is almost impossible to do. The author gave up an e-mail account on AOL, for example, because he was deluged with spam and then, a junk mailer stole his AOL name and password and used it to send mass porno solicitations. AOL seemed powerless to stop the intrusion.

The best way to handle spam is to delete it without opening it. Deletion gives a junk mailer no indication that you received it. Generally, it is easy to tell spam e-mail. The address and subject lines are usually giveaways. The address line is unfamiliar and the subject shouts promises of ways to make millions, lose weight, or get miracle cures. Spam filters are dumb and may block mail that you want. Sending e-mail back often does not work because the spammer disguises the source of the e-mail. Sending spam to the e-mail postmaster can work if the postmaster can find the site and block e-mail from it. This requires the entire message header for tracing. Inserting words into an e-mail address to confuse the automatic address harvesters that spammers use sometimes works but has its own problems. One uses an address like nospamhorton@marstonpr.com and instructs users to remove "nospam" before e-mailing. However, this can cut off people you want to hear from.

One last revenge on spammers is to **mail bomb** them. Mail bombing deluges a server with thousands of e-mails or other requests that stop a server from working. Mail bombing is a criminal act for which one can be prosecuted. There are many sites on the net that wage war against spammers. One to check is Spam.Abuse.Net (http://spam.abuse.net).

STOCK PHOTOGRAPHY

Online is the best source of stock photography that a PR practitioner could wish for. Before online, one leafed through hundreds of pages of images or sleeves of slides to find something close to what was imagined. Now, one can go to a stock photography site and find images in a hurry by the millions, or use a search engine to find images across the Web. Corbis (http://www.corbis.com), for example, offers a collection of 65 million images of which 2.1 million are available online. Stockphoto.com, a service of the Black Star photography agency (http://www.stockphoto.com), provides 2 million images online as well. There are dozens more stock photo sites in addition to these two.

Using a multimedia search engine to find images is much less accurate than visiting a stock photo site, but engines will turn up images that are not in stock photo collections. The trouble with search engines is the same that one has with any search tool. Anything labelled "feet," for example, shows up, whether it is a room 14 feet wide, a plaster model of a foot, or clay pot feet for supporting a vase. Search for "feet" on a multimedia search engine and you get 21,000+ images, most of which are not useful. On the other hand, search for "feet" on the Corbis site and you get fewer than 100 images, but they are about feet. Unlike text searching where you can define phrases, with image searches you cannot because the image is databased according to file name.

As a practical matter it is better to use a stock photo agency, even though you have to pay for the use of an image, because you are protected from charges that you used a photo without authorization.

VIRAL MARKETING

Viral marketing is a buzz phrase that debuted in 1997. It describes word-of-mouth marketing online that spreads a message with little input from the original source, other than launching the offer. Viral refers to the growth rate of viruses. First there is 1 cell that splits into 2 cells, then 4, then 8, then 16, 32, 64, and so on. The first company to exploit this word-of-mouth marketing brilliantly was Hotmail, which built a subscriber base to 12 million in just 1.5 years. Hotmail did this by appending an advertisement to each e-mail sent through its free service. The ad said simply, "Get your free e-mail at *Hotmail*."

E-mail became the viral carrier, and one person after another read the message and signed onto the service and/or told others to sign as well. An online chat software called ICQ used the same method, and Blue Mountain Arts revolutionized the online greeting card market in the same way.

Viral marketing is both automatic and proactive. Automatic viral marketing requires no effort on a customer's part. The computer sending the mail placed the message on each Hotmail e-mail. Proactive viral marketing requires users to convince other users to participate. ICQ's chat software required at least one other person to sign on so the two could chat.

Viral marketing is not easy to use. It requires a product/service that lends itself to word-of-mouth marketing, and the product/service must be easy to acquire. Usually viral marketing gives away a desirable free service that can be transmitted to others effortlessly online. Because the viral marketer relies on others to sell the product rather than the organization, the message has to be simple, clear, and easily actionable. Another challenge is that like all marketing techniques, viral marketing has been overused and abused. As one commentator noted, chain letters are a form of viral marketing with an implied threat, "Don't break the chain." So are the thousands of jokes passed around the Internet daily. The PR practitioner who considers using viral marketing should research it carefully and focus efforts sharply on what a viral message should achieve. Test carefully before launching a program and be ready to serve customers as they sign on by the thousands per day.

WEB PAGE DESIGN

Designing a Web page is equal parts science and art. It requires research and careful planning. It also requires a sense of design to present content effectively. PR practitioners will not normally design Web pages on their own, but they should be familiar with basic concepts and resources.

The driving force behind design is simplicity and usability—that is, users never have to fight the design to find information they need. Design should lead them naturally to what they are looking for, and this is not easy to achieve. It requires care and constant usability testing to find out what users want and how a site can provide it. Usability testing consists of putting real users on a site and letting them tell you what works and what does not.

Web page design starts and ends with effective presentation of content in the fastest way possible. Good design is integrated with content.

It is not applique. Animations, design elements, and assorted gewgaws have no place on a Web page unless they help deliver a message. Great Web pages can be all images or all text or all multimedia, depending on what one is doing, but more than likely, they combine images, text and multimedia into a seamless flow. An example of a tight, user-oriented design is this opening page from the MSNBC Web site:

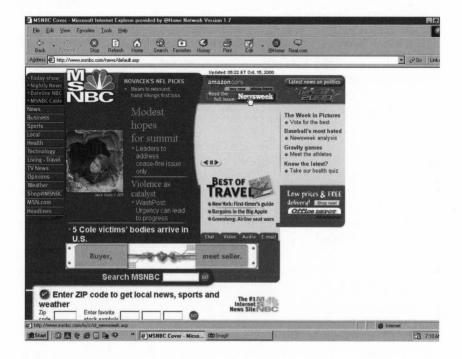

Design research begins with the target individuals for the Web page message (see Audit) and works backward to content and design. Sometimes it is self-evident what people are looking for from an organization, but just as often it is not. One of the key decisions that the PR practitioner must make is how inclusive a site will be. Will it be directed to the lowest common denominator or to a selective audience? Will it keep separate sections targeted to various levels of audience or be unified in presentation?

Multi-audience targeting is more common than not. A site with shareholder data and product/service data implicitly directs content to individuals with different interests and perhaps different demographics. A site needs to be developed in such a way to appeal to each group.

A typical corporate Web site will include the following types of information:

- General company descriptions
- Product/service descriptions
- Company news and calendars of activities
- Investor data
- Employment opportunities
- Contact information
- Office and site directory
- Feedback
- Frequently Asked Questions and Answers
- Tools: a search engine, a site map, downloads needed to use the site such as Adobe Acrobat reader
- A statement on Privacy

This does not cover all the categories of content that one might provide, but it is already complex. Increasingly, for example, global companies present sites in customer languages. This results in sites translated to four or five tongues. European sites, especially, are conscious of multilingual users.

After one has determined the categories of information that a site should carry, the next step is structuring the site—that is, how users find information they are looking for and where information needs to be placed to help them. Content structure starts with the **home page** and is in several forms:

- **Sequential**. This is a linear flow like the pages in a book.
- **Grid**. This is a spreadsheet of tables and rows.
- **Hierarchy**. This is top-down information presentation from general concepts to specific data.
- **Star**. This is a central page that routes one to bodies of hierarchical information.
- **Web**. This links all content together with little obvious underlying structure.

A Web page may use all these forms in one way or another, but the most common are hierarchical and star presentations. Sequential presentations are often associated with slide shows placed on the Web. Grid presentations are frequently used in product and service lists. Free-form Web presentation is not common because it is too easy for users to get lost in links.

The best way to proceed with information structure is to draw an actual map of what a site will contain. This is sometimes called **Web**

page cartography. Most Web page authoring tools will provide such maps to facilitate design. A typical map will look like this:

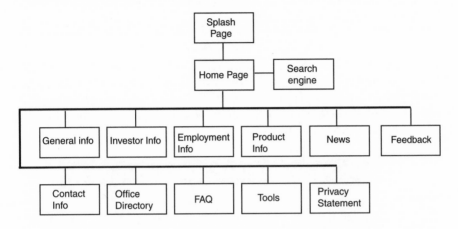

Note that this map has a **splash page** before the home page. A splash page is like a fancy book cover. It is often a graphic and/or animated presentation to advertise what the site is about before one gets to the site itself. Splash pages connect directly to home pages and may take one automatically to the home page without need for clicking, or present a single link to click. These links are often graphical and sometimes are not easy to find, which violates the first rule of good design.

The map given here is a simple representation of little depth. A true Web page map may have dozens of boxes under each separate heading, and many of these boxes may be information that is generated on demand from a database. Web page content management software from firms like Vignette (`http://www.vignette.com/`) with its Vignette V/5 Content Management Server™ integrates content management, delivery, and personalization. The benefit of the Web page map is that it diagrams links from the home page and throughout the site. It shows **information flow** and how visitors move through a site. It also provides guidance on another Web page design rule-of-thumb—in this case, the **three-click rule.** Site users get lost easily and are annoyed when they have to burrow through layer after layer to find information they need. Early on, designers realized that it is better to keep information close to the surface of a Web page. Actually, it is better to reach information in one click, but there is so much content that this is not easy to achieve.

The three-click rule shows quickly how much content needs to be on a home page, and it also tells the designer about page **navigation design.** One guideline is to place everything on the home page in a single screen—**"above the fold"**—with the most important information located near the top. (See the MSNBC illustration earlier.) However, a personal computer screen is too small to carry much information in one screen without the annoyance of scrolling. A one-screen approach leaves little space to work with. Further, one should design a Web site with emphasis on important information in order to position the site correctly with search engines—yet another complication.

Navigation design refers to the series of links that are placed on a site in bars or menus to help users move quickly to where they want to go. You can never have too much navigation on a site. A typical home page should provide navigation bars and links to a site search engine and site map. This is a navigation box.

Search   Credits   Index   About Us   Contact Us

The home page also should provide a link to send feedback to the Webmaster in case one cannot find what he or she is looking for.

The next step is site design itself, and here the designer should think of a **storyboard** and **template**. A storyboard lays out a site visually, and a template is a master design repeated on every page of a site. It gives a site a consistent look and feel that ties directly to the communications objective. This is a complex template design:

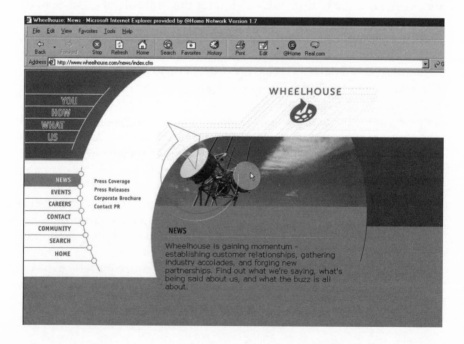

Template design is not easy because there is so much information in so many forms that consistency might seem impossible. An often-used template design is to build a graphic or actual **frame** around content. A graphic frame is part of the page and usually includes a color bar that partially or totally surrounds the text area. The color bar frequently holds navigation links to the rest of the site. An actual frame is technology that places two Web pages on the same page—one frames the other. Actual frames are hard to use well, and many designers avoid them.

Templates and interfaces should be consistent and stable with consistent and meaningful metaphors to guide users. The use for an icon, for example, should be obvious. The user should not have to think about what he or she should do. Once a template is developed, it should be distributed in a **style guide** that is enforced to keep corporate identity consistent. This is especially important on sites, such as Intranets, where multiple groups link to or are part of the main Web site and maintain their own content.

Feedback should be an integral part of any Web site, and this is usually through use of forms for e-mail or for other requests. The one principle to keep in relation to forms is simplicity. Online users do not like to enter reams of information into a screen, and often, they will not do it, even when it benefits them. Ask for the least amount of information possible in order to serve an individual. If it is necessary to learn more, ask for information in increments. Complex registrations requiring addresses, Zip codes, e-mail addresses, phone and fax numbers should be rarely required or requested.

Finding a designer who can develop an effective site is a task in itself. There are guidelines for approaching the job:

- Look for sites that you like and find out who designed them.
- Look through lists of developers in your area. Check their sites for quality.
- Determine the services that a developer can offer, including e-commerce structure, database development, content, animation, usability testing, promotion, and so on.
- Look at a company's client list and the clients' Web sites.
- Contact client companies and ask about their experience with a designer.
- Develop and send a request for proposal (RFP) to design the site to companies that you like. (The more detailed an RFP is, the better off you are.) The RFP will tell you who is in the market and who is not. Busy design shops might not take you on.
- Check price estimates against your budget. You might be shocked by how much it costs to develop a site that you need and want. If

you are shocked, you might have to make hard decisions about what your site will keep.

- Meet with the design firms to find out how you get along with them. Compatibility counts. A highly talented designer whom you cannot stand is not for you. Find one who might be slightly less talented but with whom you can work.
- Monitor the project and be there for the designer: Committees kill Web design and slow it down. There should be one point person who handles coordination with the design firm as the project develops and has the authority to make decisions.

One frequently cited guide to good design is the Yale Web Style Guide(`http://info.med.yale.edu/caim/manual/contents.html`). It provides an abundance of excellent suggestions for designing in HTML, and the PR practitioner should take time to read it. Web Pages that Suck (`http://www.webpagesthatsuck.com/`) is a good resource for learning about style through negative examples. The author of the page finds or is sent egregious examples of bad design and discusses why they are so bad. One pet peeve is the animated splash page that takes forever to download its glitzy graphics that have no real purpose.

WEB SITE LAUNCHES

Launching a Web site is difficult. With millions of Web sites in existence and millions more planned and/or coming online, gaining recognition for one site is a challenge. The days are gone when a site could win market share just through search engine registration, public relations, and word-of-mouth. That is why many commercial site launches have employed large advertising budgets. They pound awareness of their site address and content into potential users, then hope users will look and most importantly, return.

Site launches use many communications—television, radio, and print advertising; direct mail; online seeding; news releases; media tours; celebrities; events and promotions. A major launch can eat tens of millions of dollars with no guarantee of success.

A launch plan summarizes steps needed to get a site online and before target audiences. A plan does not have to be voluminous, but it should be complete, and there are both technical and media considerations that go into it. The plan should focus first on a site's technical aspects and logistics. For example, an e-commerce site is more than Web pages. It is order processing, warehousing, picking, packing, shipping, billing, re-ordering, database management, and so on.

Launch plans should include

- A crisis component.
- Time for pretesting and stress testing.
- Considerations for a "soft" launch.
- Time for site registration, Meta Tags, and keyword development or purchasing.
- Time for affiliations, partnerships, and associate programs (see Alliances).
- Time for event creation and planning.
- Time for media development and purchasing.
- An implementation schedule.
- A budget.
- Post-launch follow-up.

A crisis component in a launch plan is essential because there are continuous examples of Web sites that open before they are ready and crash. Well-known brand names have suffered this embarrassment. Part of the reason for such shortsightedness and lack of preparation is that site managers cannot predict what will happen when a site goes online. They plan for what they think will happen, but they do not know. PR practitioners developing launch plans should insist on a crisis component that discusses three scenarios:

- A site crash because of technical failure
- Overwhelming response that clogs the site
- Underwhelming response

Site **pretesting** and site **stress testing** can eliminate many technical problems, and a launch plan should include both. Loss of goodwill is so great and available substitutes for Web sites so plentiful that a poorly built or functioning site may have few means of recovery once it has failed its debut.

The launch plan also should consider a **soft launch**. Soft launches let carefully selected audiences preview a site before it opens "on Broadway." Friends and critics can tell you what they like and dislike before the rest of the world finds out, and they can ballyhoo enthusiasm to the world when the site does formally launch. A soft launch may require a nondisclosure agreement and password protection to prevent proprietary information from gaining general circulation. Sometimes, however, one can open a site and not worry about many showing up because no one has been told about it.

The launch plans should include time as well for:

- Registration with search engines and directories.
- Meta tag creation (see Meta Tags).

- Site descriptors and keyword development and/or purchasing.
- Consideration of the use of bridge pages.

Site registration with search engines used to be difficult, but there are software tools today that do registration for you. Meta tags go on the invisible portion of the Web page at the top where search engines can find them in order to classify a site properly. Site descriptors and keywords determine partially a site's ranking in search engine listings. Judicious testing of keywords in search engines will help determine the description and keywords to choose, but these are fallible. One may have to buy a keyword from a search engine in order to bring up a site first, or within the top 10, when a user searches on the pre-determined keyword. Another keyword approach is the **bridge page**. A bridge page is a beginning or "home" Web page optimized for a keyword. For example, an insurance company offers auto, health and house insurance. It might use three home pages — one optimized for auto insurance key words, a second optimized for health insurance key words and a third for house insurance key words. These three "home pages" then bridge users to the main site where information is the same.

If you plan an event to launch the site, the launch plan should detail the event and time needed to prepare. Celebrities have schedules and cannot show up overnight. Renting a large room with technical hook-ups in a major media market like Los Angeles or New York takes time. Invitations take time. Follow-up takes time. Set-up and testing takes longer than it should. Further, getting a well-known celebrity to show up for a launch may not be enough, and performing a stunt that bears little relation to the site might be a distraction. Events should highlight a site's features, functions and benefits and not divert from them. For example, a site that focuses on collectors might find a well-known celebrity who is a known collector. A site selling bicycles might concentrate on bike races, perhaps in exotic locales.

A large-scale site launch requires a detailed calendar or Gantt chart (top of next page) that lays out actions and deadlines in one place where all can follow them. The calendar back times from the launch day with slack time built in for unanticipated challenges. For example, press release/press kit preparation with screen shots of the Web site and media lists should be straightforward, but not always. Sometimes a press release is difficult to write. The act of explaining what a site is about spawns rethinking that delays site completion and compresses time needed for launch preparation. Or, it may take extra time to find the right newsgroups in which to announce the site and to post to them (see Newsgroups). Launch advertising takes time as well for design,

	A	B	C	D	E	F	G	H	I	J	K	L	M	N
1	**XYZ Web Launch**	**Gantt Chart**												
2	Sept. 00, 2000													
3														
4	**Action**	Week1	Week2	Week3	Week4	Week5	Week6	Week7	Week8	Week9	Week10	Week11	Week12	LAUNCH
5	Launch planning	■												
6	Technical Clearance	■	■											
7	Testing		■	■										
8	Registration/Meta tags/keywords	■	■	■	■	■	■	■	■	■	■	■	■	■
9	Affilation Program	■	■	■	■	■	■	■	■	■	■	■	■	■
10	Soft Launch				■	■	■	■	■	■	■	■	■	■
11	Soft Launch PR					■	■	■	■	■	■	■	■	■
12	Newsgroup posting												■	■
13	Bridge page decision	■												
14	Bridge page implementation		■	■										
15	Advertising Creation	■												
16	Media buying				■									
17	Advertising Launch													■
18	Publicity Pre-launch/Launch			■	■	■	■	■	■	■	■	■	■	■
19	Event Planning	■	■	■	■	■	■	■	■	■	■	■	■	■
20	Event launch													■

A simplified Launch Gantt Chart.

production, and media buying, especially if buying time in a high-noise period like Christmas. Another consideration is the noise itself. Launching a Web site in a medium that is already cluttered with dot-com advertising may be a waste of funds. One should consider deferring the launch.

Implementing a site plan is a sequence of technical and media rollouts. Testing, site registration, tags, keywords, bridge pages, and other housekeeping details should come first so that search engines and directories can include the site into their databases by time the launch occurs. This takes about thirty to sixty days. Media rollouts will depend on the level and extent of media campaign used. Newsgroup postings, press releases, and advertising should launch about the same time as the site opens unless there is an event. Event media buildup requires a prelaunch period of three to four weeks.

Do not be surprised if a press release/press kit carries little weight with journalists. They get hundreds of press releases for new Web sites. Look to place press releases in databases where target audiences can see them. Do not place too much weight on a launch event as well. It is hard to gain much national attention for events. Stunts have to be dramatic or celebrities world-class.

Post-launch is a time for follow-up and regrouping forces to focus on messages that are not being heard and to exploit messages that are making an impact. Media placements and press clips will provide some clue to the reach of the message, but site traffic and measurements will tell the practitioner quickly what is happening. There may be little or no correlation between what appears in the media and what happens on the site, and this can be frustrating. For example, sometimes, although rarely, word-of-mouth can swell traffic to a site with almost no media placement. Slashdot.org (http://www.slashdot.org/) is known for its "Slashdot effect." This comes from the e-zine's mention of a site that motivates thousands of its readers to look in on the site at the same time. However, PR practitioners cannot depend on such lightning strikes to occur. Launches should marshal as many technical and media forces as possible to pierce through the noise of millions of Web sites.

WEB SITE MAINTENANCE

A Web page is NEVER done. It is only as good as its content, and content gets dated, as does design. ALWAYS budget for maintenance. Maintaining sites should be done on a regular schedule. A site with low activity should be checked at least monthly for broken links and updated with news, such as company releases. A site with high activity should be checked daily. Sites with many external links should regularly scan those links to make sure they are still good. Software programs such as Linkbot (http://www.watchfire.com/) do scanning for you.

Site maintenance is as important as site creation. It is disappointing to find sites so dated that calendar items for two years prior are still listed under current events. (The author found this on a university Web site.) Such lack of maintenance indicates that a site is an orphan and/or out of control. It leaves a poor impression of the organization.

The PR practitioner should consider a Web site a work in progress. Web sites are dynamic. They are never done, and they change as organizations change in order to reflect the organizations at the moment. If understood this way, maintenance is not an after-creation activity but a task of creating and re-creating.

It happens far too often that the task of developing a site is so onerous with so many interests feeding into content and design decisions that a practitioner is wary of touching a completed entity. It is like re-opening Pandora's box. The proper attitude to take is the opposite. The practitioner should present a site in the first instance as an ongoing project that, sooner or later, will include all parties. Site planning should be calendar planning as well. One does not plan for a completion point but for a series of completion points over the expected life of the current content and design.

WEB SITE PROMOTION

Promotion online has the same purposes as promotion in traditional media. It helps maintain or build awareness, traffic, and loyalty. Promotion runs a gamut of techniques. Even long-gone promotions, such as S&H Green Stamps that rewarded frequent purchasing in the 1960s, have returned as online promotional vehicles, now called greenpoints (http://www.greenpoints.com). Today, sweepstakes, coupons, quizzes, and giveaways are common, including a search engine site that automatically enrolls one in a sweepstakes just for using the site (http://www.iwon.com/), and a company called BigBroom (http://www.bigbroom.com) that sends a daily game piece by e-mail.

Because of the competitive nature of the Web, it is wise to use more than one promotional idea, but always use them well. This requires planning that should encompass both online and traditional media. It also requires commitment to implement the plan and to keep implementing it. Promotional efforts fail when the effort is halfhearted. For example, one builds a links page to attract users by making a Web site a resource, but links are few in number, poorly categorized, and dated or broken. Unfortunately, poorly managed link pages are the rule, and well-managed pages the exception.

Promotion gives users a reason to visit a site, whether the promotion is a simple reminder or something else. There is no limit on the creativity that one can use. One ingenious ploy was a beer company that took over the Internet error alert message on a Web site (Error 404: Page not found) and offered a coupon to the frustrated Web user for a free beer.

The most basic element of a promotional plan is to place the site address (URL) on everything the company uses to communicate—business cards, letterhead, advertising, brochures, e-mails, newsletters, and the like. Consider opt-in newsletters but be sure to plan for the time it will take to produce a good newsletter continuously. Finally, do not ignore viral marketing to generate word of mouth.

Although there is no limit to creativity in promotion, activities should relate to the purpose of a site, and this may require thinking to achieve. There are far too many sweepstakes with cars or other high-value items as draws that have nothing to do with a site. Although these may be temporary traffic boosters, that is all they are because they give users no reason to hang around other than register for a sweepstakes. (On the other hand, if the purpose of the sweepstakes is to gather e-mail addresses and names for later contact, it can be useful.)

The best promotions have built-in extensions to them and longevity. They are creative ideas that can spin off into many contexts. For example, a promotion might be a study that focuses on an area of interest in an industry. The study can be introduced at a seminar, disclosed through interviews and releases, posted on a Web site, discussed in a chat room, turned into a pdf brochure and/or printed brochure, used as a marketing tool by the sales force, and repeated annually to update information. Some of the best promotions have used this approach.

Promotion on the Web has one benefit that traditional media do not have. It is immediate and interactive. A promotion can be online discussion, streaming audio and video, chats, bulletin board, and e-mail. There are individuals you can watch by Webcam as they attempt to live for a time period solely by means of the Internet. You can watch live births and surgeries. You can check the weather at the beach before you drive the fifty miles to get there because beach merchants have placed Webcams at strategic points. The television sitcom, "The Drew Carey Show," made TV history when the main character supposedly rigged his house with Webcams and the actual show Web site dovetailed with the TV episode. ABC Television saw 277,000 video segments downloaded about the Webcam episode in just three hours.

One company called Spiderdance, Inc. (www.spiderdance.com) has developed technology through which television viewers can play with TV game shows in real-time through the Web. Hosts in the studio could see answers from home viewers as quickly as they heard replies from in-studio contestants. Spiderdance has been used on Sony's Game show network, The History Channel, TBS Superstation, and MTV.

Companies have mastered the art of using Web sites for promotional purposes, especially for movies. These sites are often interactive and have games as well as downloadable software. They offer T-shirts and hats. They offer news about the course of a film's production, bios of actors and characters, film clips, and more. The sites are resources for fans and help to motivate them to see the movie, sometimes again and again. Book sites have taken the same approach. One technique that has proved useful for popular books, such as the Harry Potter series, is to let fans establish their own sites and to reward them with giveaways. Companies are careful not to pay them to avoid legal entanglements.

The J R.R. Tolkien book, *The Lord of the Rings,* for example, had more than 300 Web sites devoted to aspects of the work, including art inspired by the book. Fans ran the sites. When movie producers started filming the book, they were careful to feed production notes, cast diaries, clips, stills, online chats, and interviews to privately run sites tracking the movie. They even developed a customized browser that fans could download to track news about the movie and to chat with other fans. This is the best possible use of word-of-mouth promotion. However, it has its downside. Tolkien fans guarded the authenticity of the book and its characters zealously against tampering by Hollywood and even mounted a petition when there were hints that a character might be changed or lost. In the tradition of no-holds barred Hollywood promotion and publicity, this kind of technique can be exploited to create a "buzz," including spawning controversy where none exists.

Another clever ploy was used by Lions Gate Films to promote the movie, *American Psycho.* One could sign up for a newsletter on the film's

Web site and then the recipient would get carbons of fictitious e-mails that the film's main character was purportedly sending to his psychotherapist. Soap operas and TV series have used e-mail, Web sites, and newsletters as well to let viewers keep up with plots.

WEBCASTING

PR practitioners have adopted Webcasting enthusiastically. Go to the multimedia sections of PR Newswire (http://www.prnewswire.com), Medialink.com (http://www.medialink.com/), or other news distribution services and you will find dozens of audiovisual and slide programs on many topics. Video files are more common than live streaming media events, particularly because files are not constrained by time. Audio alerts are often used for investor communities, as are teleconferences discussing quarterly or annual results. Video covers a wide range of consumer, health, technology, public service announcements, and business news. Live streaming broadcasts include major events like the announcement of Peabody Awards Winners, fashion shows, or launch of a new Web site. Brokerage firms such as Merrill Lynch and Paine Webber place their stock analysts directly online to talk to investors rather than placing them on financial TV networks, such as CNBC.

Producing a Webcast is not for beginners. The PR practitioner should use a company that has experience in developing the short audio/video clips that are posted online and in setting up live streaming video. It is especially important for technical experts to handle live Webcasting, whether audio or video. Online technology still suffers from enough glitches that one needs technicians to keep things moving. Especially with large-scale, popular events, such as the Victoria's Secret fashion show of models in skimpy underwear, one can expect trouble, as Victoria's Secret had when its system crashed as millions of males tried to log on.

Video online is not broadcast quality or jitter-free, and it is usually the size of a large postage stamp. This means that photography for Webcasting should adjust for softness and size. It is best to use close-ups with a single establishing shot. Unfortunately, most Webcasting still treats the screen as if it were full-sized and as sharp as television, and the results can be disappointing. This apparently comes from posting TV-produced videos on Web sites as an extra distribution outlet and that does not always work well. If the practitioner can afford the editing expense, a Webcasting video should be optimized for online distribution.

Audio is different. Even though voices can have a metallic quality, audio is generally better than video. It is easier to use audio as well because one is not transmitting as much information online. Another delivery mechanism is audio combined with limited presentation such as online slide shows. This is done directly through Internet telephony or through a toll free number linked to a Web site.

Still another area in which PR practitioners can use Webcasting comes through the thousands of television and radio stations that broadcast live online. One, eYada.com (http://www.eyada.com), is live online talk radio that takes guests like any radio talk show. Visit a directory like Radio Directory (http://www.radio-directory.com), and you will find sites that offer author interviews, education videos and movies, local radio and TV, business shows, careers and employment advice, children's audio books, computers and technology shows, education, entertainment, health and fitness, personal interests, sports, and travel. Music is ubiquitous and comes from radio stations around the globe. University radio stations, especially, are finding that they can reach alumni through the Internet and listeners who are interested in their blend of unorthodox programming.

Webcasting events are frequent and draw millions. It is not uncommon for more than a million individuals to tune into a Webcast. In 1999, more than 1,000,000 tuned into the live Paul McCartney concert at The Cavern in Liverpool. More than 5,000,000 accessed the concert overall when downloading was included. More than 2.4 million tuned into a Netaid global benefit concert that same year. High-profile news events, such as hurricanes, deaths of celebrities, and major accidents also draw mass audiences.

All Webcast outlets are of use to PR practitioners trying to deliver a message. As with any media outlet, the practitioner should check to see the kind of material that each outlet uses and its reach. Do not expect a large reach for most Webcast shows. Rather, treat these media as targeted to specific audiences or as supplemental to traditional media, unless proven otherwise. The practitioner also should check into foreign language stations, depending on the message. Immigrants in the United States, for example, use the Web to listen to news and music from radio stations back home. One can experiment with sending messages in reverse from an immigrant's country of origin to the location where the immigrant dwells. One example would be for the U.S. Census to reach out to immigrants to get counted. This use of online media extends publicity techniques far beyond local and national boundaries, and it provides interesting opportunities for practitioners willing to experiment.

WRITING FOR ONLINE

Writing for online media has parallels and important differences to writing for traditional media. Get your dog-eared copy of **The Elements**

of Style (William Strunk, Jr., and E. B. White) and read the following injunction, "Omit needless words." Then reread the rest of the text, for much of it applies to online writing.

The news lead is more important than ever online. State your point in a short, clear, and credible first sentence. Online users are in a hurry. They skim information. They want to know what you are about and whether your information applies to them. After stating the point, get into details. It is in the details where writing changes because of the nonlinear nature of online media.

Commentators and usability experts hammer at the need for online writing to

- Be brief and accurate. One reason for this is that it is harder to read a computer screen. Jakob Nielsen (`http://www.useit.com`), a usability expert, has stated that reading from a computer screen is about 25 percent slower than reading from paper. He recommends that you write 50 percent less text for online to maintain reading speed and to make users feel good about reading text. Over time, this may change as resolution of computer monitors grows to match the resolution of print on paper, but it is unlikely to happen soon.
- Use short sentences and short paragraphs. Keep to one idea per paragraph. Cut and compress. Write text then edit savagely to the fewest words possible.
- Use bullets: Bullets set off points so that they can be seen better.
- Highlight keywords and use subheads. Because readers skim, help them spot information they need. Keep headlines and subheads meaningful.
- Be familiar: I am writing to you and you and yes, you too. Carry on a literate conversation among friends. Avoid jargon and promotional hype. Win the trust of your audience and appeal to their emotions.
- **Chunk** information: Group information into logical, short units and hyperlink it according to importance. Web writing is a tree of information that starts with the essential point then moves through hyperlinking to fine detail supporting the point. It is in-depth writing in a concise format. That is, the reader who wants to know everything about the topic should be able to find out by reading and clicking through the chunks of text.
- Hyperlink clearly and carefully: A reader should know what the content is that a hyperlink refers to without clicking on the link. This gives the reader a choice of whether to go to the next step or to move on. Obscure, meaningless hyperlinks are annoying and disruptive.

Text Chunking and Hyperlinking

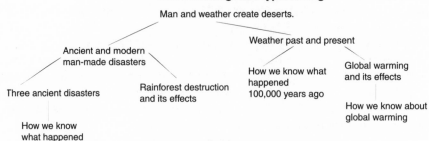

Man and weather create deserts.

Ancient and modern
man-made disasters

Weather past and present

Three ancient disasters

Rainforest destruction
and its effects

How we know what
happened
100,000 years ago

Global warming
and its effects

How we know about
global warming

How we know
what happened

**Hyperlink chunked text to the main
point to break a topic into finer detail.**

- Be credible: Give readers good reasons to believe what you are writing. Cite sources and show hyperlinks to other sites and data that support your statements so that readers can check for themselves what you have written.
- Fit screen size: Ideally, one should never have to scroll down to read online copy. A chunk should be about one screen in length. As a general rule, place important information in the first screen of text.
- Keep a readable point size: Designers in a desperate urge to cram everything into one screen have reduced type size. This is hard on readers and should be avoided.
- Use active voice and vigorous language: Writing teachers have taught this for decades, but for writing online copy, it is essential advice.
- Avoid metaphors unless you can make them clear: If you describe something as something else, use an illustration. For example, you wish to describe an organization as a machine that processes information. Show an illustration of the organization as a machine with parts of the machine changing information into useful and actionable knowledge. The reader has a visual metaphor to relate to the textual metaphor.
- Be global: Online, you are not writing for readers in the United States. You write for readers in France, India, and China, and your copy may be translated into multiple languages. Some recommend that Web content be localized rather than translated to avoid unintended gaffes and cultural differences. This requires knowing differences among languages, understanding the audience, and planning ahead for translation. One point to remember is that English speakers do not speak the same dialect of English. A British reader understands a word differently than an American. English

in India is different than English in America and the United Kingdom. Always test copy before placing it on a Web site to avoid
mistakes.

- Be interactive: Online writing should solicit reader response. Ask
  readers to react to what you have written through a forum or
  feedback form or to tell you whether he or she liked the article
  through a rating system. Even though readers will not respond
  often, just providing the option is friendlier and more open.
- Be tested for comprehension and usability. Never assume that you
  have written well. Let others tell you through controlled testing.
- Be maintained: Web sites change over time, and content changes
  with it. Write with an eye toward revision of text.

To find continuing advice for writing well online, try Contentious
(http://www.contentious.com/)—an e-zine devoted to Web writing. Jakob Nielsen's Alertbox (http://www.useit.com) is an online
newsletter about Web site functionality that archives several articles on
online writing.

4

Industries and Sources

Some industries have well-developed media and information resources online, and some do not. For example, finance and computers have information outlets that are as deep and strong as conventional print and broadcast media. On the other hand, jewelry trade topics are barely represented. PR practitioners will find working online to be uneven.

This chapter provides practitioners a baseline for eighty-five industry and general interest topics. It is not complete, and Web sites change constantly, but we reviewed key online news and information resources in each topic to determine their practical value in terms of a publicity outlet or information resource.

The Web today is primarily a library of old news rather than a source of news. It is a useful directory to traditional news media rather than a source for online news outlets. This means that PR practitioners have a way to find story placements, and stories in general have longer reach and life. Rather than disappearing into library archives or paid search sites, good and bad stories about organizations and their people live on for all to read for years at a time. In other words, because of online, PR practitioners are likely to be more captive to the past for good and ill, which makes the need to protect an organization's reptutation more important than ever.

The Web is not yet a medium in many industries where practitioners can place news. It is unclear when and if much original reporting will move online rather than remain in print, TV, and radio. Moreover, change is likely to be a slow, evolutionary trend dependent on consumers' preferences. Publishers will follow readers and viewers, and advertisers will follow publishers. New technologies will have some influence on the migration, but they will not determine it. Most publishers have not yet developed a profitable economic model for their publications online, and online news organizations have not either. Nevertheless, PR practitioners should be familiar with Web sites' content and include online in reporting publicity results.

Online stands out in one area. It is useful for publishing releases into archived databases. BusinessWire, PR Newswire, InternetWire, and the like, all maintain online databases by industry and by company that allow one to build a presence in ways that were not possible before. This is both good and bad. On the one hand, practitioners can make sure that news releases have some enduring exposure. On the other hand, practitioners can and do write dozens of news releases that have little news in them solely for the purpose of placement in these databases. The idea is to generate "buzz" about companies, many of them start-ups in search of financing. This is an abuse of online databases, and established media have caught onto the practice. Journalists and editors were annoyed at first then angered by the hype. Analysts and investors found such information flow useful for a while, until they too began to ask questions. Some companies continue flooding online archives with press releases, but it is a poor practice that harms reputations more than helps. There are only a few global companies that have daily news flows that justify such activity.

Ironically, online is useful for researching traditional print and electronic media. Publications post names and beats of editors and reporters, and reporters' stories are archived in depth. There are fewer hassles in learning a reporter's beat, likes, and dislikes. More importantly, PR practitioners have an easy way to learn about the media themselves before contacting them. This is a huge benefit to editors and reporters who constantly complain that PR practitioners call them without any idea of what their media are about.

There are trends about which PR practitioners should be aware. Large and established group publishers like Cahners Business Information and McGraw-Hill, Inc. have been successful in implementing online strategies. They have taken the time to understand and build newsworthy and resource-laden sites. Publishers with large-circulation, general interest magazines tend to have a poor online presence, whereas publishers of financial media, such as *Fortune*, *Forbes*, and *Business Week* are well represented. Electronic media show the same variance. CNN has a powerful Web site with archived and original reporting. On the other hand, some other major networks are weak.

News aggregators are abundant. Aggregation sites list stories from other media's Web sites and link one directly to the stories. News aggregation sites have made daily industry tracking easier for PR practitioners, but they too are variable. Some industries have no news aggregation sites, and others have several. Here is a news aggregation site:

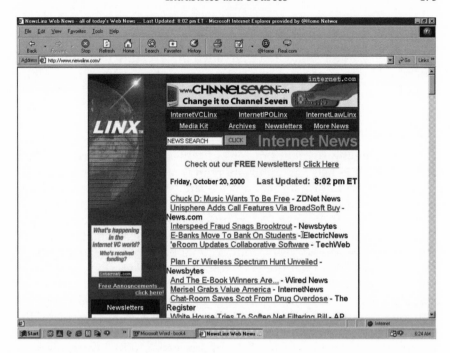

PR practitioners also will find online used as a distribution network for some media, such as limited circulation journals with a small advertising base. Publishers have found that they can dispense with a printing press to get articles to well-defined audiences such as physicians in medical specialties, but such sites are locked off and by subscription only. Moreover, subscriptions tend to be expensive.

It is important to note that what is written here will change—and sometimes quickly—because online is dynamic. We cite sources that we judge to be long-term, but there is no guarantee that a well-developed resource today will exist tomorrow.

The chapter is designed so that you can dip into a topic quickly and get an idea of where you should go and what you should do. Web sites are listed in tables under each heading with key features summarized in boxes next to them for your convenience. We follow the same industry and topic classifications used for traditional print and electronic media because established media use online as an additional distribution outlet.

ACCOUNTING TOPICS

There is a rich resource of accounting information and associations online, but media outlets are sparse. Many accounting associations have linked their sites throughout the world. For example, see The Institute of Internal Auditors at http://www.theiia.org/). There is a printed guide available as well called the Accountant's Guide to the Internet. There is at least one active accounting newsgroup—alt.accounting.

Reading the Tables

In this chapter, there are dozens of tables listing hundreds of Web sites. Each table lists the publication and/or Web site name, the URL of the site, and information about the site. The "Daily News "column indicates whether the Web site offers daily or at most, weekly reports. This is important because PR practitioners will want to contact these Web sites to cover their news. "Archive News" means that publishers have simply reprinted news from original print, TV, or radio sources. In such cases, PR practitioners should continue working with journalists in print, TV, or radio and use online as a research tool and publicity extender. That is, publicity picked up in original print, TV, and radio sources have an extended life on a Web site. The "Resources," column is where the author lists other features that PR practitioners might find useful, including new product tests, resource directories, link sites and industry event calendars. At the least, practitioners will want their products tested, their companies listed and their events in calendars.

Now, on to the tables.

Publication/Medium	URL	Daily news	Archive news	Resources
Accountant's Home Page	http://www.computercpa.com		•	Abundant resources
Anet (Australian)	http://www.csu.edu.au/anet/lists/index.html			30 online mailing lists on accounting topics
Businessfinancemag.com	http://www.businessfinancemag.com/		•	•
Camagazine (for Canadian accountants)	www.camagazine.com/		•	•
CPAnet	http://www.cpalinks.com/index.asp		•	Abundant resources
Electronicaccountant (Faulkner & Gray)	http://www.electronicaccountant.com		•	•
ITAudit Forum	http://www.itaudit.org/		•	Solicits authors for its page on internal auditing
Journal of Accountancy	http://www.aicpa.org/index.htm		•	
Strategic Finance	http://www.mamag.com/strategicfinance/)		•	•
The American Accounting Association	http://www.rutgers.edu/Accounting/raw/aaa/links/			Extensive list of U.S. and

Publication/Medium	URL	Daily news	Archive news	Resources
	natassoc.htm			International accounting organizations from public accounting through internal auditing; a good place for PR practitioners to start finding basic accounting resources
The American Institute of Certified Public Accountants (AICPA)	http://www.aicpa.org/index.htm	•	•	AICPA resources for public accountants
The CPA letter	http://www.aicpa.org/index.htm		•	
The Tax Adviser	http://www.aicpa.org/index.htm		•	

ADVERTISING AND MARKETING TOPICS

The PR practitioner does not have to work hard to find advertising and marketing resources and media online. Online is a primary medium for advertising and marketing news. Weekly publications use online's immediacy to report stories that would be old news by the next print edition. What is listed here skims the surface of available resources. Practitioners working with advertising and marketing organizations should develop their own detailed lists.

Publication/Medium	URL	Daily news	Archive news	Resources
Advertising Age	http://www.adage.com	•	•	Has Interactive Daily, a newswire of online stories; posts online critiques of major Web sites and marketing programs
AdWeek Online	http://www.adweek.com	•	•	Newswire—daily advertising and marketing stories under advertising, media, and interactive
American Demographics	http://www.demographics.com/		•	Marketing tools sourcebook, events and seminars directories, marketing tools, forecasts
Catalog Age	http://industryclick.com/	•	•	Event calendars

Publication/Medium	URL	Daily news	Archive news	Resources
Customer Support Management	http://industryclick.com/	•	•	Sourcebook
Direct Magazine	http://industryclick.com/	•	•	Annual forecast, sourcebook, supplier profiles
Promo	http://industryclick.com/	•	•	Promo 100, trends, sourcebook
BrandWeek (AdWeek sister publication.) BrandWeek and MediaWeek are tied closely online.	http://www.brandweek.com	•	•	
BtoB (Advertising Age's tabloid publication reporting on online business-to-business marketing)	http://www.netb2b.com/	•	•	
DM News (Part of DM News, industry trade for direct marketing)	http://www.dmnews.com/	•		Offers free daily newsletters
IQ Interactive Report			•	Daily newswire subset of BrandWeek and AdWeek focused on online market
Media Central (Part of Direct Magazine)	http://www.mediacentral.com/	•	•	Covers more than the direct industry
MediaWeek				Daily newswire with different content
The Clickz Network	http://www.clickz.com/	•	•	Compendium of counsel and services for marketing and e-commerce
The Internet Advertising Resource Guide	http://www.admedia.org/			Not-for-profit site from a professor at Michigan State University; provides useful resources and links
The University of Texas	http://advertising.utexas.edu/world/			Extensive links page for advertising and marketing
Wilson Internet	http://www.wilsonweb.com/webmarket		•	Compendium of counsel and services for marketing and e-commerce

AGRIBUSINESS

There are a few large sites serving farming and agribusiness that carry in-depth news, information, and resources. These are useful for PR practitioners. There are many more specialty sites and subscriber-only sites that will appeal to practitioners focused on specific areas, such as dairy and horse breeding. Practitioners serving agribusiness organizations will need to develop lists by specialty. Agribusiness publishing firms own the large sites. There are at least three newsgroups—alt.agriculture, sci.agriculture, and uk.business.agriculture.

Publication/Medium	URL	Daily news	Archive news	Resources
@griculture online (from Meredith Corporation that also publishes Successful Farming)	http://www.agriculture.com/	•	•	Markets, weather, and Link Ranker that solicits votes on the worth of the sites from readers
Ag link site/resource	http://www.aaea.org/resources .html			Extensive link collection
Ag link/resource site	http://www.encyberpedia.com/ agri.htm			Extensive link collection
Ag link/resource site	http://www.wisc.edu/ dairy-profit/ag.html			Extensive link collection
Ag link/resource site	http://asae.org/hotlist/abe/			Extensive link collection
Ag link/resource site	http://www.tumpline.com/ stackyard/			Extensive link collection
Agweb	http://www.agweb.com/	•	•	News from five separate publications, including *Farm Journal*; weather reports by U.S. county, livestock and grain market price reports, and analysis; a complete news resource for farmers and related agricultural interests
Crop-Net (Crop Protection Magazine)	http://www.crop-net.com/	•	•	Focuses on all aspects of crop growth and protection from weeds, insects, and diseases.
DirectAg	http://www.directag.com/	•		Marketplace and news source
Farmbid.com	http://www.farmbid.com/	•		Marketplace and news source
Homefarm.com	http://www.homefarm.com/	•	•	Contents of nine different farming and livestock publications from Intertec Publishing Corp.

Publication/Medium	URL	Daily news	Archive news	Resources
Progressive Farmer	http://www.progressivefarmer.com/	•	•	Related to Progressive Farmer today; similar to Agweb
Progressive Farmer Today	http://www.progressivefarmer.com/today/	•	•	Similar to Agweb
Rooster.com	http://www.rooster.com/news/	•		Marketplace and news source

APPLIANCE TOPICS

Overall, there are few resources for PR practitioners to use, and the field appears to be best handled in print media.

Publication/Medium	URL	Daily news	Archive news	Resources
Appliance.com	http://www.appliance.com/			Consumer directory
Dealerscope	http://www2.dealerscope.com/		•	

ARCHITECTURE

At this point, architecture and architects are not well served online, and PR practitioners should continue working more with traditional media. There are at least two newsgroups—alt.building.architecture and alt.architecture. There are a number of architectural e-zines worldwide, but none appear to be dominant. The link sites point to a large number of resources that PR practitioners might find helpful, including historical resources and awards.

Publication/Medium	URL	Daily news	Archive news	Resources
Archinect	http://www.archinect.com/	•	•	•
Archiseek (Irish site)	http://www.archiseek.com/			Directory
Architectural link site	http://www.riceinfo.rice.edu/projects/RDA/links.html			Link site
Architectural Record (McGraw-Hill magazine)	http://www.archrecord.com/	•	•	•
Buildingteam (joint venture of *Cahners Business Information,Building Design & Construction* magazine, and *Consulting-Specifying Engineer* magazine)	http://www.buildingteam.com/	•		

Publication/Medium	URL	Daily news	Archive news	Resources
Cyburbia.org	http://cyburbia.ap.buffalo.edu/pairc/			Link site
Design/Build Business	http://www.dbb-online.com/	•	•	•

ART TOPICS

Fine arts are poorly covered on the Web. There are few general news sources, and many of the magazines that cover the field have a small or no online presence. PR practitioners will find that remaining with a print strategy is the better way to go. There are abundant arts links sites. Many of them are not useful, but some are close to portals for the fine arts. There are at least twenty-five separate newsgroups under rec.arts.

Publication/Medium	URL	Daily news	Archive news	Resources
Absolute Arts	http://www.absolutearts.com/	•	•	•
Art News	http://www.artnewsonline.com/	•		
Arts Journal	http://www.artsjournal.com/	•	•	Aggregated news from various sources; e-mail newsletter, links
Arts links	http://artsnet.heinz.cmu.edu/arts_links.html			Links
Arts Scope	http://www.artscope.net/		•	News aggregated from various sources; forum
Arts Wire	http://www.artswire.org/		•	Links
Folk Art Messenger	http://www.folkart.org/messenger/folkmessenger.html		•	
Gadfly	http://www.gadfly.org		•	Reviews
Performing Arts links	http://www.theatrelibrary.org/links/index.html			Links
World Wide Arts Resources	http://world-arts-resources.com/			Links

AUDIO-VIDEO TRADES

The audio-video trade segment is poorly covered in terms of daily news but has abundant resources. PR practitioners should follow a print stategy in this segment.

Publication/Medium	URL	Daily news	Archive news	Resources
AudioVideo News	http://www.audiovideonews.com/	•	•	New products, events calendar

Publication/Medium	URL	Daily news	Archive news	Resources
AV Video Multimedia Producer	http://www.kipinet.com/av_mmp/issues.htm		•	Industry associations, trade show calendar
DV: Digital Video Magazine	http://www.dv.com/	•	•	Weekly video newsletter, forums, product reviews, buyers guide
Etec	http://www.etecnyc.net		•	
Mixonline	http://www.industryclick.com		•	
Presentations	http://www.presentations.com/		•	Buyers guide, associations, trade show calendar, tutorials
Sound & Video Contractor	http://www.svconline.com/		•	Selected editorial; buyer's guide
Video Age International	http://www.videoageinternational.com/		•	Selected editorial
Video Systems	http://www.videosystems.com/html/Homeset1.htm	•	•	Product reviews; user forum
Visual Convergence (Canadian)	http://www.visualconvergence.com/		•	Selected editorial
VNU Net (U.K.)	http://www.vnunet.com/	•	•	Covers a broad range of news in addition to audiovideo

AUTOMOTIVE AND TRUCKING

Car culture is well represented in cyberspace, so well represented that this synopsis barely scratches the surface of Web sites, bulletin boards, and e-zines. PR practitioners working in the auto and truck industries have a broad array of online news outlets and resources and should have defined online publicity and research strategies. Trucking and fleet management publications are extensive and have in-depth news and resources. The Web is overflowing with facts and figures about autos and the auto industry. We have not covered magazines and resources in languages other than English, but there are many of those as well. There are numerous newsgroups devoted to autos—too many to list more than a few—rec.autos.makers, alt.autos, rec.autos.sport.info, and rec.autos.tech. Truck newsgroups include misc.transport.trucking and rec.outdoors.rv-travel.

Publication/Medium	URL	Daily news	Archive news	Resources
American Motorcyclist Association	http://www.ama-cycle.org/	•	•	•
American Trucker	http://www.trucker.com/		•	Manufacturer's links, trade show calendar

Publication/Medium	URL	Daily news	Archive news	Resources
Automobile Magazine	http://www.automobilemag.com/	•	•	Links, message boards, chat rooms, auto guides, and more
Automotive Aftermarket World	http://www.aftermarketworld .com/		•	•
Automotive Marketer	http://www.autonews.com/html/ main/amarketer/index.htm	•	•	•
Automotive News (tied to Autonews Europe, Automotive News International, and Automotive Marketer	http://www.autonews.com/html/ main/index.html	•	•	•
Automotive News International	http://www .autonewsinternational.com/	•	•	•
Automotive Week (aftermarket parts and repair)	http://www.auto-week.com/	•	•	•
AutonewsEurope	http://www.autonewseurope .com/	•	•	•
Autoweb	http://www.autoweb.com/			Car specifications
Car and Driver	http://www.caranddriver.com/	•		
Edmunds	http://www.edmunds.com/			Essential resources for new and used cars
eTrucker.net	http://www.etrucker.net/	•		
Fleet Central (combines several fleet management publications from Bobit Publishing)	http://www.fleet-central.com/	•	•	•
Fleet Owner	http://www.fleetowner.com/	•	•	•
Hemmings	http://hemmings.com/			Central resource for auto collectors
Hemmings (Auto clubs)	http://clubs.hemmings.com/index .cfm			Information on thousands of car clubs
Kelley Blue Book	http://www.kbb.com/			Essential resource for new and used cars
Land Line Magazine	http://www.landlinemag.com/	•		
Motor Trend	http://www.motortrend.com/	•		Emphasizes services for car owners
NASCAR Racing News	http://www.nascar.com	•	•	•
National Automobile Dealers Association	http://www.nada.org/			Industry data
Off-road	http://www.offroad.com	•		
Road & Track	http://www.roadandtrack.com/	•		
Trailer Life (RV news)	http://www.trailerlife.com	•	•	•
Trailer/Body Builders	http://industryclick.com	•	•	

Publication/Medium	URL	Daily news	Archive news	Resources
Transport Topics	http://www.ttnews.com/	•	•	Message board; includes *Light & Medium Truck Magazine*
Truckinginfo.com	http://www.truckinginfo.com/	•	•	Product guide
Wards Auto World	http://www.wardsauto.com/	•	•	•

AVIATION AND AEROSPACE

PR practitioners will find that online news sources are slim in number, except for the overpowering Aviation Week site. On the other hand, resources are in depth and link sites deep and useful. There are at least six aviation newsgroups—alt.disasters.aviation, alt.aviation.safety, rec.aviation.student, rec.aviation.piloting, rec.aviation.military, and aus.aviation. There are at least two aerospace newsgroups—sci.space.policy and rec.models.rockets.

Publication/Medium	URL	Daily news	Archive news	Resources
Aviation Week (McGraw-Hill)	http://www.aviationnow.com/	•	•	Covers the global aviation and aerospace industry with staff-generated copy; news is divided into 11 categories; includes contents of more than 10 publications and newsletters; it has a forum, polling on issues, reference books and technical documentation, careers center, events calendar, and shopping
AVweb	http://www.avweb.com/	•	•	•
Landings	http://www.landings.com/	•	•	•
Spaceviews	http://www.spaceviews.com/	•	•	•
Space.com	http://www.space.com/	•	•	Maintains a roster of 5,000 links on space topics
Arjen's Aviation links	http://www.ameijer.demon.nl/airlinks.htm			More than 1,500 sites
Caltech link site	http://www.alumni.caltech.edu/~padam/htmls/AeroLinks.html			Aerospace links
X-CD Business Technologies	http://www.x-cd.com/			Database of 7,000 aerospace, aviation, and defense companies

BAKING

PR practitioners who work in the baking industry will find that online options are sparse. In addition, there are few link or resource sites. Two Web sites serve the baking industry. Both are owned by trade publications that serve commercial bakers, and both strive to be news and information resources.

Publication/Medium	URL	Daily news	Archive news	Resources
Bakingbusiness.com	http://www.bakingbusiness.com/	•	•	•
Bakery-Net	http://www.bakery-net.com/	•	•	•
Modern Baking Magazine	http://www.bakery-net.com /rdocs/modern/modbak .html		•	Recipes, industry calendar

BANKING AND FINANCE

The number of banking and finance news outlets and financial information resources online are overwhelming. This brief collection does not include general financial and economic information. Any PR practitioner working in these areas should have a well-developed strategy for using them. At best we can provide a glimpse of some of the largest media and resource sites. There are dozens of free resource sites that provide information on stocks, bonds, companies, commodities, and more. There are dozens more sites that are by subscription.

Financial information is so abundant that some investor relations strategies, particularly for start-up companies, depend on online exposure. PR practitioners should surf resources to get an idea of information that is readily and freely available.

Publication/Medium	URL	Daily news	Archive news	Resources
American Banker	http://www.americanbanker .com/	•	•	Has a members only section
Bank Technology News (Faulkner & Gray)	http://www.electronicbanker .com/		•	
Bloomberg	http://www.bloomberg.com/	•	•	Comprehensive news and financial site with huge resources
Bridge (Bridge news service)	http://www.bridge.com/	•	•	•
CBS Marketwatch	http://www.cbsmarketwatch.com/ news/newsroom.htx	•	•	•
CNBC (Part of CNBC cable TV channel)	http://www.cnbc.com/	•	•	•
CNNfn (Part of CNNfn cable TV channel	http://www.cnnfn.com/	•	•	•

Publication/Medium	URL	Daily news	Archive news	Resources
Dismal Science (Economics)	http://www.dismal.com/			Economic data
Dow Jones	http://www.dowjones.work.com/	•	•	•
Economics	http://.economics.miningco.com/finance/economics/			Economic data
Family Money (from Better Homes and Gardens: Personal Finance)	http://www.familymoney.com/	•	•	•
Financial Service Online (Faulkner & Gray)	http://fso.faulknergray.com/	•	•	Covers a broad range of banking and Wall Street issues
Free Edgar	http://www.freeedgar.com/			EDGAR, the Securities and Exchange Commission's online database of corporate filings; a primary source for public company information
Hoovers Online	http://www.hoovers.com/			Company profiles, information on initial public offerings, stock screens, and more
Ino	http://www.ino.com/	•	•	Information for futures, options, and equity traders
Intellifact	http://www.intellifact.com/			Provides information on 300,000 companies worldwide
Money (Part of Money Magazine; Personal finance.	http://www.money.com/money/	•	•	•
Morningstar	http://www.morningstar.net/			Mutual fund information
News Alert	http://www.newsalert.com/	•		For breaking financial news
Quote.com	http://www.quote.com/			Stock information
Registered Representative	http://industryclick.com	•	•	Forum, links, commentary
Smartmoney (Personal Finance)	http://www.smartmoney.com/	•	•	•
The Motley Fool (Started on AOL and moved to Web; Personal finance)	http://www.fool.com/	•	•	•
TheStreet.com (Financial news e-zine)	http://www.thestreet.com/	•	•	•
The Wall Street Journal	http://wsj.com			Interactive edition; subscription-based

Publication/Medium	URL	Daily news	Archive news	Resources
Trusts & Estates	http://www.trustsandestates.com		•	
Wall Street Research Net	http://www.wsrn.com/	•	•	Research on more than 29,000 companies, mutual funds, and indexes; claims more than 500,000 links to SEC documents, company home pages, annual reports, press releases and other investor information, stock quotes, graphs, audio, and more
Yahoo! Finance (comprehensive digest of news and stock information)	http://finance.yahoo.com/	•	•	•

BEAUTY AND COSMETICS TRADES

Though e-commerce and manufacturers sites related to beauty and cosmetics are abundant, news sites about the industry are not. At the time of writing, we could not find a single site that was a news or resource site for the industry at large. PR practitioners working in beauty and cosmetic trades should rely on traditional print publications.

BEVERAGE INDUSTRY—BEER, WINE, SOFT DRINKS

Overall, the industry does not appear to be well covered from a trade perspective.

There are many links pages for beer and wine, which PR practitioners can use to build a list of resources, and there are many e-commerce and winery Web sites as well as usenet (.news:alt.food.wine) and discussion groups focused on food and wine. The industry is fragmented online, and this makes the practitioner's job harder.

Publication/Medium	URL	Daily news	Archive news	Resources
Beverage World	http://www.beverageworld.com/	•	•	Reports on the soft drink industry as well

Publication/Medium	URL	Daily news	Archive news	Resources
Beveragenet	http://www.beveragenet.net/	•	•	Combined site for several magazines in the beer, wine, and spirits industry; provides daily news and resources
Robin Garr's Wine Lovers' Page	http://www.www .wine-lovers-page.com/	•	•	Industry and wine news that PR practitioners know about
Smart Wine	http://smartwine.com/	•	•	Daily news from several wine industry publications
Wine Spectator	http://winespectator.com/	•	•	Carries a broad range of news on the wine industry

BOOK, JOURNALISM, AND PUBLISHING TRADES

The book, journalism, and publishing trades are covered in depth online, and PR practitioners should have little trouble finding news outlets. What is listed here scratches the surface of resources available. Consult Online Public Relations (http://www.online-pr.com) for other links resources, of which there are many.

Publication/Medium	URL	Daily news	Archive news	o	Resources
American Booksellers Association	http://www.bookweb.org/	•	•		News about independent bookstores nationwide
American Journalism Review (AJR)	http://ajr.newslink.org/	•	•		Journalism news and resources in great depth; more than 18,000 links to newspapers, magazines, broadcasters, and news services worldwide; a powerful voice examining and promoting online journalism
Bookwire(Publishers Weekly)	http://www.bookwire.com/	•	•		Comprehensive online news resource for the industry
Circulation Management	http://industryclick.com	•	•		Awards, forum
Columbia Journalism Review	http://www.cjr.org/		•		

Publication/Medium	URL	Daily news	Archive news	Resources
Editor and Publisher Online	http://www.mediainfo.com/	•	•	Comprehensive news and resource site
Electric Library	www.elibrary.com			Searches the contents of hundreds of magazines and newspapers
Ezine-Universe	http://ezine-universe.com/			Tracks e-zines and e-mail newsletters
Folio Magazine	www.industryclick.com	•	•	Daily newsletter
Jim Romenesko's Daily Media News	http://www.poynter.org/ medianews/index.cfm	•	•	Bulletin board
Kidon's media links	http://www.kidon.com/ media-link/index.shtml			Lists media by country worldwide
Library Journal	http://www.ljdigital.com/	•	•	Informative site with news and resources focused on publishing and libraries
Mediaweek Daily	http://www.mediaweek.com/	•		Daily events in publishing
Operations & fulfillment	http://www.industryclick.com	•	•	Sourcebook
Publist	http://www.publist.com/			More than 150,000 magazines, journals, newsletters, and other periodicals
School Library Journal Online	http://www.slj.com/	•	•	Serves librarians working with young people in school and public libraries

BUILDING AND CONSTRUCTION TOPICS

Most information in this segment is republished from print media. The building and construction segment overall appears to have in-depth resources for suppliers and for events such as trade shows. Some of these, however, are by subscription only. If one is looking for resources globally, there are several link sites available. When searching for building and construction links, it is best to search both on combined and individual terms—"building and construction links," "building links," and "construction links."

Publication/Medium	URL	Daily news	Archive news	Resources
Builder Online	http://www.builderonline.com/	•	•	Comprehensive news and resource site
Building Design & Construction	http://www.bdcmag.com/		•	

Publication/Medium	URL	Daily news	Archive news	Resources
HousingZone	http://www.housingzone.com/	•	•	Comprehensive news and resource site; combines the news content and resources of several magazines
International Construction	http://industryclick.com		•	

BUSINESS AND COMMERCIAL

This category encompasses major business magazines and newspapers. Some have separate online editorial staffs or publish news online at the same time or before it reaches print columns.

Online newsrooms are not unusual for media like the *Wall Street Journal*, which has long had the Dow-Jones newswires. For the most part, magazine Web sites have the same editorial focus as the magazines themselves and often feature the same columnists.

The magazines listed here are a fraction of what is available, and sites change frequently. Most business and commercial Web sites maintain deep resources in many topic areas that are useful for research. In addition, there are hundreds of local and national general business link sites—far too many for practitioners to use effectively.

Publication/Medium	URL	Daily news	Archive news	Resources
American City Business Journals	http://bizjournals.bcentral .com		•	A central site for its 41 city journals that provides a broad resource of local business information; PR practitioners who need to research information from different locales should find it a good resource
BizReport	http://www.bizreport.com/		•	Focuses on the Internet
Business 2.0	http://www.business2.com/	•	•	Bills itself as a publication for the new economy
Business Week Online	www.businessweek.com	•	•	Divided into BW Daily, open to anyone, and magazine for

Publication/Medium	URL	Daily news	Archive news	Resources
				subscribers only; "Video Views" section interviews experts and others and backlogs audio interviews; provides media opportunities for PR practitioners
Crain's Chicago Business	http://www.crainschicagobusiness.com/		•	•
Crain's Cleveland Business	http://www.crainscleveland.com/		•	
Crain's Detroit Business	http://www.crainsdetroit.com	•	•	•
Crain's New York Business	http://www.crainsnewyorkbusiness.com/	•	•	•
Employee Benefit News	http://benefitnews.com		•	
Entrepreneur	http://www.entrepreneur.com/		•	
Fast Company	http://www.fastcompany.com/homepage/	•	•	Lifestyle Web page that focuses on broad themes with a different theme each week; there is opportunity for PR practitioners to fit news into the themes
Financial Times	http://news.ft.com/	•	•	Divided into world news, business news, market news, and market prices; search engine looks for articles in more than 3,000 publications; general resource business directory, business reports by industry segment; among the most ambitious offerings in general business news
Forbes	http://www.forbes.com/	•	•	Broad range of news, personal investing, and online resources; has content republished from the magazine and Digital Tool
Fortune	http://www.fortune.com/fortune/	•	•	Provides daily column on technology; aspires to be a broad resource for businesspeople,

Publication/Medium	URL	Daily news	Archive news	Resources
				including leisure and investing advice
Inc	http://www.inc.com/		•	Aspires to be a general resource for the small businessperson, including the magazine, newsletters, products, and services
Industry Standard	http://www.thestandard.com/	•	•	A broad news and feature site with republished material, investor information, and newsletters
IndustryWeek	http://www.industryweek.com/		•	
Pensions & Investments	http://www.pionline.com/	•	•	Locks off daily news page to all but subscribers
Quality Digest	http://www.qualitydigest.com/		•	
Red Herring	http://www.redherring.com/		•	Has video archive and subscriber only services
The Economist	http://www.economist.com/		•	Offers newsletters, access to its archives, and access to its surveys of industries and countries
The Journal of Commerce	http://www.joc.com/	•	•	A full news site focusing on transportation and trade
The Wall Street Journal	http://interactive.wsj.com/home.html	•	•	One of the few successful subscriber sites; offers three views of its editions— Europe, Asia, and the United States; offers special section on technology news and access to archives of past editions, as well as customized personal portfolio page
Upside	http://www.upside.com/	•	•	•

CERAMICS AND GLASS TRADES

The ceramic and glass industries republish content from print editorial. *Glass Magazine*, from the National Glass Association, provides a good resource directory that PR practitioners might find useful. There is an abundance of links resources for glass and ceramics, primarily collector oriented, and for e-tailers and manufacturers. Practitioners working in the ceramics and glassware trades are better off with print publications.

Publication/Medium	URL	Daily news	Archive news	Resources
Glass Magazine	http://www.glass.org/		•	Trade show calendar, industry links
UK Glass Magazine	http://www.glassage.com/		•	Trade show calendar
US Glass Magazine	http://www.usglassmag.com/		•	Newsgroup, seminar listings, links

CHEMICAL TRADES

In the chemical trade industry, print publications dominate. PR practitioners working in this field may find that there is little need for an online strategy. There is at least one newsgroup focusing on chemicals—sci.chem.

Publication/Medium	URL	Daily news	Archive news	Resources
Chemical & Engineering News (American Chemical Society)	http://www.acs.org/	•	•	Locks off daily news to all but subscribers; massive resources
Chemical Engineering	http://www.che.com/		•	Offers a suppliers/buyers guide and calendar of trade shows
Chemical Market Reporter	http://www.chemexpo.com/	•		Profiles of manufacturers and information about the chemical products they manufacture
Chemical Week	http://www.chemweek.com/			Useful links from the Environmental Protection Agency (http://www.epa.gov/c eppo/cameo/links

Publication/Medium	URL	Daily news	Archive news	Resources
				.htm) and Chemfinder.com (http://www.chemfinder .camsoft .com/), which provides links, searches in chemical databases and its own news, Chemnews (http://www.chemnews . com/)

CHILDREN AND YOUTH

This is a category dominated by games, activities, and republished content. However, it is also the segment that has been exploited more than any other for online public relations through skillful use of chat rooms, bulletin boards, games, and other interactivity. Many of the major teen publications have little or no exposure online. There are thousands of kids', children, and youth news sites. Most are of no value to PR practitioners. The same can be said for links for kids, children, and youth. There are several portals that are built just for young people with approved links that keep them out of trouble. They are not listed here, but practitioners should be aware of them. Both AOL (America Online) and CompuServe have youth and teen sections that are of value. PR practitioners working in this area need an online strategy.

Publication/Medium	URL	Daily news	Archive news	Resources
American Cheerleader	http://www.americancheerleader. com/		•	Directory
American Girl	http://www.americangirl.com/ homepage2.html		•	Calendar, games
AOL (America Online) Teens		•	•	Music, movies, fan club, games, sports girls, chat, and style
Classroom Connect	http://www.classroom.com/home .asp		•	Online lesson plans and resources for K–12 teachers in cooperation with major content suppliers; also has Ed's Oasis, a similar resource: http://www.classroom .com/edsoasis/
CompuServe Kids				TV, movies, music, games, sports, activities for little kids

Publication/Medium	URL	Daily news	Archive news	Resources
Connect for Kids	http://www.connectforkids.org/ homepage1535/index.htm		•	E-mail newsletter for kids
Cricket Magazine Group	http://www.cricketmag.com/		•	Includes Cricket, Spider, Ladybug, Babybug, Click, and Muse
Dinosaur Interplanetary Gazette	http://www.dinosaur.org/ frontpage.html		•	Reviews, message board
Dosomething.org	http://www.dosomething.org/		•	Contests, forum
Dragonfly	http://www.muohio.edu/ dragonfly/		•	
e-Pals	http://www.epals.com/			Classroom exchange and community connecting two million students in 182 countries
Family World	http://family.go.com/			Activities for parents and kids
Freewheelin' (Canadian)	http://www.freewheelin.com/		•	Forum
Generation Next	http://www.gennext.com/		•	
Girls' Life	http://www.girlslife.com/		•	Q and A, contests
Heckler	http://www.heckler.com/		•	Video gallery
Hip	http://www.hipmag.org/		•	
Inkspot	http://www.inkspot.com/			Writing help for kids, links list
Jump	http://www.jumponline.com/ jump-main.cfm			Quiz
Kid City	http://www.ctw.org/		•	Games
Kidnews	http://www.kidnews.com/		•	
Kidsworld	http://www.kidsworld-online.com/pages/main.html			Games, poll
Lollipop	http://www.lollipop.com/		•	
Magical Blend	http://www.magicalblend.com/		•	
Mamamedia	http://www.mamamedia.com/			Games, contests
Mirror	http://www.mirrormirror.com/		•	Survey, reviews, calendar, club; for Puget Sound teenagers in Washington State
NandoNext	http://www.nando.net/links/ nandonext/next.html		•	New York Times Learning Network
Nickelodeon	http://www.nick.com/		•	TV schedule, games, music, activities, chat room, horoscope, weather
Owlkids online (Canadian)	http://www.owlkids.com/		•	Games, lots of games; includes Chickadee
Pencil News	http://www.msnbc.com/local/ pencilnews/	•	•	

Publication/Medium	URL	Daily news	Archive news	Resources
Puddler	http://puddler.ducks.org/ puddler/index.html		•	Games
Ranger Rick	http://nwf.org/rangerrick/index .html		•	Games, activities, stories
Scholastic	http://www.scholastic.com/kids/ index.htm	•	•	Activities, games, parent and teacher sections, Web guide, forum
Shift	http://www.shift.com/	•	•	Web radio and TV
Sports Illustrated for Kids	http://www.sikids.com/	•	•	Fantasy sports, digital sports cards
Teen People	http://teenpeople.com/ teenpeople/flashhome	•	•	Poll
Teen Voices	http://www.teenvoices.com/		•	
Time Magazine for Kids	http://www.timeforkids.com/TFK/ index.html	•	•	Toolbox, games
Turtle	http://www.turtlemag.org/		•	
Twist	http://www.twistmag.com/		•	Mail, games, quizzes, polls, links
Urb	http://www.urb.com/home.html		•	
Wrestling World for Kids	http://www.wwforkids.com/		•	
YO! Youth Outlook	http://www.pacificnews.org/yo/		•	
Y-Press	http://www.ypress.org/	•	•	Reviews of books, games, movies, and music

CHURCHES AND RELIGION

Churches and religions use online intensively. Not surprisingly, Web sites are segmented by religions, and few are interactive. Almost all sites reprint content from publications. One publication only reaches across denominational lines, *Chistianity Today*. PR practitioners will find online a barrier when attempting to reach broad groups of churches or religions. On the whole, it is better to stay with print.

Publication/Medium	URL	Daily news	Archive news	Resources
Christianity online (*Christianity Today*)	http://www.christianitytoday .com/		•	News by demographic groups, book reviews, resources, and a search engine for Christian sites; attempts to serve all Christian denominations

CLEANING, DYEING, AND LAUNDRY TRADES

There were no Web sites at the time of writing that covered news from these industries, and most online representation came from associations representing the industries, such as the Coin Laundry Association (http://www.coinlaundry.org/), and the International Fabricare Institute (http://www.ifi.org/). The PR practitioner looking to reach these industries will find little help online.

COMPUTER, DATA PROCESSING, AND SOFTWARE TRADES

As practitioners would expect, these industries are covered in-depth online, although there is a still plenty of content republished from print publications. A few publishing groups have an enormous presence, whereas others are modest, but even the modest Web sites are more informative than most industries. The Usenet has forty-six separate newsgroups focused on all aspects of computing under the extension "comp." There are hundreds of link sites. PR practitioners should be able to find just about anything online related to computer, data processing, and software news and resources, and they should have a well-developed online strategy.

Publication/Medium	URL	Daily news	Archive news	Resources
2600: The Hacker Quarterly	http://www.2600.org/	•	•	
@stake Security News	http://www.atstake.com/security_news/	•	•	Events
AllEC.com	http://www.allec.com/	•	•	Products/services guide, message board, calendar
Andover News Network	http://www.andovernews.com/index.html	•	•	Newswire covering sectors of the industry
Asiabiztech	http://www.nikkeibp.asiabiztech.com/	•	•	
AtNewYork	http://www.atnewyork.com/	•		Forums, events calendar
Bizreport	http://www.bizreport.com/	•	•	Events calendar
Boardwatch	http://www.boardwatch.com/	•	•	ISP directory, buyer's guide, events calendar
Byte Magazine	http://www.byte.com/	•	•	Tools, downloads, newsletter
CMP media's Techweb	http://www.techweb.com/	•	•	More than 30 company and affiliated magazines, content web sites, and

Publication/Medium	URL	Daily news	Archive news	Resources
				newswires into a gigantic site that the PR practitioner can surf for hours at a time; many outlets for news
Computer News Daily	http://www.computernewsdaily.com/	•		Discussion groups
Computerwire	http://www.computerwire.com/	•		
Computerworld	http://www.computerworld.com/	•	•	Poll, white papers, field reports, reviews
CNET.com	http://www.cnet.com/	•	•	Huge news and resource e-zine; many outlets for news
CompInfo-Center.com	http://www.www.compinfo-center.com/			List of dozens of computer publications that have online Web sites
Computer Hope	http://www.computerhope.com/			Hundreds of links and resources that practitioners can use
CRM Daily	http://www.crmdaily.com/	•	•	
Davenetics	http://www.davenetics.com/	•		
Dr. Dobb's Journal	http://www.ddj.com/	•	•	News and content on programming topics
Earthweb	http://intranetjournal.earthweb.com/		•	E-mail newsletters
Ecommerce Times	http://www.ecommercetimes.com/	•	•	Industry guide, message board
E-commerce news	http://www.internetnews.com/ec-news/	•	•	E-mail newsletters
Ecompany Now	http://www.ecompanynow.com/	•	•	E-mail newsletters, product guides.
EDTN Network	http://www.edtn.com/	•	•	E-cyclopaedia
Electric News (Ireland)	http://www.electricnews.net/	•	•	Events, reviews, survey
Electronic Commerce	http://www.ecommerce.internet.com/	•	•	Webopaedia, discussion list, reviews
ENT	http://www.entmag.com/	•	•	Product reviews, buyer's guide.
Federal Computer Week	http://www.fcw.com/	•	•	Focused on government computing and government contractors
Government Computer News	http://www.gcn.com/	•	•	Focused on government

Publication/Medium	URL	Daily news	Archive news	Resources
				computing and government contractors
Hotwired	http://hotwired.lycos.com/	•	•	E-mail newsletters
iBoost	http://www.iboost.com/	•	•	E-mail newsletters, forums
IDG.net	http://www.idg.net/	•	•	Links to publisher's magazines (including Computerworld, CIO, and The Industry Standard); links to research and books and up-to-the-minute news; access to 15 distinct channels of information from financial news to technical development; PR practitioners can access news in 15 distinct global regions and in several languages
Information Security Magazine	http://www.infosecuritymag.com/	•	•	Vendor links
Information Today	http://www.infotoday.com/			Combines magazines and information resources into one large links page
Information Week	http://www.informationweek.com/	•	•	Event calendars, e-mail newsletters, resources
Interactive Week	http://www.zdnet.com/intweek/	•	•	Downloads, events
Internet.com	http://www.internet.com/home-d.html	•	•	Internet industry portal
Internet Week	http://www.internetwk.com/	•	•	Reviews, case studies, resource center, event calendars
Internet World	http://www.internetworld.com/	•	•	Newsletters, events, conferences, resources
Internet News	http://www.internetnews.com/	•		
IT Director	http://www.it-director.com/	•	•	Events calendar, conference calendar, glossary
IT World	http://www.itworld.com/	•	•	Product reviews, e-mail newsletters,

Publication/Medium	URL	Daily news	Archive news	Resources
				white papers, web casts
IT World Canada	http://www.itworldcanada.com/	•	•	Calendar, interviews, expert help
Line 56	http://www.line56.com/	•	•	B2B directory, e-mail newsletters
Linux Journal	http://www.www2.linuxjournal.com/	•	•	User groups, career center, speaker's bureau
Linux.com	http://www.linux.com/	•		
Markets and Exchanges B2B (International focus)	http://www.marketsandexchanges.com/		•	Newsletters, industry directory, events calendar
Microsoft	http://www.microsoft.com/			Hundreds of links and resources that practitioners can use
Netmarketers Magazine	http://www.netmarketmakers.com/	•	•	Events, e-mail newsletters, knowledge base
New Media	http://www.newmedia.com/	•	•	Focuses on digital content creators
Newsbytes	http://www.newsbytes.com/	•	•	Online wire service that covers a broad range of computer technology
Newsfactor Network	http://www.newsfactor.com/	•	•	E-mail newsletters
Newslinx	http://www.newslinx.com/	•		Aggregation site that pulls Internet and Web-related stories from dozens of publications
On Magazine	http://www.onmagazine.com/on-mag/	•	•	Reviews, forum
OS Opinion	http://www.osopinion.com/	•	•	Commentary, chat rooms
PC World	http://www.pcworld.com/	•	•	Discussion groups, e-mail newsletters, reviews, downloads
SD Times	http://www.sdtimes.com/		•	Links
Security Focus	http://www.securityfocus.com/	•	•	Mailing list, calendar, links
Siliconvalley.com	http://www.siliconvalley.com/	•	•	
Silicon Alley Reporter	http://www.siliconalleyreporter.com/main.html		•	
Slashdot	http://www.slashdot.org/	•		A news site combined with bulletin board
Smart Business Magazine	http://www.zdnet.com/smartbusinessmag/	•	•	
Softletter	http://www.softletter.com/		•	Awards

Publication/Medium	URL	Daily news	Archive news	Resources
Streaming Media	http://www.streamingmedia.com/	•	•	Product reviews, e-mail newsletters
Tech TV	http://www.techtv.com/techtv/	•	•	Product reviews
The Chronicle of Higher Education Information Technology page	http://chronicle.com/infotech/	•	•	
Unix Insider	http://www.sunworld.com/unixinsideronline/home.html		•	White papers.
URL Wire	http://www.urlwire.com/	•		
Webreview	http://webreview.com/		•	
Winmag	http://www.winmag.com/	•	•	Discussion groups, e-mail newsletters, reviews
Winplanet	http://www.winplanet.com/winplanet			Hundreds of links and resources that practitioners can use
Wired	http://www.wired.com/	•	•	Maintains online wire service
Wired News	http://www.wired.com/news	•	•	Product reviews, e-mail newsletters, webcasts
Yahoo Daily Technology News	http://dailynews.yahoo.com/headlines/technology	•		
Zdnet.com	http://www.zdnet.com/	•	•	Combines all ZD Inc. publications and resource sites into a gigantic news and information resource site for computer professionals and amateurs; many outlets for news
ZDNet E-commerce	http://www.zdnet.com/enterprise/e-business/	•	•	Reviews, downloads, e-mail newsletters

CONSERVATION, ENVIRONMENTAL, AND NATURE

All major environmental, conservation, and nature associations and magazines have an online presence, but only one or two do more than republish content from print columns. On the whole, online news outlets for conservation, environment, and nature are skimpy. Link sites and resources are scattered, but there are many of them. There are dozens of conservation and environment newsgroups on the Usenet, but they are spread through major discussion group headings. The PR practitioner should be prepared to dig when looking for resources and to work with print publications first.

Publication/Medium	URL	Daily news	Archive news	Resources
Eelink	http://eelink.net/			A catalog of environmental educational sites and materials
Environment Canada	http://www.ns.ec.gc.ca/links.html			Maintains a lengthy link site
National Audubon	http://www.audubon.org/		•	•
Sierra Club	http://www.sierraclub.org/	•	•	•
Trout Unlimited	http://www.tu.org/		•	Aggregates news weekly from multiple sources
World Wide Web virtual library	http://earthsystems.org/ Environment.shtml			A list of environmental lists

COUNTRY/WESTERN LIVING AND LIFESTYLE SITES

Few country lifestyle magazines have made it to the Web, and those that have tend to republish content. *Country Living* (http://www.countryliving.com/) maintains an elegant site with a daily tip but not much more. *Mother Earth News* (http://www. motherearthnews.com/) offers a range of self-help tips but no online news, and Yankee (http://www.newengland.com/yankee/index.html) is primarily an e-commerce site.

There are some resource sites, but not many, and they are widely scattered. PR practitioners working in this arena should stick to print publications.

DAIRY PRODUCTS AND TRADES

The dairy industry has several sources of news and information. Internationally, there are many dairy sites worth checking, especially in the United Kingdom and Australia. Link site resources, unfortunately, tend to be scattered, and the practitioner will need to look broadly.

Publication/Medium	URL	Daily news	Archive news	Resources
Dairy Business	http://www.dairybusiness.com/	•	•	Combines six publications; features a daily radio program that can be downloaded by radio stations or directly—Dairyline radio; has industry

Publication/Medium	URL	Daily news	Archive news	Resources
				resources, including ag expos, a farm direct mail list service, and colleges and their dairy programs
Dairy Foods	http://www.dairyfoods.com/	•	•	Has a supplier sourcebook and other resources, such as dairy associations and industry calendar
Dairy Max Linx	http://www.dairymax.org/	•	•	Sponsored by dairy farmers in Oklahoma, New Mexico, Texas, and western Tennessee; a news and link site
DairyBiz	http://www.dairybiz.com/		•	Uses infomercials from ag companies
Moomilk	http://www.moomilk.com/			A site for kids; features recipes

DENTAL TRADES

Online resources for dentistry are abundant. Overall, there are hundreds of dental sites, most which belong to practicing dentists. There are many dental journals, but almost all are republished content or peer-reviewed e-zines that do not publish news. PR practitioners will find that news outlets for dental trades are scarce, and conventional print trade media are still the prime resource for publicity.

Publication/Medium	URL	Daily news	Archive news	Resources
ADA News Daily (American Dental Association)	http://www.ada.org/	•		•
American Dental Hygienist's Association	http://www.adha.org/	•		•
Dental Related Internet Resources	http://www.www .dental-resources.com/			Link site
Dental Review Online	http://www.dentalreview.com/			Abundance of resources and a large link site
Southern Illinois University at Carbondale	http://www.lib.siu.edu/hp/ divisions/sci/health/dental.html			Large dental link site
The Dental Net	http://www.thedentalnet.com/ d-link1.htm			Links to online resources
The University of Pittsburgh	http://www.hsls.pitt.edu/intres/			Large dental link site in health section

DEPARTMENT, CHAIN, AND SPECIALTY STORE TRADES

Whereas every major department, chain, and specialty store has a presence online, the same cannot be said for news and resources covering the industry. They are sparse. PR practitioners will find that the traditional print publications are still the most important news outlet in this industry.

Publication/Medium	URL	Daily news	Archive news	Resources
Chain Store Age Online	http://www.chainstoreage.com/	•	•	News, technology, operations, e-commerce, real estate, people, financial, and research
Chain Store Guide	http://www.csgis.com/			Database that tracks over 300,000 retailers, distributors, and wholesalers in the United States and Canada; a subscription site
Drug Store News	http://www.drugstorenews.com/	•		News site divided into industry, cosmetics and fragrance, chains, personal and beauty care, health, and general merchandise
DSN Retailing Today (Discount Store News)	http://www.discountstorenews.com/	•	•	
National Home Center News	http://www.homecenternews.com/	•		Home improvement stores
SCWonline (Shopping Center World)	http://www.scwonline.com/	•	•	Retail real estate news

DRUG TRADES

By comparison to the number of print publications serving the drug and pharmacy field, online news offerings are few. For the most part, PR practitioners working in the drug industry should concentrate on print publications for news outlets. Resource sites are few in number, and search engines mix them in with sites dealing with illegal drugs and drug prevention. Sci.med.pharmacy is a newsgroup focused on pharmacy issues.

Publication/Medium	URL	Daily news	Archive news	Resources
Drug Topics	http://www.drugtopics.com/		•	•
FDC Reports	http://www.fdcreports.com/		•	Republishes news with a one-week delay from eight newsletters, including the Pink Sheet, Health News Daily, and Pharmaceutical Approvals Monthly
Health News.com	http://www.drugs.healthnews.com/	•	•	An aggregation of stories about the industry, mixed in with stories about illegal drugs
Pharmacy Times	http://pharmacytimes.com/	•	•	•
PharmInfoNet	http://pharminfo.com/			Database of information on drugs and article archives
PharmWeb	http://www.pharmweb.net/			A global resource site from the University of Manchester in the United Kingdom
The Pharmacy virtual library	http://www.cpb.uokhsc.edu/pharmacy/pharmint.html			A comprehensive link site to pharmacy schools, links and other resources
U.S. Pharmacist	http://www.uspharmacist.com/		•	

ELECTRICAL TRADES

PR practitioners will find an abundance of online resources but a scarcity of news outlets online. There is not much need for an online strategy for the electrical trade Web sites. There is an online newsgroup site at alt.engineering.electrical.

Publication/Medium	URL	Daily news	Archive news	Resources
Builders Data	http://buildersdata.com/diy/electrical/index.html			Comprehensive links section
CEE News	http://www.ceenews.com/		•	
Electrical Construction & Maintenance	http://industryclick.com/		•	
Electrical Contractor	http://www.ecmag.com/	•	•	
Electrical Marketing (subscription only)	http://www.electricalmarketing.com/		•	

Publication/Medium	URL	Daily news	Archive news	Resources
Electrical Wholesaling	http://industryclick.com/		•	
Electrical Zone	http://www.electricalzone.com/	•	•	News and articles reprinted from four trade magazines
Lightforum.com	http://www.archlighting.com/	•		General resource site with links to industry associations and regulation sites
Lighting News	http://www.lightingnews.com/	•	•	News and information for electrical and lighting divided into product, corporate, trade, and feature news sections
Lightsearch.com	http://www.lightsearch.com/	•		Directory and links to manufacturers
Transmission & Distribution World	http://industryclick.com		•	

ELECTRONICS TRADES

The depth of online news sources and information indicate that PR practitioners should have an online media strategy when working in the electronics trades. In addition, at least three separate newsgroups focus on electronics at sci.electronics.

Publication/Medium	URL	Daily news	Archive news	Resources
Cahner's Semiconductor International	http://www.semiconductor.net/	•	•	Bills itself as "The Definitive Internet Resource for the Semiconductor Manufacturing Industry"
Circuits Assembly	http://www.circuitsassembly.com/	•	•	
EDN magazine	http://www.ednmag.com/	•	•	
Electronic Business	http://www.eb-mag.com/	•	•	
Electronic Design	http://www.elecdesign.com/		•	
Electronic Design, Technology and News (EDTN) network (CMP Publishing)	http://www.edtn.com/	•	•	Links all CMP publications in the sector including Electronic Buyers' News (http://www.ebnonline.com/) and Electronic

Publication/Medium	URL	Daily news	Archive news	Resources
				Engineering Times (http://www.eetimes.com/)
Electronic News	http://www.electronicnews.com/	•	•	
Electronic Products	http://www.electronicproducts.com/		•	Maintains a comprehensive products directory
Evaluation Engineering	http://www.evaluationengineering.com/		•	
IEEE Spectrum	http://www.spectrum.ieee.org/		•	Subscribers only
Laser Focus World (part of Penwell Publishing's PennNET community)	http://lfw.pennwellnet.com/home/home.cfm	•	•	
Microwave Journal	http://www.mwjournal.com/	•	•	Subscribers only
Microwaves & RF (EDTN network)	http://www.thecircuitboard.com/	•	•	•
PennNET	http://www.pennnet.com/	•	•	News Web sites on advanced electronics manufacturing, communications/broadband, electronic systems, and computer graphics

ENGINEERING TRADES

PR practitioners will find that engineering trades are poorly covered online in terms of news but heavily laden with resources. In fact, resources are encyclopedic, and there are many more link and resource sites than what are listed here. From a news perspective, the practitioner would be better off with print media.

Publication/Medium	URL	Daily news	Archive news	Resources
CE News	http://www.cenews.com/		•	
Civil Engineering	http://www.pubs.asce.org/ceonline/		•	
Engineering News Record	http://www.enr.com/	•	•	
Equipment World	http://www.equipmentworld.com/			Directory to 600 industry Web sites
Nuclear engineering links	http://www.ne.uiuc.edu/links.html			The University of Illinois at Champagne-Urbana
The International Directory of Chemical Engineering	http://www.ciw.uni-karlsruhe.de/chem-eng.html			Abundant resources; German site
The virtual library of structural engineering	http://www.virtualengineer.com/vengvlib1.htm			Information on earthquake design

Publication/Medium	URL	Daily news	Archive news	Resources
Virtual Engineering library	http://www.eevl.ac.uk/wwwvl .html			Abundant resources (University of Edinburgh)

ENTERTAINMENT INDUSTRY

This category has two dominant Web sites—Variety and Hollywood Reporter. The rest of the trade media are republished content for the most part. There are dozens of local and regional entertainment sites, entertainment guides and dozens of movie review sites (far too many of all three to list here). Practitioners should develop specific lists as needed. Newsgroups are plentiful as well. Look under rec.arts for several web sites on various entertainment topics. Practitioners working in this segment should have an online strategy.

Publication/Medium	URL	Daily news	Archive news	Resources
American Cinematographer	http://www.cinematographer .com/magazine/index.htm		•	Online is subscriber only
Amusement Business	http://www.amusementbusiness .com/		•	
Animation Magazine	http://www.animationmagazine .net	•	•	Industry directory, links; events calendar
Back Stage	http://www.backstage.com/	•	•	Show guide, links
Bingo Bugle	http://www.bingobugle.com/	•	•	Links
Bomb	http://www.bombsite.com/		•	
Box Office	http://www.boxoffice.com/		•	Movie reviews
Cinescape	http://www.cinescape.com/	•	•	
Coming Soon	http://www.comingsoon.net/			Forums, reviews
Cover	http://www.covermag.com/	•	•	
Dance Magazine	http://www.dancemagazine .com/		•	Reviews, calendar of events, directory of dance schools
Dance Spirit	http://www.dancespirit.com/		•	Selected editorial; chat, message board
Dance Teacher	http://www.dance-teacher.com/		•	Selected editorial; chat, message board
Entertainment News and Views	http://www.entnews.com/		•	Chatroom, contests, e-mail newsletter
Entertainment News Daily	http://www.www .entertainmentnewsdaily.com/	•	•	Reviews, listings
Entertainment Today	http://www.ent-today.com/		•	Links
Eye (Toronto)	http://www.eye.net/		•	Event listings, links
Film Comment	http://www.filmlinc.com/		•	Movie reviews

Publication/Medium	URL	Daily news	Archive news	Resources
Hollywood Reporter	http://www.hollywoodreporter.com/	•	•	Events calendar, TV schedules
Illinois Entertainer	http://www.illinoisentertainer.com/		•	
Ink 19 (Georgia, Florida)	http://www.ink19.com/		•	Concert calendar
In Motion	http://www.inmotiononline.com/		•	Chat, message board
Los Angeles Film and Music Magazine	http://www.lafm.com/		•	Movie reviews
Moviemaker	http://www.moviemaker.com/		•	Calendar of events, links
Opera News	http://www.operanews.com/		•	Subscription only
Playbill	http://www.playbill.com/	•	•	Chat, message board, play listings
Pointe	http://www.pointemagazine.com/		•	Message board, chat
Premiere	http://www.premiere.com/		•	Forum
Soap Opera Digest	http://www.soapdigest.com/		•	
Stage Directions	http://www.stage-directions.com/		•	Chat, message board
Theatre Direct	http://www.theatredirect.com/	•	•	E-mail newsletter
Variety	http://www.variety.com/	•	•	Movie reviews
What's On Stage (U.K.)	http://www.whatsonstage.com/	•	•	Reviews, calendar, e-mail newsletter

ETHNIC LIFESTYLE

This area is poorly covered, and PR practitioners should stay with a print strategy. There are dozens of ethnic newsgroups. Look under soc.culture to find at least 138 separate discussions.

Publication/Medium	URL	Daily news	Archive news	Resources
AOnline (Asian American)	http://www.aonline.com/	•	•	Chat, forum, e-mail newsletter
Asian Week	http://www.asianweek.com/		•	Forum
The Boston Irish Reporter	http://www.bostonirish.com/		•	
Brazzil	http://www.brazzil.com/		•	Chat, forum, calendar
Latino.com	http://www.latino.com/		•	Chat, forums, calendar; portal for Latinos
German Life	http://www.germanlife.com/		•	
Herencia (New Mexican Hispanics)	http://www.herencia.com/online/index.html			Links, newsgroup
Masala (South Asian)	http://www.masala.com/Masala/index.html	•	•	Chat, WebTV

Publication/Medium	URL	Daily news	Archive news	Resources
Native Peoples	http://www.nativepeoples.com/		•	Forum, directory to communities
The Black World Today	http://www.tbwt.com/	•	•	Links, chat, forums

EXPORT/IMPORT TRADES

The export/import trades are poorly covered. Inside U.S. Trade (http://www.insidetrade.com/) carries a range of daily news focused on trade bills and activities in Washington, D.C., and Latin Trade (http://www.latintrade.com/news/index.cfm) aggregates daily trade news from several newswires, but there is little else in terms of news or resource availability. The PR practitioner seeking news outlets for import/export news will need a print strategy.

FITNESS AND PERSONAL HEALTH

Much health and medicine information is republished from print media or evergreen content. PR practitioners will find that a print publicity strategy is more important than an online approach unless one is placing basic content on fitness and personal health. There are thousands of personal health and e-commerce sites for weight watching and nutrition. Few are useful for PR practitioners. There are at least two newsgroups for fitness—misc.fitness.weights and rec.running.

Publication/Medium	URL	Daily news	Archive news	Resources
Alternative Medicine	http://www.alternativemedicine.com/		•	Database and message boards
CNN	http://www.cnn.com/HEALTH/index.html	•	•	
Efit	http://www.efit.com/		•	Online health and fitness network and resource site
Fitness Link	http://www.fitnesslink.com/		•	A compendium of articles on fitness
Fitness Management magazine	http://www.fitnessworld.com/index_main.html		•	E-commerce
Fitness online (content from six Weider Publications)	http://www.fitnessonline.com/	•	•	•
Health Magazine	http://www.healthmag.com/		•	Includes discussion room and Q&A's
iVillage.com (women's portal)	http://www.ivillage.com/			Panel of experts for fitness, food and health

Publication/Medium	URL	Daily news	Archive news	Resources
Justmove (American Heart Association)	http://www.justmove .org/fitnessnews/	•	•	Daily health newswire from Reuters, also accessible at http://www.www .reutershealth.com/
Men's Health	http://www.menshealth.com/ index.html		•	Republishes content in seven sections and adds daily tips along with Web site feedback, contests, and surveys
NewsRX	http://www.newsrx.com/	•	•	Broad coverage of health and health industry topics
The Medical News	http://www.themedicalnews .com/		•	Stores hundreds of articles on healthcare subjects
We Magazine	http://www.wemagazine.com/	•	•	•
Women.com network (20 publications)	http://women.com/index.html		•	Web sites for Healthy Living and Prevention

FLORIST, LANDSCAPING, AND GARDENING

PR practitioners will find that floral, landscaping, and gardening sites combine the editorial of multiple magazines. Almost all content is republished, but the publication collections make the sector easy to navigate. There are numerous gardening newsmagazines by region as well, which merit attention. Universities run several of them. Resources are extensive, and there are dozens more link sites in addition to those listed here. There is at least one newsgroup—rec.gardens. Practitioners should not have difficulty finding resources, but for publicity, they should use a print media strategy.

Publication/Medium	URL	Daily news	Archive news	Resources
Country Living Gardener (part of women.com)	http://cl-gardener.com/		•	•
Garden WebHYPERLINK	http://www.gardenweb.com/vl/			Virtual library of gardening links
Greenbeam.com	http://www.greenbeam.com/	•	•	Daily online newswire and synthesizes editorial of four nursery and garden center magazines

Publication/Medium	URL	Daily news	Archive news	Resources
GreenNet	http://www.greenindustry.com/		•	Combines the editorial of eight nursery and landscaping magazines. links to news about gardening and landscaping
Horticultural Magazine	http://www.hortmag.com/		•	Chat rooms
Hortworld (HortDigest)	http://www.hortworld.com/		•	Large resource site for the horticultural industry
Landscape Group	http://www.landscapegroup .com/		•	Combines the content of four magazines devoted to turf and landscaping
Master Gardeners	http://www.mastergardeners.org/ links.html			From the University of California Cooperative Extension department; a good list of sources
The National Council of State Garden Clubs	http://www.gardenclub.org/links .htm			A comprehensive link site that a PR practitioner will find immediately useful

FOOD INDUSTRY AND PROCESSING TRADES

Overall, PR practitioners should find an abudance of food industry news and information. Practitioners also should be aware of sites devoted to individual foods such as avocados (http://www.avocado.org/), tomatoes (http://www.tomato.org/), and eggs (http://www.enc-online.org/). There are several of them. Resources are abundant, and there is at least one newsgroup—sci.bio.food-science. Practitioners should consider an online strategy in this category.

Publication/Medium	URL	Daily news	Archive news	Resources
Food Distributor	http://www.fdi.org			Links site oriented to supermarkets
Food Explorer (Cahners publishing)	http://www.foodexplorer.com/	•	•	A combination of seven magazines (one in Spanish)
Food Online	http://www.foodonline.com/	•	•	An e-zine and news site for the food processing industry
Food Processing	http://www.foodprocessing.com/		•	

Publication/Medium	URL	Daily news	Archive news	Resources
Food Product Design	http://www.foodproductdesign.com/		•	
Michigan State University	http://www.msu.edu/~foodmark/links.htm			Large and useful resource links site
Prepared Foods	http://www.preparedfoods.com/	•	•	Provides a large number of industry resources
Stagnito Communications	http://www.stagnito.com/		•	Master site for its nine food industry magazines
Wayne State University	http://www.science.wayne.edu/~nfs/nfslinks.htm			Lists food science programs and resources

FOOD—CONSUMER NEWS

Food is a heavily covered topic online, and PR practitioners will find plenty of news sites and hundreds of links and resources. Practitioners should have an online strategy for food news and publicity. There is at least one newsgroup devoted to food at rec.food.cooking.

Publication/Medium	URL	Daily news	Archive news	Resources
Cooking Light	http://www.cookinglight.com/		•	
Cooks Illustrated	http://www.cooksillustrated.com/		•	Provides useful ratings
Cuisine	http://www.cuisinemagazine.com/	•	•	Provides a webcam that broadcasts from its test kitchens so that one can watch recipes being prepared
Food TV	http://foodtv.com/		•	
Food and Wine	http://www.pathfinder.com/FoodWine/		•	Chat, bulletin board
Good Cooking	http://www.goodcooking.com/			Major resource site with links to many places
Gourmet and Bon Appetit	http://www.epicurious.com/		•	Deep in resources; daily food recipes and weekly
				food/dining report that PR practitioners might find useful
Internet Chef (Women's Forum)	http://www.ichef.com/index.html		•	Part of the Women's Forum channel (http://www

Publication/Medium	URL	Daily news	Archive news	Resources
				.womensforum .com/); primarily a recipe site
IVillage (women's portal)	http://www.ivillage.com/		•	Food section seems to be warmed-over content
Kitchen Link	http://www.kitchenlink.com/	•	•	Massive news and resource site that connects to other media that do food reporting; links to food columns of daily U.S. newspapers and to cable TV sites, such as BH&G TV (http://www.bhglive .com/tv/)
Meals for You	http://www2.mealsforyou.com/			Recipe site, but it has hundreds that may be a useful resource for PR practitioners
The Global Gourmet	http://www.globalgourmet.com/	•	•	Online staff writes about food; has abundant resources
The Internet Epicurean	http://internet.epicurean.com/			Extensive links collection of e-zines along with features and recipes
Wine Today (New York Times)	http://www.winetoday.com/	•	•	

FURNITURE AND INTERIORS TRADES

This is a sparse category. Home Retail Network (http://www.
homeretailnetwork.com/) is a Cahners Business Publishing site
that combines nine of its magazines into a channel that carries breaking
news as well as news republished from the magazines. Other sites are
little more than advertisements for print publications. Newsgroup discussions are consumer or small woodworking shop oriented.

GAY TOPICS

There are hundreds of gay forums and gay links sites. PR practitioners should develop their own lists as appropriate. Gay magazines,
however, still outnumber online gay news sites. Gay-oriented daily

news is still scarce and often oriented to local or regional communities. Practitioners should have an online strategy when working in this segment.

Publication/Medium	URL	Daily news	Archive news	Resources
365gay.com (Canadian)	http://365gay.com/	•	•	
Baltimore Alternative	http://www.baltalt.com/		•	
Baltimore Gay Paper	http://www.bgp.org/	•		
Bay Area Reporter	http://www.ebar.com/	•	•	
BLK	http://www.blk.com/blkhome.htm			Links page for black gays; calendar
Curve	http://www.curvemag.com/		•	Forum
Front Page	http://www.frontpagenews.com/		•	Forum, calendar, resources
Frontiers	http://www.frontiersweb.com/		•	
Gay.com	http://www.gay.com/	•		Portal for the gay community
Gaynews (United Kingdom)	http://www.gay-news.org.uk/	•	•	Chat room, calendar
Gaywired.com	http://www.gaywired.com/	•	•	
Genre	http://www.genremagazine.com/		•	Calendar
Girlfriends	http://www.gfriends.com/		•	Forum
Houston Voice	http://www.houstonvoice.com/houstonvoice/index.html		•	Forum, calendar, directory of organizations
In the Life	http://www.inthelife.com/		•	
LGNY—Lesbian & Gay New York	http://www.lgny.com/		•	
New York Blade News	http://www.nyblade.com/	•	•	
The Advocate	http://www.advocate.com/	•	•	Reviews, forum, polls
The Washington Blade	http://www.washblade.com/	•	•	
XY Magazine	http://www.xymag.com/index2.html		•	

GENERAL INTEREST CONSUMER NEWS AND FEATURE SOURCES

This is a broad and undifferentiated category—a catchall—but it mirrors print media that own most of the sites in the category. PR practitioners will find that most sites republish material and add useful resources and interactivity, such as newsgroups. National Geographic is an exception.

National Geographic (http://www.nationalgeographic.com/) is perhaps the most developed of the general interest news and feature sources online. Its enormous site includes daily news, maps, features from the current magazine, webcams, photo features, games for kids, news dispatches from explorers and scientists in the field, and more. The site shows the astonishing depth to which a publisher can go online. Other general interest news sites pale by comparison.

E-zines fit into the catchall category for PR practitioners because there are hundreds of them and they wink in and out of existence quickly. E-zines are alternative media. They are quirky, sometimes juvenile and sometimes authoritative. Their readership is generally small and not too useful unless one is aiming to send a message to a specific niche. To get a flavor of what e-zines are like, look at Zines (http://www.www.zinebook.com/), which provides a directory to the e-zine world, and Zinos (http://www.zinos.com/), which republishes writing from e-zines.

Publication/Medium	URL	Daily news	Archive news	Resources
Atlantic Monthly	http://www.theatlantic.com/		•	
Betnetworks	http://www.betnetworks.com/	•	•	General news and resource site for African Americans
Brill's Content	http://www.brillscontent.com/		•	
Consumer Reports	http://www.consumerreports.org/		•	Locks off much of its site to all but subscribers
Ebony	http://www.ebony.com/		•	
Entertainment Weekly	http://www.ew.com/ew/	•		Focused on celebrities and the popular arts
Hispanic	http://www.hispaniconline.com		•	
Inside.com	http://www.inside.com	•		Focused on celebrities and the popular arts
Jet	http://www.jetmag.com/		•	
National Geographic	http://www.nationalgeographic.com/	•	•	Daily news, maps, features, webcams, photo features, games for kids, news dispatches from explorers and scientists
People	http://people.aol.com/people/daily/	•	•	
Readers Digest	http://www.readersdigest.com/		•	Offers selections from other publications in multiple languages
Salon	http://www.salon.com/	•	•	general interest e-zine
Slate	http://slate.msn.com/	•	•	general interest e-zine
Smithsonian Magazine	http://www.smithsonianmag.si.edu/		•	

Publication/Medium	URL	Daily news	Archive news	Resources
The HistoryNet	http://www.thehistorynet.com/		•	Combines the content of 15 general interest history magazines, including American History and Civil War Times Illustrated
The Onion	http://www.theonion.com/		•	Humor e-zine, provides weekly satire on the news
Town & Country (Women.com network)	http://www.tncweddings.com/		•	Focuses on weddings and wedding planning
Upscale Magazine	http://www.upscalemagazine.com/		•	
Utne Reader	http://www.utne.com/		•	Alternative magazine; has a bulletin board

GENERAL INTEREST NEWS

These are sites that are closely associated with news magazines and television networks. The magazines mostly republish content from print versions. PR practitioners will need to be selective in using them for news outlets, but on the whole, they are excellent resources for news and information. The list provided here is a small part of what is available. News links are plentiful and deep.

Publication/Medium	URL	Daily news	Archive news	Resources
ABC News	http://www.abcnews.go.com/	•	•	Similar to CNN but not as deep in daily news reporting
CBS News		•	•	A portal to its news and information sites; news from wire services, links to its entertainment, personal finance, sports, health, and entertainment sites; incorporates stories from eight news and magazine shows that the news division produces
CNN	http://www.cnn.com/	•	•	Deep news site with multimedia, video, and audio; its daily

Publication/Medium	URL	Daily news	Archive news	Resources
				almanac combines a calendar of events and a record of past events
Fox News	http://www.foxnews.com/			Similar to CBS News in layout but not quite as deep
Insight Magazine	http://www.insightmag.com/		•	Audio commentary, discussion forum, and chat room
Maclean's (Canadian)	http://www.macleans.ca/		•	
MSNBC	http://www.msnbc.com/ news/default.asp	•	•	Extraordinary for usability with drop-down menus that let one review the news quickly
Newsweek	http://www.newsweek.com/	•	•	Features "Web exclusives" that integrate with weekly columns and reporting; weekly live chat focused on cover topic with editors and writers
The Economist	http://www.economist.com/		•	
Time Magazine	http://www.time.com/time/	•	•	Close to a portal for brand extensions, such as Time Digital and Time for kids; "Newsfiles" section collects stories on a topic into one location; ties directly to CNN news for updating; CNN ties to Time for news analysis
U.S. News & World Report	http://www.usnews.com		•	

GENERAL INTEREST NEWSPAPER LINK DIRECTORIES

Nearly every daily newspaper worldwide has a Web site. The sites vary in quality from extraordinary to barely acceptable and their usability from easy to difficult. It is useless to review any of them here, but it is important to know how to find them. PR practitioners will find that the directories listed here are good for researching reporters and interests, for clipping stories, for monitoring news by locale, and for planning publicity by region. There is little need any more to send for a copy of a newspaper. Any practitioner anywhere has the same access to world newspapers as anyone else. This provides an important advantage to practitioners located outside of major media markets.

Publication/Medium	URL	Daily news	Archive news	Resources
AJR Newslink	http://ajr.newslink.org/			Maintains more than 18,000 links to newspapers, magazines, broadcasters, and news services worldwide
Publist	http://www.publist.com/			Logs more than 150,000 magazines, journals, newsletters, and other periodicals
Electric Library	www.elibrary.com	•	•	News aggregator; searches contents of hundreds of magazines and newspapers
Kidon	http://www.kidon.com/media-link/index.shtml			Lists media by country worldwide
Editor & Publisher's Mediainfo	http://www.mediainfo.com/			Lists newspapers around the world
Ezine-Universe	http://ezine-universe .com/			Tracks e-zines and e-mail newsletters

GENERAL INTEREST POLITICAL MEDIA

This is an area where activists and political commentators of all persuasions take to cyberspace. There are hundreds of such sites, and we cover a few here. Sites change regularly, so PR practitioners should develop and update their own lists. Online has become a powerful tool in campaigning and activism.

Publication/Medium	URL	Daily news	Archive news	Resources
Adbusters	http://www.adbusters.org/home/		•	Campaigns against mass media advertising and public relations; although located in Canada, keeps a close eye on U.S. activities

Publication/Medium	URL	Daily news	Archive news	Resources
AllPOLITICS	http://cnn.com/ALLPOLITICS/	•	•	Joint site from CNN and Time magazine that digests political news
Campaigns and Elections	http://www.campaignonline.com/		•	Provides an elections handicapping service for U.S. elections.
C-Span	http://www.c-span.org/	•	•	
Foreign Affairs	http://www.foreignaffairs.org/		•	Excellent link site to international news and policy resources
Grassroots.com	http://www.grassroots.com/		•	Commentary and resources on a large number of political and social issues
Speak Out	http://www.speakout.com/			Political discussion site
The American Spectator	http://www.spectator.org/	•	•	Politics and the arts
The Nation	http://www.thenation.com/		•	Offers Web features
The New Republic	http://www.thenewrepublic.com/	•		
WebActive	http://www.webactive.com/	•	•	Political news aggregation site targeted to activists; audio commentary, links

GENERAL INTEREST REGIONAL SITES

PR practitioners should be aware of hundreds of regional, state or province, and city sites that can be useful for news and publicity. These sites often carry the most up-to-the-minute calendars available and can reach a broad local audience quickly. Most are associated with newspapers or magazines, but others are freestanding. Regional sites vary widely in content and quality. PR practitioners need to check each individually. But the good sites should be a part of publicity strategy. Here is a sampling of sites:

Publication/Medium	URL	Daily news	Archive news	Resources
Arborweb	http://www.arborweb.com/			Calendar and city guide for Ann Arbor, Michigan
Baltimore Magazine	http://www.baltimoremag.com/			A series of city guides that are immensely useful

Publication/Medium	URL	Daily news	Archive news	Resources
Boston.com (Boston Globe)	http://www.boston.com/	•	•	An umbrella site incorporating the newspaper's Web site; packed with news and information
Chicagomag (Chicago Magazine)	http://www.chicagomag.com/			Calendars, columns, and message boards
CTCentral.com	http://www.zwire.com/site/news.cfm?brd=1773	•	•	Combines content of five central Connecticut newspapers; adds broad resources; includes highway webcams so that drivers can check traffic conditions
Digital City	http://home.digitalcity.com/			Covers more than 200 U.S. cities with directories and guides
NJO	http://www.njo.com/	•	•	Massive news, resource, and portal site to just about everything in the state of New Jersey; webcams, city links, local New Jersey radio, and chat rooms
San Diego	http://www.sandiego-online.com/			
Vancouver	http://www.vanmag.com/	•	•	•
Washingtonian	http://www.washingtonian.com/	•	•	Washington, D.C.

GIFTS, ANTIQUES, AND COLLECTIBLES

This online category includes consumer and trade-oriented sites. For the most part, sites do a poor job of news coverage. Calendars are abundant, however. There are hundreds of link sites for gifts, antiques, and collectibles. Most are parochial, which makes research difficult for PR practitioners. Overall, the number of print publications for gifts, antiques, and collectibles outweighs Web sites of worth.

Publication/Medium	URL	Daily news	Archive news	Resources
AmericanStyle	http://www.americanstyle.com/		•	Links to museums and galleries by state; datebook for events

Publication/Medium	URL	Daily news	Archive news	Resources
Antique Week	http://www.antiqueweek.com/	•	•	Aggregates news from Wired (http://www.wired.com), calendar of shows, auctions, and flea markets
Antiques and the Arts Weekly	http://www.antiquesandthearts.com/		•	Auction calendar
Collectors Journal	http://www.collectorsjournal.com/			Subscribers only
Doll Reader	http://www.dollreader.com/		•	
Maine Antique Digest	http://www.maineantiquedigest.com/			Weekly calendar of auctions and antiques events
Teddy Bear and Friends	http://www.teddybearandfriends.com		•	E-mail newsletter, e-mail postcards, events calendar

GROCERY AND FOOD MARKETING

There are ample news outlets for PR practitioners in the grocery and food market segment, but Web site quality varies from excellent to mediocre. The total number of Web sites is a fraction of the available print media. PR practitioners should make use of online in their publicity strategies but not rely too heavily on it. Resources are scarce. We could find no newsgroups focused on grocery and food marketing.

Publication/Medium	URL	Daily news	Archive news	Resources
Convenience Store News	http://csnews.com/index.shtml	•		
Food Logistics	http://www.foodlogistics.com/index.html	•		
Food People	http://www.foodpeople.com/Home.html	•		Events calendar, assocation listings
Food Service	http://www.foodservice.com/	•		Recipes, forum, school listings, manufacturer listings, trade show listings
Gourmet Retailer	http://www.gourmetretailer.com/home.htm		•	
Progressive Grocer	http://www.progressivegrocer.com/			
Supermarket Business	http://www.supermarketbusiness.com/index.html		•	
Supermarket News	http://www.supermarketnews.com/		•	E-mail newsletter
The Food Institute	http://www.foodinstitute.com/			Subscribers only
Western Michigan University	http://www.hcob.wmich.edu/~fmk/food_links.htm			Link site

HOME AND SHELTER TOPICS

This segment includes home decorating and rebuilding or remodeling. It is a diverse category and disappointing. Many of the largest magazines have little more than subscription information, and much of the category is republished content. On the other hand, there are at least three excellent resource sites that PR practitioners should know about when working in this topic area. They are listed here.

Publication/Medium	URL	Daily news	Archive news	Resources
Better Homes & Gardens	http://www.bhglive.com/		•	Resource site with house and home, food, garden, health, food, crafts and travel sections; forums
Canadian Living	http://www.canadianliving.com/		•	Resource site with house and home, food, garden, health, food, crafts and travel sections; forums
Coastal Living	http://www.coastallivingmag.com/		•	Resource site with house and home, food, garden, health, food, crafts and travel sections
Good Home	http://www.goodhome.com/		•	Resource and how-to site
Good Housekeeping (Part of women.com; http://www.women.com/index.html)	http://www.goodhousekeeping.com/	•		
House Beautiful (Part of women.com; http://www.women.com/index.html)	http://www.housebeautiful.com/	•		
Homestore	http://www.homestore.com/		•	Home decorating and improvement
Martha Stewart	http://www.marthastewart.com/		•	Directory and link site to the many enterprises that Martha Stewart runs
Sunset Magazine	http://www.sunsetmagazine.com/		•	Selected editorial excerpts; mostly subscriber only
The Paint and Decorating Retailers Association	http://www.pdra.org/		•	Home decorating questions and challenges

HOME BUILDING, BUYING, AND REMODELING

This category is replete with how-to informational features that PR practitioners can use for product placement and case studies. It lacks, however, in daily news outlets. Resource sites are abundant and deep. Alt.home.repair and alt.building.construction are busy newsgroup sites. There are web-based forums as well such as Home Repair Forum (http://www.homerepair.about.com/homegarden/homerepair/). There are also many link sites that PR practitioners can use.

Publication/Medium	URL	Daily news	Archive news	Resources
Better Homes & Gardens (also on AOL)	http://www.bhg.com/househome/		•	How-to features; message boards
BuildNet	http://www.abuildnet.com/			Links lists, resources
Consumer World	http://www.consumerworld.org/pages/home.htm			Links lists, resources
Home Tips	http://www.hometips.com/		•	Built around a television personality
Housing Zone (Cahners Publishing)	http://www.housingzone.com/	•	•	Integrates 13 magazines
Old House Journal	http://oldhousejournal.com/		•	Part of the Home Building Remodeling Network (http://www.hbrnet.com/) that includes seven magazines, all with deep resources
Popular Mechanics	http://popularmechanics.com/		•	
Rebecca's Garden	http://www.rebeccasgarden.com/home.html		•	E-mail newsletter
Repair Place	http://www.repairplace.com/index.htm		•	Monthly e-mail newsletter on home repair topics
The Old House Network	http://www.oldhouse.com/			Links lists, resources
This Old House	http://www.pbs.org/wgbh/thisoldhouse/home.html		•	Webcam, resource directory
Today's Home Owner	http://www.todayshomeowner.com/		•	Snippets of advice
Woman's Day on AOL (America Online)			•	Home and garden advice, forums, chat room, e-mail newsletter
Women.com on AOL (America Online)			•	Home and garden advice; Message boards
Work Bench	http://www.workbenchmagazine.com/		•	

HOME ELECTRONICS TOPICS

There are many more print magazines in this category than Web sites, but unlike other topic areas, there are daily and weekly news sites. PR practitioners working in home electronics should have an online strategy. Alt.video.dvd, rec.video.desktop, rec.audio.pro, rec.audio.car, and rec.audio.opinion are just five of the available newsgroups. Newsgroups found on Web sites include Home Theater Forum (http://www.hometheaterforum.com/) and Car Audio Forum (http://www.audiomarket.com/forum/). The Consumer Electronics Association (http://www.ce.org/index.asp) provides an interesting resource site, which is beyond the usual association sites. There are thousands of audio and video links pages, most of which are not useful for PR practitioners.

Publication/Medium	URL	Daily news	Archive news	Resources
Audiophile Audition	http://www.audaud.com/	•	•	e-zine for sophisticated listeners with articles and reviews
Car Audio and Electronics	http://www.caraudiomag.com/		•	
Car Stereo Review			•	America OnLine (AOL); reviews
Computer Video	http://www.computervideo.net/		•	
Equip	http://equip.zdnet.com/		•	Home electronics test results in depth
MP3	http://www.mp3.com/			Newsgroup where one can report on events in the music world
Stereo Review			•	America OnLine (AOL); reviews
Stereophile	http://www.stereophile.com/		•	
Stereophile Guide to Home Theater	http://www.guidetohometheater.com/		•	
This Week in Consumer Electronics	http://www.twice.com/		•	Abundant resource information and statistics
Video Business	http://www.videobusiness.com/	•		
Wide Screen Review	http://www.widescreenreview.com/	•	•	Daily news aggregated from various sources; Digital Video Disks (DVD) reviews, weekly industry news releases, and industry statistics

HOSPITAL AND HEALTHCARE ADMINISTRATION TOPICS

The lack of coverage online for hospitals and for healthcare administration topics is surprising. There are many small print publications in the field, but they have not transferred successfully to online, and PR practitioners working in this area will find online superfluous. Even Healthcare PR and Marketing News is a subscription solicitation site.

Publication/Medium	URL	Daily news	Archive news	Resources
American Hospital Association	http://www.aha.org/	•		Member only; resource center
Catholic Health Association	http://www.chausa.org/			Members only
Healthcare Financial Management Association	http://www.hfma.org/			Members only
Healthcare Informatics	http://www.healthcare-informatics.com/		•	
HospitalWeb	http://.neuro-www. mgh.harvard.edu/ hospitalweb.shtml			Links
Hot Topics in Healthcare	http://www.ahcpub.com /ahc_root_html/hot/index.htm		•	Selected editorial
Modern Health Care	http://www.modernhealthcare .com/	•		

HOTEL, MOTEL, AND RESORT TRADE TOPICS

PR practitioners will find few news outlets and resources online that focus on hotel, motel, and resort management and technology. This is a segment that has few print publications as well. PR practitioners should be aware of online, but there is little need to formulate a strategy for it.

Publication/Medium	URL	Daily news	Archive news	Resources
Bottomline	http://www.hftp.org/		•	
Hospitality Technology	http://www.htmagazine.com/		•	
Hotel & Motel Management	http://www.hmmonline.com/		•	
Hotels	http://www.hotelsmag.com/	•	•	Aggregates daily news from several sources
Lodging Hospitality	http://www.lhonline.com/	•	•	
Lodging News	http://www.lodgingnews.com/	•	•	Aggregates press releases from industry sources and mixes them with editorial copy
Club Industry	http://www.industryclick.com/	•	•	

INDUSTRIAL TOPICS

Many industrial topics are covered online through reprinted editorial. There are some daily news sections, but they are scarce. PR practitioners should not depend on the segment as a news outlet. However, resources are plentiful except in design and product engineering. Two publishers dominate the area—Penton and Cahners. Sci.engr.mech is an active newsgroup focused on mechanical engineering and industrial topics. Industrial resources are plentiful. Most magazine Web sites have directories, and industrial link sites are numerous, although many are of limited value.

Publication/Medium	URL	Daily news	Archive news	Resources
Assembly Magazine	http://www.assemblymag.com/		•	Buyer's guide
Bizlink (Rogers Media Business Magazines of Canada)	http://www.bizlink.com/		•	Eight industrial publications with resource directories
Cleanrooms (part of PennNet)	http://cr.pennnet.com/home/home.cfm	•	•	Product reviews, calendar of events
Computer-Aided Engineering (Penton Publishing)	http://www.caenet.com/	•	•	Resources are locked off to all but subscribers
Consumer Goods Technology	http://www.consumergoods.com/		•	
Designfax	http://www.designfax.net/	•		
Engineering Automation Report	http://www.eareport.com		•	
Engineering News Record	http://www.enr.com/industrial/		•	
Engineer's Digest	http://www.mroindustry.com/ed/		•	
Fastener Industry News	http://www.fastenernews.com/			Subscribers only
Flow Control	http://www.flowcontrolnetwork.com		•	Daily news is subscriber only
Industrial Maintenance & Plant Operation	http://www.impomag.com/		•	Product directory
Job Shop Technology	http://www.jobshoptechnology.com/		•	Resource directory
Machine Design (Penton Publishing)	http://machinedesign.com		•	
Managing Automation	http://www.managingautomation.com/		•	Resource directory
Manufacturing.net (Cahners Publishing)	http://www.manufacturing.net/	•	•	E-mail newsletter; manufacturers directory; includes Design News, Product Design and Development (http://www.pddnet.com/), and four other design magazines

Publication/Medium	URL	Daily news	Archive news	Resources
Materials Handling Engineering	http://www.mhesource.com/	•	•	
Plant Services	http://www.plantservices.com/ps/index.html		•	
PT Design	http://www.ptdesign.com/		•	
Quality	http://www.qualitymag.com/		•	
Quality in Manufacturing	http://www.qualityindustry.com/qm/		•	
Standardization News (American Society for Testing and Materials)	http://www.astm.org/		•	Standards section
Industry Log	http://www.usindustrialnews.com			Links

INSTRUMENTATION AND CONTROL SYSTEM TOPICS

There is at least one outstanding Web page in this category that PR practitioners will find useful, but overall, it is disappointing. Outlets are few and resources thin.

Publication/Medium	URL	Daily news	Archive news	Resources
Control Engineering	http://www.controleng.com/	•	•	Tutorials, new product releases and Web features
Control Magazine	http://www.controlmagazine.com		•	
Electronic Tech	http://www.electronictech.com/weblinks/index.html			Newsgroup listing
Experimental Mechanics	http://www.sem.org/		•	Tutorials
Experimental Techniques	http://www.sem.org/		•	Tutorials
IEEE Control Systems	http://www.computer.org/		•	
Instrumentation and Automation News Online	http://www.ianmag.com/		•	Product releases in news section; buyer's guide; new product directory
International Society for Measurement and Control	http://www.isa.org/	•	•	Daily news aggregated from various sources
Virtual Instruments	http://www.virtual-instruments.com/links-Instrumentation.htm			Links
VXI Journal	http://www.vxijournal.com/		•	

INSURANCE INDUSTRY TOPICS

The insurance industry receives spotty coverage online. Much daily information is by subscription or aggregations of stories from other news sources. On the other hand, PR practitioners will find an abundance of resources for researching information. There are thousands of sites purporting to offer insurance news that are little more than news-letters for agents and brokerages or temporary Web sites around disasters. For the most part, these are of little value to practitioners.

Publication/Medium	URL	Daily news	Archive news	Resources
Best's Review, BestLine and BestWeek (A.M. Best Company)	http://www.ambest.com/	•	•	BestLine provides daily news but it is subscriber only; Best's Review site is reprinted editorial; Best's Week is a subscription solicitation site
Business Insurance	http://www.businessinsurance.com/	•	•	
Crittenden	http://www.crittendennews.com/	•	•	Subscription only e-mail and online newsletters
Insurance Industry Internet Network	http://www.iiin.com/			Links
Insure.com	http://www.insure.com/		•	Comprehensive news and resource site, primarily targeted to consumers
International Risk Management Institute	http://www.irmi.com/		•	Outlet for byliners
NAIFA, the National Association of Insurance & Financial Advisors	http://www.naifa.org/index.html	•	•	Members only e-mail and online newsletters
NAMIC, the National Association of Mutual Insurance Companies	http://www.namic.org/	•	•	Aggregates daily insurance news from Moreover.com (http://www.w.moreover.com/)
National Underwriter Company (Life/Health and Property & Casualty/Risk & Benefits)	http://www.nuco.com/	•	•	Selected editorial; industry calendar; industry and government links
NewsRe	http://www.newsre.com/	•	•	Daily news aggregated from various sources
Risk and Insurance	http://www.riskandinsurance.com/		•	A subscription site with teaser editorial
Rough Notes	http://www.roughnotes.com/		•	
Thompson's News (Canadian)	http://www.thompsonsnews.com/		•	
Ultimate Insurance Links	http://www.barryklein.com/			Links

JEWELRY INDUSTRY TOPICS

Only two publications cover the industry online. There are hundreds of links related to jewelers who are selling their products on the Web, but these have little value to PR practitioners as news outlets or as resources.

Publication/Medium	URL	Daily news	Archive news	Resources
National Jeweler	http://www.national-jeweler.com/	•	•	
Professional Jeweler	http://www.professionaljeweler.com/		•	
American Watchmakers-Clockmakers Institute	http://www.awi-net.org/			Link site on horology
Lapidary Journal	http://www.lapidaryjournal.com/			Resources and tutorials

LEGAL AND LAW TRADE TOPICS

PR practitioners will find that a few sites dominate legal news, whereas legal resources are comprehensive across the web. Several local state and city legal publications distribute news online by subscription only. Law.court and Law.listserv are a newsgroup and listserv focusing on legal topics. UK.legal is a newsgroup focused on British law.

Publication/Medium	URL	Daily news	Archive news	Resources
ABA Journal (American Bar Association)	http://www.abanet.org/		•	
Association of Trial Lawyers of America	http://www.atlanet.org/			Members only
Commercial Law League of America	http://www.clla.org/		•	Bulletins on the status of legislation in Washington, D.C.
Corporate Legal Times	http://www.corporatelegaltimes.com/		•	
Court TV	http://www.courttv.com/	•	•	Selective trial coverage from around the world
Environmental Law Reporter (Environmental Law Institute)	http://www.eli.org/		•	
FINDlaw	http://legalnews.findlaw.com/	•	•	Aggregates daily news from various sources
Glasser Publications Inc.	http://www.legalwks.com/			Links

Publication/Medium	URL	Daily news	Archive news	Resources
International Centre for Commercial Law	http://www.icclaw.com/			Directory covering several countries; some legal news as well
Internet Lawyer	http://www.internetlawyer.com/			Links
Internet Legal Resource Guide	http://www.ilrg.com/			Links
Journal of Internet Law	http://www.gcwf.com/			Links
Jurist	http://jurist.law.pitt.edu/	•	•	Aggregated news from various sources; resources for legal education
Law.com (includes The American Lawyer and The National Law Journal (http://www.nlj.com/)	http://www.law.com/index.html	•	•	Daily e-mail digest of news to subscribers; some news aggregated from various sources
Lawlinks	http://www.lawlinks.com/			Access to opinions published online
Legal News France	http://www.legalnews.fr/	•	•	(In French)
Los Angeles Law Online	http://lalawonline.net/			Local links
Sidebar.com	http://www.sidebar.com/links.htm			Links
The Institute of Management & Administration	http://www.ioma.com/			Resource site and discussion groups that includes law office management and administration; e-zine is subscriber only

LUMBER AND FORESTRY TRADE TOPICS

News in this category is dominated by one site—Forestindustry.com. No other site comes close to its editorial depth. There are hundreds of link sites and associations, but most focus on regional forestry issues, especially Canadian government and industry Web pages. PR practitioners will find an abundance of lumber and forestry information online for research.

Publication/Medium	URL	Daily news	Archive news	Resources
Crows Weekly Market Report	http://www.crows.com/	•	•	Subscription only
Forestindustry.com	http://www.forestindustry.com/	•	•	Link site to 22 separate industry magazines; in-depth resources; directory of logging, forestry companies, and forestry products

Publication/Medium	URL	Daily news	Archive news	Resources
Logging and Sawmilling Journal	http://www.forestnet.com/		•	
Pallet Enterprise	http://www.palletenterprise.com/		•	Bulletin board
Random Lengths	http://www.randomlengths.com/	•	•	Selected archival editorial
The Journal of Forestry	http://www.safnet.org/		•	Abstracts only
Timber Processing	http://www.timberprocessing.com/		•	Selected editorial
TimberWeb	http://www.timberweb.co.uk/			Directory of logging, forestry companies, and forestry products
Wood Technology	http://www.woodtechmag.com/		•	

MARINE TOPICS

This broad category covers commercial and consumer-oriented news and resource sites, including commercial fishing. Trade-oriented news is poorly represented online, although resources are available. Consumer-oriented news is deep and varied. Some sites print journals from traveling sailors; others print columns from their writers; still others post press releases, calendars, and product reviews. The bulk of information is focused on pleasure craft, but at least one commercial fishing site, National Fisherman, is first rate. There are hundreds of link sites, some of which PR practitioners will find useful. PR Practitioners working in marine topics need an online strategy.

Publication/Medium	URL	Daily news	Archive news	Resources
48 Degrees North	http://www.48north.com/		•	Selected editorial
Boat & Motor Dealer and Marina Dock Age	http://www.boatdealer-marina-info.com/recreational.htm		•	
Boat/U.S.	http://www.boatus.com/	•	•	Resources for businesses and consumers, directories
Boatershub	http://www.boatershub.com/			Links
Boating Industry	http://boatbiz.com/	•	•	
Canoe & Kayak	http://www.canoekayak.com/		•	Calendar of events; newsgroups
DiveWeb	http://www.diveweb.com/			Resource directory for the diving industry
Go Boating	http://goboatingamerica.com/		•	Product tests; forums; calendar of boat shows; buyer's guide

Publication/Medium	URL	Daily news	Archive news	Resources
Latitude 38	http://www.latitude38.com/		•	Calendar of Northern California boating; journals from sailors visiting exotic ports
Marine Log	http://www.marinelog.com/		•	
Marine News	http://www.marinelink.com/	•	•	Daily online news is subscriber only; marine contract news reports are free
Massachusetts Institute of Technology	http://web.mit.edu/seagrant/ advisory/fishfolkfaq.html			Listserv—fishfolk devoted to fishery issues
Motor Boating and Sailing	http://www.www .motorboatingandsailing.com/ index.html			Newsgroup, calendar
National Fisherman	http://www.nationalfisherman .com/	•	•	Resources; weather for commercial fishermen; links
Northern Breezes	http://www.sailingbreezes.com/		•	Calendars, other listings
Paddler (American Canoe Association)	http://www.acanet.org		•	
Personal Watercraft Illustrated	http://www.watercraft.com	•		
Professional Boatbuilder	http://www.proboat.com/			Resource directory
Sailnet	http://www.sailnet.com/	•		Resources for sailors
Seaology (Italian)	http://www.sealogy.com/line.htm			Links
United States Sailing Association	http://ussailing.org/	•	•	Sailing-related press releases; calendar
World Publications	http://www.worldpub.net/ wpubfdoor.html		•	Product reviews from 10 magazines,
				including Boating Life and WaterSki
Sail Magazine	http://www.sailmag.com/	•	•	Weather, industry links
Yachting Magazine	http://www.yachtingnet.com/	•	•	Product reviews, Resources
Yachtworld	http://www.yachtworld.com/		•	Editorial from Sea, Go Boating, and Great Lakes Boating magazines.

MATURE ADULTS

This is a difficult category for PR practitioners. Most of the magazines in the segment do not have Web sites, yet there are many senior-related links, news sources, and forums. Seniors have proven to be active online users because it allows them to stay in touch with family and others. Most news in the category is republished content, so practitioners do not need an online strategy. On the other hand, resources on senior issues and interests are abundant. There are many newsgroups as well. See Friendly4Seniors.

Publication/Medium	URL	Daily news	Archive news	Resources
AARP	http://www.aarp.org/	•	•	Channels on computers, health, leisure, legislation, and money
Age Venture News Service	http://www.demko.com/	•	•	
AgeofReason.com	http://www.ageofreason.com/			More than 5,000 links for senior citizens
Fifty-Plus.Net (Canadian)	http://www.fifty-plus.net/		•	
Friendly4Seniors	http://www.friendly4seniors.com/			Excellent links list, especially for chat and newsgroups
Olderandwiser.com	http://www.olderandwiser.com/		•	Calendar
Senior	http://www.senior.com/	•	•	Chat, forums, games
Senior Focus Radio	http://www.seniorfocusradio.com/New.html	•	•	Internet radio
Senior World	http://www.seniorworld.com/		•	
Seniorcitizens.com	http://www.seniorcitizens.com/	•	•	
Seniornet.org	http://www.seniornet.org/			Resources for seniors—online and computer help, financial planning
SeniorSite News	http://www.seniorsite.com/news/index.htm	•	•	Chat rooms, forums
Third Age	http://www.thirdage.com/	•	•	Chat, bulletin board, tools, activities
Today's Senior News	http://todaysseniors.com/		•	
Today's Seniors	http://www.todaysr.com/		•	
Worldwide Seniors	http://www.wwseniors.com/cgi-bin/index.pl		•	For Arizona Senior Citizens

MEDICAL TOPICS

Medical topics are a huge category, and PR practitioners have long needed an online strategy for it. They were part of online discussion before the Web was developed. Groups existed on commercial services such as AOL and CompuServe as well as Internet bulletin boards. Discussion forums were and are mostly disease-related. Individuals afflicted with a disease, or caring for someone with health problems, can share concerns, get advice, and read about the latest treatments. The power and speed of newsgroups has been such that word of new drugs and potential treatments circles the world well before researchers or the Food and Drug Administration are ready to approve their use. This has created pressure on pharmaceutical companies and governmental agencies to release potential cures before they are thoroughly tested for efficacy.

Pharmaceutical firms and medical device manufacturers such as Lifescan (http://www.lifescan.com/), a maker of diabetes monitoring equipment, have developed into resource sites for sufferers as well. These sites help offset erroneous information that sometimes finds its way into newsgroups.

Because the medical category is large, we focus mainly on large sites. Most content on Web pages is republished from print sources, and PR practitioners may find few of them useful as news outlets. What is written here hardly covers the medical and resource sites available worldwide. PR practitioners working in this field should do their own surveys based on the specialties they are representing.

Publication/Medium	URL	Daily news	Archive news	Resources
American Diabetes Association	http://www.diabetes.org/	•	•	Aggregates daily news from a variety of sources; journal access with free registration
American Family Physician (American Academy of Family Physicians)	http://www.aafp.org/		•	Definitions
American Psychiatric Association	http://www.psych.org/		•	Subscription only
Annals of Internal Medicine (American College of Physicians - American Society of Internal Medicine	http://www.acponline.org/		•	Directory of quotes about medicine; links
APA Monitor monthly	http://www.apa.org/monitor/		•	
Association of periOperative Registered Nurses	http://www.aorn.org/			Links
BioWorld	http://www.bioworld.com/	•	•	Biotechnology topics
CenterWatch	http://www.centerwatch.com/main.htm	•	•	Clinical trials listing service
Chiroweb	http://www.chiroweb.com/	•	•	Chiropratic
Critical Care Nurse (American Association of Critical Care Nurses)	http://www.aacn.org/		•	Forums

Publication/Medium	URL	Daily news	Archive news	Resources
Diabetes Self-Management	http://www.diabetes-self-mgmt.com/			Links
Drug Topics	http://www.drugtopics.com/		•	
Essential Links	http://www.el.com/elinks/medicine/			Links
Good Medicine (Physicians Committee for Responsible Medicine)	http://www.pcrm.org/		•	
Healthgate	http://www.healthgate.com/	•	•	Message board; consumer oriented
HealthyNet	http://www.healthy.net/		•	Alternative medicine
Home Healthcare Consultant	http://www.mmhc.com/hhcc/		•	
Hospital Practice	http://www.hosppract.com/		•	
ISC Publications	http://www.iscpubs.com/			Clinical laboratory products directory
JAMA (American Medical Association)	http://www.ama-assn.org/		•	Reprints text and/or abstracts of all publications online, including E-letter on health professions career and education; some parts members only
Joslin Diabetes Center	http://www.joslin.harvard.edu/		•	For consumers
Juvenile Diabetes Foundation	http://www.jdf.org/index.html		•	Reports on recent research; consumer resources
Managed Care	http://www.managedcaremag.com/	•	•	Aggregates daily news from various sources
Mayo Clinic Health Oasis	http://www.mayohealth.org	•	•	Glossary of medical terms
Mayo Clinic medical resources	http://www.mayo.edu/healthinfo/resources.html		•	
Medical Economics	http://www.pdr.net/memag/index.htm		•	
Mediconsult	http://www.mediconsult.com/		•	
MedInfoSource (CME, Inc.)	http://www.medicineandbehavior.com/		•	Psychiatric
Medline	http://www.nlm.nih.gov/		•	Government-sponsored; Content from 4,300 medical journals
Medscape	http://www.medscape.com/	•	•	Portal for physicians
Medsite	http://www.medsite.com/	•	•	Medical news from Reuters; portal for physicians
Medstat	http://www.medstat.com/	•	•	
Merion Publications	http://www.merion.com/	•	•	Daily news for 19 Advance publications

Publication/Medium	URL	Daily news	Archive news	Resources
Micromedex	http://www.mdx.com/	•	•	Reprints news releases
Multimedia HealthCare/Freedom	http://www.mmhc.com/			Selective editorial from five magazines on geriatrics
Nurseweek	http://www.nurseweek.com/		•	New articles every Monday and Thursday
Nursing Center	http://www.nursingcenter.com/journals/		•	Reprinted content of 23 nursing journals
Nursing Spectrum	http://www.nursingspectrum.com/			Search engine and directory for nursing-relate d sites
P&T	http://www.www.pharmacyandtherapeutic.com/		•	Formulary news
PDR.Net	http://www.pdr.net/	•	•	For physicians
Physician's Practice Digest	http://www.ppdnet.com/		•	
Postgraduate Medicine	http://www.postgradmed.com/		•	
PsycPORT (American Psychological Society)	http://www.psycport.com/	•	•	Aggregates daily news from various sources
RNWeb	http://www.rnweb.com/		•	
SpringNet	http://www.springnet.com/		•	Selected editorial from journal
Summary statistics on medical education and medical schools (Association of American Medical Colleges)	http://www.aamc.org/	•	•	Statistics
Surgical Products	http://www.surgprodmag.com/		•	Directory of products and manufacturers; product reviews
Telemedicine Today	http://www.telemedtoday.com/			Links list telemedicine resources online
The American Journal of Clinical Pathology	http://www.ajcp.com/		•	
The American Society of Clinical Pathologists	http://www.ascp.org/			Subscription e-mail newsletter
The Physician and Sports Medicine	http://www.physsportsmed.com/		•	
Today's Chiropractic	http://www.todayschiropractic.com/		•	
Turner White Communications	http://www.turner-white.com/		•	Selected editorial from Hospital Physician

Publication/Medium	URL	Daily news	Archive news	Resources
U.S. Medicine	http://www.usmedicine.com/		•	
Webmedlit	http://webmedlit.silverplatter.com/index.html		•	Aggregates articles from medical journals in 10 topic areas

MEDICAL AND DIAGNOSTIC EQUIPMENT TOPICS

PR practitioners will find this segment to be poorly covered. Overall, the sector offers newsletter and magazine subscriptions online or locks off content to subscribers only.

Publication/Medium	URL	Daily news	Archive news	Resources
Biomedical Products	http://www.bioprodmag.com/scripts/default.asp			Product directory
Diagnostic Imaging	http://www.dimag.com/	•	•	
Medical Device and Diagnostic Industry	http://www.devicelink.com/			
Medical Imaging	http://www.healthtechnet.com/			

MEN'S INTEREST AND ENTERTAINMENT

PR practitioners have little to work with in this segment. Most editorial is reprinted from magazines, and pictures are as one would expect from men's magazines. Several adult publications are hard- to soft-core porn sites. There are hundreds of men's link and forum sites that range from spirituality to porn. PR practitioners will find this category difficult to use for online news outlets and men-related resources.

Publication/Medium	URL	Daily news	Archive news	Resources
Esquire	http://www.esquiremag.com/		•	Advice for men and pinup pictures
Maxim	http://www.maximonline.com/		•	Sex-oriented editorial; pinups; newsgroups
Men's Journal	http://www.mensjournal.com/		•	Outdoor-oriented editorial
New Man	http://www.newmanmag.com/		•	Spiritually oriented copy
Playboy	http://playboy.com/		•	
Popular Mechanics	http://www.popularmechanics.com/		•	Product reviews

METALWORKING AND MACHINERY TOPICS

PR practitioners will find that metalworking and machinery topics online are primarily useful for researching resources. The number of news sites is slim, and most editorial is reprinted. That said, resources are deep.

Publication/Medium	URL	Daily news	Archive news	Resources
Abrasives Magazine	http://www.abrasivesmagazine.com/home.htm		•	Selected editorial
American Machinist (Penton Publishing)	http://www.americanmachinist.com/		•	Directory of manufacturers and products
American Metal Market	http://www.amm.com/index2.htm	•		
Canadian Metalworking	http://www.canadianmetalworking.com/		•	Links
Cutting Tool Engineering	http://www.cuttingtoolengineering.com/		•	Manufacturers' guide
Gardner Publications	http://www.gardnerweb.com/		•	Reprinted editorial from Modern Machine Shop, Products Finishing, Automotive Manufacturing & Production and Automotive Finishing; links
Gear Technology	http://www.geartechnology.com/		•	
Industrial Heating	http://www.industrialheating.com/index.html			E-mail news updates, buyer's guide, calendar
Manufacturing Center	http://www.manufacturingcenter.com/	•	•	
Metal Powders Industries Federation	http://www.mpif.org/		•	Calendar, glossary, selected editorial
Metal Working Industry	http://www.metalworkingindustry.com/	•	•	Links to 15 magazines
Metalworking Digest	http://www.metalwdigest.com/		•	Trade show calendar, links
Modern Machine Shop	http://www.mmsonline.com/	•	•	Forums
Products Finishing	http://www.pfonline.com/		•	
The Society of Manufacturing Engineers	http://www.sme.org/	•	•	Editorial is members only

MILITARY

PR practitioners working in military topics will find plenty to work with. For one, the U.S. Department of Defense and the military services have been diligent about building and maintaining useful and informative Web sites. Secondly, commercially run Web sites have worked hard to be news and resources suppliers. Practitioners should have an online strategy when working in this area. There are hundreds of military link sites and many are duplicates. Newsgroups and forums appear to be mostly Web-related.

Publication/Medium	URL	Daily news	Archive news	Resources
About.com	http://usmilitary.about.com/		•	Forum, links
Air Force Crossroads	http://www.afcrossroads.com			Links
Air Force Technology	http://www.airforce-technology.com/			Resources on Air Force equipment
Armed Forces Journal International	http://www.afji.com/		•	
Army Forces Command	http://www.forscom.army.mil/			Intranet for U.S. Army with links to news, publications, forms, and army organizations and installations
Army Magazine (Association of the U.S. Army)	http://www.ausa.org/		•	
Defence Systems Daily (U.K.)	http://defence-data.com/	•	•	
Defense Daily	http://www.defensedaily.com/		•	Subscriber only
Defense News	http://www.defensenews.com/		•	Selected editorial; rest is subscriber only
Defense-aerospace (French-based)	http://www.defense-aerospace.com/	•	•	
DefenseLINK	http://www.defenselink.mil/news/	•	•	News from the American Forces Press Service; audio from Defense press conferences; transcripts of news briefings; news archive; daily activities summary
Janes Defence Weekly	http://www.janes.com/		•	
Leatherneck Magazine and Marine Corp Gazette	http://www.mca-marines.org/		•	
Marine Corp	http://www.usmc.mil/	•	•	
Militarycity.com	http://www.militarycity.com/	•	•	In-depth daily reporting from the Army Times, Air Force Times, Navy Times, and Marine Corp Times; resources; online

Publication/Medium	URL	Daily news	Archive news	Resources
				subscriptions to 10 newsletter and briefing areas
National Defense	http://www.ndia.org		•	
National Guard	http://www.ngaus.org/		•	
Naval Institute Proceedings	http://www.usni.org/		•	
Sea Power (The Navy League)	http://www.navyleague.org/		•	
Soldiers Magazine	http://www.dtic.mil/soldiers/		•	
The Fleet Reserve Association	http://www.fra.org/		•	
The Retired Officer	http://www.troa.org/		•	
United States Airforce Online News	http://www.af.mil/newspaper/	•	•	Official online news source for the Air Force
United States Coast Guard	http://www.uscg.mil/news/ cgnews.html	•	•	
United States Navy	http://www.ncts.navy.mil/ newsinfo/index.html	•	•	

MINING AND MINERAL

Mining and mineral topics provide a surprising number of news outlets and resources for PR practitioners, considering the low number of print publications in the field. There are several newsgroups related to mining and metallurgy under sci.engr.

Publication/Medium	URL	Daily news	Archive news	Resources
Coal Age	http://industryclick.com/		•	Runs product releases
Coal Outlook	http://www.ftenergyusa.com/ coaloutlook/	•	•	Subscription only
E&MJ—Engineering & Mining Journal	http://industryclick.com	•	•	Links; calendar of events
Goldsheet Mining Directory	http://goldsheet.simplenet.com/			Links
Infomine	http://www.infomine.com/	•	•	Portal for mining
J.T. Boyd Company	http://www.jtboyd.com/links.htm			Links
Mining Technology	http://www.www .mining-technology.com/			Descriptions of mining projects; company index; industry organizations; calendar of activities; equipment catalogs

Publication/Medium	URL	Daily news	Archive news	Resources
Mining USA	http://www.miningusa.com/	•	•	Aggregates daily news from various sources
Platt's Global Energy newsletters	http://www.platts.com/index.html	•	•	Free and subscriber sections
Prospector News	http://www.www.prospector-news.com/	•	•	Daily e-mail newsletter
The National Mining Association	http://www.nma.org/		•	
The Northern Miner (Canadian)	http://www.northernminer.com/	•	•	Daily news subscription only
The Pittsburgh Society for Mining, Metallurgy and Exploration	http://www.smepittsburgh.org/			Links
Yahoo!'s mining page	http://biz.yahoo.com/news/mining.html	•	•	

MUNICIPAL, COUNTY, AND NATIONAL GOVERNMENT

This is a rapidly growing area of news and resources. Government entities at all levels in the United States have moved online. Entrepreneurs have launched sites that make government services to citizens easier. Lobbyists are online. Political reporting is online. Parties and candidates have web pages. The U.S. Congress and the U.S. Senate both maintain Web pages. There are thousands of municipal and county news and links pages. Online news reporting varies in quality; resources are deep. PR practitioners working in government areas should have well-developed online strategies. The following is a fraction of what is available.

Publication/Medium	URL	Daily news	Archive news	Resources
All Politics (CNN and Time Magazine)	http://www.cnn.com/ALLPOLITICS/	•	•	Election links to information on candidates, races, polls, and delegate counts
American City & Country	http://industryclick.com/		•	Events, supplier links
Better Roads	http://www.betterroads.com/			Links to state/country departments of transportation
Congress.org	http://www.congress.org/			Congressional directory

Publication/Medium	URL	Daily news	Archive news	Resources
Council of State Governments	http://www.statesnews.org/	•	•	Aggregates states' news from various sources; in-depth resources on states' officials and Web sites
CQ	http://www.cq.com/	•	•	Subscriber only
C-Span	http://www.c-span.org/	•	•	
ElectNet	http://www.electnet.org/			State-by-state election returns
Essential Information	http://www.essential.org/			Group of activist sites
E-ThePeople	http://www.e-thepeople.com/	•	•	Political/govt news from several hundred sources; petitions on dozens of topics
Etown	http://www.etown.edu/vl/			Link site library on international affairs
Federal Election Commission	http://www.fec.gov/			Federal Election Commission information, including contributors' reports; format not as usable
Federal Times	http://www.federaltimes.com/		•	
Fedstats	http://www.fedstats.gov/			Statistics from 70 agencies
Fedworld	http://www.fedworld.gov/			Switch page to all Federal government Web sites
FPMI Communications	http://www.fpmi.com/		•	Selected editorial on Federal employee relations; Fed News Online, a brief news survey
Freedomchannel	http://www.freedomchannel.com/		•	Video reports on candidates' races
Global Computing	http://www.globalcomputing.com/states.html			Links to state Web sites
Governing	http://www.governing.com/	•	•	Aggregates daily news from a variety of sources
Government Executive	http://www.govexec.com/	•	•	
Govworks	http://www.govworks.com/			Links
Grassroots	http://www.grassroots.com/			Site to help activists
International Affairs	http://www.internationalaffairs.com/home.html			Link site for global politics and economics
Municipal World (Canadian)	http://www.municipalworld.com/		•	Forum

Publication/Medium	URL	Daily news	Archive news	Resources
Munisource	http://www.munisource.org/			Resource for municipal government related information
National Journal	http://nationaljournal.com/		•	Subscribers only; joint site for 5 congressionally oriented publications
National Political Index	http://www.politicalindex.com/			Links
Nonprofit	http://www.nonprofit.gov/			Links to govt for nonprofits
Official City Sites	http://officialcitysites.org/			Ambitious effort to list and track municipal Web sites the world over
Oregon State University	http://govinfo.kerr.orst.edu/			Government information sharing project
Political Resources	http://www.politicalresources.net/home.htm			Links to political sites around the globe
Politics Online	http://www.politicsonline.com/			Source for fund raising and Internet tools
Politics.com	http://www.politics.com	•	•	Aggregates news from varoius sources; resources on candidates, funding, and polls
Roll Call	http://www.rollcall.com/		•	Congressional news and opinion 2x a week
Speakout	http://www.speakout.com/			Place to express opinions
Stateline.org (Pew Charitable Trusts)	http://www.stateline.org/	•	•	News from the states
The Center for Responsive Politics	http://www.opensecrets.org/			
The Hill	http://www.hillnews.com/	•	•	Daily news aggregated from
				key newspapers; Federal/state campaign news, links; Federal govt. links, Hill Links, guide to congressmen and districts
The Hill Times (Canadian)	http://www.thehilltimes.ca/	•	•	Similar to The Hill
The Local Government Group (Primedia/Intertec Publishing)	http://www.localgov.com/		•	Combined site for eight magazine and television sites for city and county

Publication/Medium	URL	Daily news	Archive news	Resources
				governments, fire and police forces and emergency medical services; calendars of events, forums, links
Thomas (Library of Congress)	http://thomas.loc.gov/		•	Legislative information
Tray.com	http://www.tray.com/			Analyzes Federal Election Commission information, including contributors' reports
Vote Smart	http://www.vote-smart.org/			Directory to candidates and issues
Vote.com	http://www.vote.com/			An odd site that lets one vote on political and other issues
Webactive	http://www.webactive.com/			Site for activists
Yahoo!'s government page	http://dir.yahoo.com/government/index.html			Useful resources for PR practitioners

MUSIC AND MUSIC TRADES

This segment is one of the better known because of the downloadable and file-sharing music sites, streaming music, audio and video interviews of artists, live links to performances, and more. Bands and singers know the art of publicizing their materials on the Web. Studio Web sites publicize established singers, and homegrown Web sites publicize lesser-known talents. Specialty firms seed youth-oriented newsgroups with information about new artists and releases. Orchestras feed their performances live on the Web. The music industry has been a leader in adapting to online, and PR practitioners working in music publicity should be aware of online strategies in use. There are thousands of music link sites and many newsgroup forums, often associated with e-zines. PR practitioners will need to research these independently by music type.

Publication/Medium	URL	Daily news	Archive news	Resources
7Ball Magazine	http://www.7ball.com/		•	
Access Magazine	http://www.accessmag.com/		•	Concert calendar
Acoustic Guitar	http://www.acguitar.com/		•	Selected editorial
Alternative Press	http://altpress.com/		•	Alternative music scene; reviews new releases

Publication/Medium	URL	Daily news	Archive news	Resources
Bass Player	http://www.bassplayer.com/		•	
Billboard Magazine	http://www.billboard.com/	•	•	Charts of top songs, including music rankings from 16 Web sites
Black Beat	http://www.blackbeat.com/	•		Fan bulletin board
Blues Revue	http://www.bluesrevue.com/			Calendar of Blues-related musical events
CDNow	http://www.cdnow.com/		•	
Chart (Canadian)	http://www.chartattack.com/	•	•	
Clickmusic (United Kingdom)	http://www.clickmusic.co.uk/	•	•	Aggregates music news from other sites; directory
CMJ New Music Monthly	http://www.cmj.com/	•	•	Listings of upcoming CDs and link list of Internet broadcasts
Contemporary Christian Music	http://www.ccmmagazine.com/news/		•	
Country Weekly	http://www.countryweekly.com/		•	Tour schedules
Down Beat	http://www.downbeat.com/	•	•	Calendars, live interviews with artists, message boards , music downloads
Drum!	http://www.drumlink.com/		•	Product reviews
Electronic Musician	http://industryclick.com		•	Supplier directory
Exclaim! (Canadian)	http://www.exclaim.ca/		•	
Gig Magazine	http://www.gigmag.com/			Forums
Guitar Magazine	http://www.guitaronemag.com/		•	Selected editorial; tutorials; MP3 downloads
Guitarplayer	http://www.guitarplayer.com/		•	Tutorials and product tests
Jam Magazine (Florida)	http://floridajam.com/		•	
Keyboard Magazine	http://www.keyboardmag.com/			Tutorials for keyboard players; reviews
Mad Rhythms	http://www.madrhythms.com/		•	
Modern Drummer	http://www.moderndrummer.com/		•	Select editorial and press releases
Murder Dog	http://www.murderdog.com/		•	Selected editorial
Music Connection	http://www.musicconnection.com/			Forums
Musician Magazine	http://www.musicianmag.com/			The Musician's Guide with comprehensive resources
New Media Music	http://www.newmediamusic.com/	•	•	E-zine; regular audio interviews with industry leaders

Publication/Medium	URL	Daily news	Archive news	Resources
Rolling Stone	http://www.rollingstone.com/	•	•	Web casts; CD reviews; message boards; tour calendars; contests; games
Spin	http://www.spin.com/	•	•	
The Music Trades	http://www.musictrades.com/		•	Access to back issues
The Source	http://www.thesource.com/		•	
Vibe	http://www.vibe.com/	•	•	Music samples from CDs; audio/video interviews; discussion groups; chat room

OCCUPATIONAL HEALTH AND SAFETY

This field is poorly covered online with just one publication that provides daily reporting and two others that provide regular posting of news and events. PR practitioners will find deep resources, however. There is a newsgroup covering occupational health issues at sci.med.occupational and another covering repetitive strain injuries at misc.health.injuries.rsi.

Publication/Medium	URL	Daily news	Archive news	Resources
American Industrial Hygiene Association	http://www.aiha.org/			Resources and health links
Association for Worksite Health Promotion	http://www.awhp.org/			Resources and health links
Compliance magazine	http://www.compliancemag.com/		•	
Industrial Hygiene	http://www.rimbach.com/		•	
Industrial Safety & Hygiene News	http://www.ishn.com/		•	Weekly news summary
National Safety Council	http://www.nsc.org/			Resources and health links
Occupational Hazards (Penton Publishing)	http://www.occupationalhazards.com/	•	•	
Occupational Health & Safety	http://www.ohsonline.com/		•	
Risk Management Internet Services	http://rmis.com/			Claims more than 13,000 resources and hundreds of thousands of pages on occupational health and a broad range of risks

Publication/Medium	URL	Daily news	Archive news	Resources
The National Council on Compensation Insurance	http://www.www5.ncci.com/ncciweb/	•	•	Postings and updates on worker's compensation issues

OPTICAL

This category is of little use for PR practitioners online, except for research and some discussion groups. Content is largely reprinted except for subscription-based, peer-reviewed journals. There is no daily news online, but there are calendars. Sci.med.vision is a newsgroup that discusses eye issues.

Publication/Medium	URL	Daily news	Archive news	Resources
20/20	http://www.2020mag.com/		•	
All About Vision	http://www.allaboutvision.com/			Consumer advice on eye care issues
European Optical Newsnet	http://www.eon-jobson.com/EON/default.cfm		•	
Eyecare Business	http://www.eyecarebiz.com/		•	
Eyecareinfo	http://www.eyecareinfo.com/			Links
Eyesearch	http://eyesearch.com/			Links
Medhelp	http://www.medhelp.org/			Discussion groups on eye diseases and eye care
Ocular Surgery News	http://www.ocularsurgerynews.com/		•	
Primary Care Optometry News	http://www.slackinc.com/eye/pcon/pconhome.asp		•	
Review of Optometry	http://www.revoptom.com/		•	
Vision Monday	http://www.visionmonday.com/default.cfm		•	

PACKAGING

The PR practitioner will find that the packaging industry is reasonably well represented online with news appearing at least weekly, if not daily. Most sites have calendars and industry resources useful for research. There are thousands of packaging link sites. Most are affiliated with businesses and are not of much use to PR practitioners. Forums or newsgroups on packaging topics are scarce.

Publication/Medium	URL	Daily news	Archive news	Resources
Boxboard Containers International	http://industryclick.com		•	Updates news twice weekly

Publication/Medium	URL	Daily news	Archive news	Resources
Canadian Packaging	http://www.canadianpackaging.com/		•	
Converting Magazine (Cahners Publishing)	http://www.convertingmagazine.com/			News updates about twice a week; multiyear calendar of industry events
Netsourcing	http://www.netsourcingmag.com/		•	Listing of business-to-business packaging sites
Packaging Digest	http://www.packagingdigest.com/	•	•	Aggregates daily news from various sources; calendar; machinery and materials guide
Packaging World	http://www.packworld.com/	•	•	Web exclusives; calendar of events, listings of associations and packaging schools
Packaginginfo.com	http://www.packaginginfo.com/		•	Reprinted editorial from Brand Packaging, Flexible Packaging and Food and Drug Packaging; free login; prints news releases; trade show calendar and listing of associations
Packexpo	http://www.packexpo.com/	•		Portal for packaging resources

PARENTING AND FAMILY

There is plenty about parenting and family issues online. PR practitioners will find in-depth resources but little news. Most of the material is evergreen or features, but there is a lot of it. In addition to national sites, there are many regional, city, and local parenting sites that PR practitioners should investigate, depending on the issue. In addition, there are thousands of parenting and family link sites, most of which are not useful for practitioners. There are many parenting and family forums such as alt.parenting.solutions, alt.support.single-parents, and misc.kids.pregnancy in addition to numerous forums associated with Web sites. PR practitioners will need to research.

Publication/Medium	URL	Daily news	Archive news	Resources
Alternative Family Magazine	http://www.altfammag.com/		•	Lesbian and Gay family issues

Publication/Medium	URL	Daily news	Archive news	Resources
America OnLine (AOL)			•	
American Baby	http://www.americanbaby.com/		•	For new parents
Child Magazine (part of Parents.com— http://www.parents.com/)	http://www.childmagazine.com/		•	Resource site for new parents; chat, newsgroup
Christian Parenting	http://www.christianityonline .com/cpt/current/		•	
City Family	http://www.cityfamily.com/		•	For immigrant families
Education Update	http://www.educationupdate .com/		•	New York City education; links list
Exceptional Parent	http://www.eparent.com/		•	Newsgroup
Family Digest	http://www.familydigest.com/		•	
Family Fun	http://www.familyfun.com/		•	Activities for kids
Family.com	http://family.go.com/		•	Message boards
Healthykids.com (Primedia Publishing)	http://www.healthykids.com/		•	Children's health issues and family fitness; chat room, newsgroup
Home Education Magazine	http://www.home-ed- magazine.com/		•	
Localmom.com	http://www.localmom.com/		•	Local parenting magazines from seven cities
Los Angeles Family	http://www.childrenmagazine .com/		•	
Netfamilynews	http://www.netfamilynews.org/		•	
Parent Soup (iVillage)	http://www.parentsoup.com/		•	
Parenthoodweb	http://www.parenthoodweb.com/		•	Content from nearly 30 city magazines
Parenting	http://www.parenting.com/ parenting/		•	The Parenting.com group—Healthy Pregnancy, Baby Talk, Parenting and Family Life
Parenttime (co-owned by Time Inc. and Procter & Gamble Productions)	http://www.parenttime.com/		•	For pregnant women; forums
Practical Homeschooling	http://www.home-school.com/		•	
Scholastic	http://www.scholastic.com/index .asp		•	Three subsections for teachers, kids, and parents; on the
				kids site, it reports weekly news
Sesame Street Parents	http://www.sesamestreet.org/		•	
Today's Parent	http://www.todaysparent.com/		•	
Working Mother	http://www.womenconnect.com/		•	

PAPER AND PAPER PRODUCT TRADES

This is a small category online and PR practitioners would do better with a print-based strategy. There are many paper link sites that are of

little use for practitioners and no newsgroups or forums that appeared
to be of importance.

Publication/Medium	URL	Daily news	Archive news	Resources
Paper Age	http://www.paperage.com/	•		Links
Paper Exchange	http://www.paperexchange.com/	•	•	Aggregates news from press releases and from various sources; in German, Italian, Spanish, Swedish, and Finnish
Pulp & Paper	http://www.pponline.com/	•		Editorial for subscribers only; links, calendar, chat room
Technical Association of the Pulp and Paper Industry	http://www.tappi.org/	•	•	Daily news aggregated from various sources

PETROLEUM AND GAS TRADES

PR practitioners will find useful media outlets in this segment and
research material as well. However, most publications have not gone
online, or if they have, they are largely subscriber-only. Sci.geo.petro-
leum is an active newsgroup devoted to oil exploration and recovery.
For the most part, PR practitioners can stay with a print-based strategy.

Publication/Medium	URL	Daily news	Archive news	Resources
American Association of Petroleum Geologists	http://www.aapg.org/		•	
Bloomberg Natural Gas Report and Oil Buyers' Guide	http://www.bloomberg.com/energy/	•	•	Mostly subscriber only
Energy Markets	http://www.energy-markets.com/	•		
Gas Daily (part of FTEnergy)	http://www.ftenergyusa.com/gasdaily/		•	Most copy for subscribers only
Gas News	http://www.gas.com/	•	•	Worldwide news aggregation for gas, petroleum, hydroelectric, and energy
Gulf Publishing Company	http://www.gulfpub.com/		•	Combines several energy publications; selected editorial
Hart's E&P	http://www.eandpnet.com/ep/		•	
Journal of Petroleum Technology	http://www.spe.org/	•	•	Publishes Oil & Gas Executive Report

Publication/Medium	URL	Daily news	Archive news	Resources
National Petroleum News	http://www.petroretail.net/npn/		•	Provides access to NPN International, Fuel Oil News, and Station & Store with free registration
Oil and Gas Investor	http://www.oilandgasinvestor.com/	•		
Oil Field Directory	http://www.oilfielddirectory.com/	•	•	Vertical portal (vortal) for petroleum and gas topics; links and forums
Penwell Publishing's PennNet site	http://www.pennet.com/	•	•	Energy news and resource community built around Oil & Gas Journal, Oil & Gas Petroleum Equipment and Offshore magazines; industry calendar; product guide
Pipeline & Gas Journal	http://www.undergroundinfo.com/	•	•	Picks up energy industry news releases from PR Newswire
Scandinavian Oil-Gas Magazine	http://www.scandoil.no/		•	Links
The Institute of Petroleum	http://www.petroleum.co.uk/prnib.htm	•		

PETS AND PET SUPPLY

PR practitioners will find that pet and pet supply topics vary by the type of pet and interests of pet owners. Virtually all material is reprinted from magazines except for pet forums. Practitioners should search the Web by pet type when developing media outlets and research. Associations for animal breeds will have news about the breed and events that practitioners should not ignore. There are hundreds of pet links pages on the Web. Most are not useful for practitioners. There are numerous pet forums as well by breed and type, including at least three newsgroup forums—rec.pets.dogs.breeds, rec.pets.dogs.behavior, and rec.pets.cats.health+behav. The list of sites given here is far from complete. PR practitioners will find abundant resources throughout the Web, and they should have an online strategy.

Publication/Medium	URL	Daily news	Archive news	Resources
AKC Gazette (American Kennel Club)	http://www.akc.org/index.html		•	

Publication/Medium	URL	Daily news	Archive news	Resources
America OnLine (AOL)				Sponsored forum for pet owners
Bird Dog & Retriever News	http://bird-dog-news.com/		•	Resources and forums
Birdtimes (Pet Business, Inc.)	http://www.birdtimes.com/		•	
Cats	http://www.catsmag.com	•	•	
Cats & Kittens (Pet Business, Inc.)	http://www.catsandkittens.com/		•	
CompuServe				Useful links page in its Family Channel
Dog & Kennel (Pet Business, Inc.)	http://www.dogandkennel.com/		•	Breed profiles
Dog News	http://www.dognews.com/		•	Selected editorial
Dogworld	http://www.dogworldmag.com		•	
Equisearch	http://www.equisearch.com	•		Links
Fancy Publications	http://www.animalnetwork.com/		•	11 magazines focused on birds, cats, dogs, ferrets, fish, horses, rabbits, and reptiles
Pet Business	http://www.petbusiness.com/		•	Selected editorial
Pet Life	http://www.petlifeweb.com/		•	Extensive resources
Prodogs	http://www.prodogs.com/			Forums
The Pet Channel	http://www.thepetchannel.com/			A vertical portal (vortal) for pet owners

PHOTOGRAPHY

Photography is a well-covered topic online. Part of the reason has to do with the Internet's ability to transmit images and the rise of digital photography. PR practitioners working in this area should have an online strategy. There are thousands of photo news, photo links, and photo forum sites on the Web. Most are of little use to practitioners. There are at least five news groups as well—rec.photo.digital, fr.rec.photo, rec.photo.equipment.35mm, rec.photo.technique.people, and rec.photo.technique.nature.

Publication/Medium	URL	Daily news	Archive news	Resources
America OnLine (AOL)				Forums and other resources
Outdoor Photographer	http://www.outdoorphotographer.com/		•	Equipment reviews, links
PEI	http://www.peimag.com/		•	Tutorials
Photo District News	http://www.pdn-pix.com/	•	•	Awards, new product reviews,

Publication/Medium	URL	Daily news	Archive news	Resources
				business resources, and a glossary of terms
Photo Insider	http://www.photoinsider.com/		•	
Photo Marketing	http://photomarketing.com/newsline.htm	•	•	
Photo News	http://www.photo-news.com/		•	Selected editorial; online newsletters to subscribers; database of suppliers
Photo Retailer (Canadian)	http://www.photolife.com/		•	
Photodo (Swedish)	http://www.photodo.com/			Links to six magazines in multiple languages and provides product testing information
Photographic Processing	http://www.labsonline.com/	•	•	Industry calendar of events
Popular Photography	America Online			Equipment reviews and photographic galleries
Shutterbug	http://www.shutterbug.net/		•	Test reports, forums and a buyer's guide; press releases from manufacturers and others
TechPhoto	http://www.techphoto.org/	•	•	Interactive e-zine; product reviews
The Rangefinder	http://www.rangefinder-network.com/		•	Selected editorial; calendar of events; suppliers directory
Today's Photographer International	http://www.aipress.com/			Tutorials and resources

PLASTICS AND RUBBER TOPICS

PR practitioners will find that the plastics and rubber segment is well represented online, especially for daily news. In addition, resources are provided in-depth. This is an area in which the practitioner should consider an online strategy, although a print-based strategy might be sufficient. There are hundreds of plastics and rubber links sites, of which most are of little use, and there are few forums or newsgroups.

Publication/Medium	URL	Daily news	Archive news	Resources
Canadian Plastics	http://www.canplastics.com/			Buyers guide

Publication/Medium	URL	Daily news	Archive news	Resources
Commerx PlasticsNet	http://www.commerxplasticsnet.com/		•	B-to-B site that lists suppliers, events, and news releases
IAPD magazine	http://www.iapd.org/			Editorial calendar
Injection Molding Magazine	http://www.immnet.com/		•	Directory, forum
Modern Plastics, Modern Plastics International, and Modern Mold & Tooling	http://www.modplas.com/		•	Glossary
Plastics Distributor & Fabricator	http://www.plasticsmag.com/		•	
Plastics Machining & Fabricating	http://www.plasticsmachining.com/		•	
Plastics News (Crain Communications)	http://www.plasticsnews.com/	•	•	Product news, calendar, directories to manufacturers and links
Ray Publishing	http://www.raypubs.com/			Two magazines, *High-performance Composites* and *Composites Technology*; editorial calendars
Rubber & Plastics News	http://www.rubbernews.com/	•	•	Directory to rubber product manufacturers, industry calendar, links
Rubber World	http://www.rubberworld.com/	•		Links, suppliers' index
The Society of Plastics Engineers	http://www.4spe.org/			Event calendar

PLUMBING, HVAC, AND REFRIGERATION

PR practitioners will find in-depth resources on plumbing, HVAC, and—less so—refrigeration; but little editorial. News is mostly aggregated from other sources, but link sites are useful. There is at least one newsgroup dedicated to this segment—alt.HVAC. Practitioners can stay with a print strategy in this segment.

Publication/Medium	URL	Daily news	Archive news	Resources
Air Conditioning, Heating, and Refrigeration News	http://www.achrnews.com/		•	Links
ASHRAE Journal (American Society of Heating, Refrigerating, and Air-Conditioning Engineers)	http://www.ashrae.org/		•	Resources

Publication/Medium	URL	Daily news	Archive news	Resources
Consulting-Specifying Engineer	http://www.csemag.com/	•	•	Aggregates daily news from multiple sources, including Buildingteam.com (
Contractor	http://www.contractormag.com/	•	•	Aggregates daily news from various sources; product features; resource directory
Engineered Systems	http://www.esmagazine.com/		•	Weekly news updates
Heating/Piping/Air Conditioning	http://www.hpac.com/		•	Industry calendar and roundtable
HVAC News	http://www.hvacnews.com/		•	Industry directory
Plumbing Links	http://www.plumbinglinks.com/			Links
PlumbingWeb	http://www.plumbingweb.com/			Links
Plumbnet	http://www.plumbnet.com/			Forum
Supply House Times	http://www.supplyht.com/	•	•	Aggregates daily news from various resources
The Plumber	http://www.theplumber.com/			Resource site for plumbers; forum

POLICE, LAW ENFORCEMENT, AND FIRE PROTECTION

There is scant police and fire news online but a wealth of police and fire resources. PR practitioners working in law enforcement and fire protection areas will find that online is primarily useful for research. There are hundreds of police links sites and several newsgroups, most of which are locked off. Security is of concern to policemen.

Publication/Medium	URL	Daily news	Archive news	Resources
Fire Chief	http://www.industryclick.com/	•	•	Forum, awards, links
Fire Engineering	http://fe.pennnet.com/home.cfm		•	Firehouse Magazine
Law Enforcement News	http://www.www.law-enforcement.com/	•	•	Aggregates police news from various sources
Law Enforcement online	http://www.pima.edu/dps/police.htm			Links site to city, county, state, and federal government law enforcement and courts sites
Leolinks	http://www.leolinks.com/			Directory of law enforcement sites
National Fire & Rescue	http://www.nfrmag.com/		•	
Officer.com	http://www.officer.com/		•	Aggregates news from other sites; forums
Police	http://policemag.com/		•	Resources

Publication/Medium	URL	Daily news	Archive news	Resources
Policeone	http://www.policeone.com/			Directory of law enforcement sites; forums
The Official Directory of State Patrol and State Police sites	http://www.statetroopersdirectory.com			Links

POWER, ENERGY, AND UTILITIES

Power, energy, and utility topics are well-covered online with abundant news, resources, and links. PR practitioners should have an online strategy when working in this segment. There is at least one newsgroup—alt.energy.renewable.

Publication/Medium	URL	Daily news	Archive news	Resources
Diesel & Gas Turbine Publications (Seven publications)	http://www.dieselpub.com/		•	Industry events calendar; emissions regulations center; industry directory
ElectricNet	http://www.electricnet.com/	•	•	Product center
Energy Ideas	http://www.energyideas.org/	•	•	E-zine for Washington State Energy/utility professionals
Financial Times Energy (seven newsletters)	http://www.pasha.com/		•	Reprints selected editorial from newsletters and rest is subscriber only: Coal outlook, Energy Insight, The Energy Report, Gas Daily, Generation Week, Megawatt Daily, Transportation, and Storage Hub; industry calendar
Infocast	http://www.informationforecast.com/			Industry Conferences on power issues
Platts Global Energy (McGraw-Hill)	http://www.platts.com/index.html	•	•	10 sections: Oil, natural gas, coal, electric power, nuclear, petrochemicals, information technology, engineering, regulatory and business; has

Publication/Medium	URL	Daily news	Archive news	Resources
				Industry conference calendar; includes Power Magazine and T&D World Magazine
Power Engineering (Part of PennNet)	http://pe.pennwellnet.com/home/home.cfm	•	•	Daily news aggregated from other sources; product showcase, discussion group, e-mail newsletter, industry event calendar, virtual events, and webcasting
Power Engineering International (Part of PennNet)	http://pei.pennwellnet.com/home/home.cfm	•	•	Daily news aggregated from other sources; product showcase, discussion group, e-mail newsletter, industry event calendar, virtual events, and webcasting
Power Expert	http://www.powerexpert.com/	•	•	Extensive links
Powervalue	http://www.powervalue.com/	•	•	Aggregates daily news from other sources; new products, buyers guide, discussion forum, industry conference calendar, association listing
Public Utilities Reports (Public Utility Fortnightly)	http://www.pur.com/	•	•	Much of it subscriber only; includes PUR Utility Regulatory News
The Energy Daily	http://kingpublishing.com/publications/ed/	•		Subscriber only
Utility & Telephone Fleets	http://www.utfmag.com/index.shtml	•	•	Product guide
Utility Automation (Part of PennNet)	http://ua.pennwellnet.com/home/home.cfm	•	•	Daily news aggregated from other sources; product showcase, discussion group, e-mail newsletter,
				industry event calendar, virtual events
Utility Business	http://telecomclick.com		•	
Utility Connection	http://www.utilityconnection.com			Link site

Publication/Medium	URL	Daily news	Archive news	Resources
Utility Fleet Management (part of Transport Topics)	http://www.ttnews.com/ufm/		•	•
Utility Week	http://www.utilityweek.com/	•	•	Subscriber only
Water Online	http://www.wateronline.com/content/homepage/	•	•	Product center

PRINTING, GRAPHICS, AND COMMERCIAL ARTS

Resources are abundant in this segment, but news and publicity outlets are sparse. Most content is reprinted from magazines or other sources. PR practitioners are better off remaining with a print strategy for publicity.

Publication/Medium	URL	Daily news	Archive news	Resources
American Printer	http://industryclick.com	•	•	Technology directory, buyer's guide
Applied Arts Magazine (Canadian)	http://www.appliedartsmag.com/		•	
Booktech	http://www.napco.com/btm/		•	
Communication Arts	http://www.commarts.com/		•	Forum, exhibits, links, and product directory
Converter	http://www.industryclick.com	•	•	White papers
Dealer Communicator	http://www.dealercommunicator.com/		•	
Digital Graphics	http://www.nbm.com/digitalgraphics/	•		Active bulletin board
Digital Output	http://www.digitalout.com/		•	Industry calendar, product directory
Document Processing Technology	http://www.dptmag.com/		•	
Flash Magazine	http://www.flashweb.com/		•	
Form	http://www.formmag.com/	•	•	
Graphic Arts Monthly	http://www.gammag.com/	•	•	New products, event calendar, e-mail newsletter, newsgroup, sourcebook
Graphic Exchange (Canadian)	http://www.gxo.com/		•	
Graphics bibliography	http://ira.uka.de/bibliography/Graphics/index.html			Large site with thousands of references to graphics articles
How	http://www.howdesign.com/		•	
Micro Publishing News	http://www.micropubnews.com/		•	Hardware and software reviews

Publication/Medium	URL	Daily news	Archive news	Resources
Modern Reprographics	http://www.modrepro.com/		•	
Prepress Technology	http://www.prepresstechnology.com/		•	Includes Newspapers & Technology and Online Technology
Print On Demand Business	http://www.podb.com/		•	
Printing News	http://www.printingnews.com/		•	
Printwear	http://www.nbm.com/printwear/		•	Graphics resource center, bulletin board
Quick Printing	http://www.quickprinting.com/		•	
Renderosity	http://www.poserforum.com/			Online graphic artists community; forum, exhibits, calendar, galleries, tutorials
Screen Printing	http://www.screenweb.com/		•	Tutorials, products, message boards, association directory
The Press	http://industryclick.com		•	
U&LC Online	http://www.itcfonts.com/itc/ulc/index.html		•	

PUBLIC RELATIONS

Public Relations resources online are extensive, and PR practitioners should be familiar with them. Online-PR.com (http://www.online-pr.com) provides more than 150 links to associations, magazines and newsletters, news media directories, news clipping services, measurement resources, and vendors. This scratches the surface of what is available. On the other hand, news is scarce. Practitioners distributing PR news should continue to rely on a print strategy.

Publication/Medium	URL	Daily news	Archive news	Resources
A Public Relations Bookshelf	http://www.theprnetwork.com/			Listing of PR books in print
Communications Briefings	http://www.combriefings.com/		•	
Communications World Online	http://www.iabc.com/cw/index.htm	•	•	Member-only
CyberPulse	http://www.webcom.com/impulse/			Listing of PR agency Web sites
Internet Public Relations Discussion List	http://www.audettemedia.com/i-public_relations/			PR strategy and implementation for the Internet, online media relations, internet PR tools

Publication/Medium	URL	Daily news	Archive news	Resources
				and resources, industry articles, news from major trade shows and seminars
IR Magazin (German)	http://www.ir-magazin.com/		•	
Marketing, PR, and Public Relations in Germany	http://www.marketing-webguide.de/			Links
Media Insider (PR Newswire and Profnet)	http://www.mediainsider.com/	•	•	**Media Wire**—Media intelligence, by industry segment; profiles of journalists and publications, contact information and pitching tips **News Break**—events of interest to the PR community **IR Focus**—News and events of relevance to the investor-relations community **Trade Talk**—Reports and reflections on the practice of public relations; Q&As with PR experts; calendar of events
Michael Driscoll's Online PR Sources	http://www.gsu.edu/~wwwpra/links.html			Links
O'Dwyer's PR Daily (includes Washington, DC PR News and PR Services Report)	http://www.odwyerpr.com/	•	•	Directories of PR firms, PR practitioners, and PR services; firm rankings, media news
Online-PR.com	http://www.online-pr.com/		•	Links and resources for PR practitioners
PR and Marketing News (includes Healthcare PR and Marketing News	http://www.prandmarketing.com/cgi/catalog/info?PRN		•	Industry calendar, awards and contests, industry links
PR Place	http://www.prplace.com/			Resources for PR Practitioners
PR Tools & Resources	http://www.weinkrantz.com/aw&ctools.html			Links
PR Watch (Center for Media & Democracy)	http://www.prwatch.org/		•	Dated material

Publication/Medium	URL	Daily news	Archive news	Resources
PR Week US	http://www.prweekus.com/us/index.htm		•	Selected editorial; industry calendar, awards
PRSA Silver Anvil	http://silveranvil.org/			Awards site
PRSIG	http://forums.compuserve.com/vlforums/default.asp?SRV=PublicRelations	•	•	The longest-running PR and marketing forum online
Public Affairs Monitor (Public Affairs Council)	http://www.pac.org/	•		Members only
Public Relations Tactics	http://www.prsa.org/prpubs.html		•	
Ragan Newsletters (Employee Communications)	http://www.ragan.com/		•	Selected editorial; seven newsletters: Ragan Report, Journal of Employee Communication Management, Stategic Employee Publications, Business Intelligence, Intranet Report, Speechwriter's Newsletter Institute and First Draft; conferences
Ragan Newsletters (Public Relations)	http://www.ragan.com/		•	Selected editorial; e-mail forum for Interactive PR; six separate newsletters: Annual Report Review, Interactive Public Relations, Media Relations Report, PR Intelligence, Public Relations Journal and Web Content Reportl; conferences
The PR Network	http://www.theprnetwork.com/			Links and resources
West Coast PR	http://www.westcoastpr.com/			Subscriber only

PURCHASING TOPICS

This is a poorly covered segment online from both news and resource perspectives. PR practitioners are better off remaining with a print strategy.

Publication/Medium	URL	Daily news	Archive news	Resources
Canadian Purchaser	http://www.copa.ca/		•	
Health Care Purchasing News	http://www.hpnonline.com/index.html	•	•	Industry guide and resources

Publication/Medium	URL	Daily news	Archive news	Resources
Purchasing Magazine	http://www.manufacturing.net/magazine/purchasing/		•	Procurement resources, pricing news, supply strategies

RADIO, TV, CABLE, AND RECORDING TRADE TOPICS

These industry segments are among the few where online has become an integral part of news. There is an abundance of daily online reports, and resources are deep. PR practitioners working in the radio, TV, cable, and recording trades should have well-developed online stategies. In addition, there are hundreds of link and newsgroup sites—too many for this book to cover. PR practitioners should develop their own lists, as appropriate.

Publication/Medium	URL	Daily news	Archive news	Resources
Baseline	http://www.pkbaseline.com/	•	•	Aggregates daily news from other sources; offers in-depth data and charts on the entertainment industry
BE Radio (for radio professionals)	http://www.beradio.com/		•	Product finder
Billboard	http://www.billboard-online.com/	•	•	Charts
BMI Music World	http://www.bmi.com/musicworld/	•	•	
Broadband Systems & Design	http://www.broadbandmag.com/scripts/default.asp		•	Buyer's guide
Broadcast Engineering	http://www.broadcastengineering.com/html/HomeSet1.htm	•	•	Buyer's Guides
Broadcasting & Cable	http://www.broadcastingcable.com/	•	•	Industry calendar
Cable Today	http://www.cabletoday.com/	•	•	Industry links and event calendar
Cablevision	http://www.cvmag.com/	•		
Cable World	http://www.telecomclick.com/	•	•	Supplier directory, newsletters
Cabling Installation & Maintenance (part of PennNet)	http://cim.pennnet.com/home/home.cfm	•	•	New products
CED—Communications Engineering & Design	http://www.cedmagazine.com/		•	Includes Plant Management
CMJ New Music Report	http://www.cmj.com/		•	Directory
CQ-Amateur Radio	http://www.www.cq-amateur-radio.com/	•	•	Forums
Current (PBS and National Public Radio)	http://www.current.org/		•	Selected content

Publication/Medium	URL	Daily news	Archive news	Resources
Dotmusic (International music)	http://www.dotmusic.com/		•	
Electronic Media	http://www.emonline.com/	•	•	
EQ Magazine	http://www.eqmag.com/		•	Active discussion board
Gavin	http://www.gavin.com/	•	•	Charts
Hitmakers	http://www.hitmakers.com/	•	•	
Kidscreen	http://www.kidscreen.com/		•	
Millimeter	http://www.millimeter.com/ HTM/HomeSet1.htm		•	
Mix	http://www.mixonline.com/	•	•	Industry calendar
Mobile Radio Technology	http://www.telecomclick.com/		•	Supplier directory, newsletters
Multichannel News	http://www.tvinsite.com/ multichannelnews.com/	•	•	Industry calendar
Music Row	http://www.musicrow.com/	•	•	
News Blues—A forum for TV Newsroom Whiners	http://www.newsblues.com/	•	•	Station directory; salary information
NRB—National Religious Broadcasters	http://www.nrb.org/magazine .htm		•	
Playback (Canadian)	http://www.playbackmag.com/		•	
Pro Sound News	http://www.prosoundnews.com/	•	•	
QST	http://www.arrl.org/arrlletter/	•	•	Product directory
R&R: The Industry's Newspaper	http://www.rronline.com/	•	•	Industry directory
Radio and Production	http://www.rapmag.com/		•	
Radio Ink	http://www.radioink.com/	•	•	
Real Screen (Canadian)	http://www.realscreen.com/		•	
RF design	http://www.telecomclick.com/		•	Supplier directory, newsletters
Rick on TV	http://www.rickontv.com/	•	•	Message board
Satellite Today	http://www.satellitetoday.com/	•	•	News is subscriber only; satellite database
Satellite Broadband	http://www.telecomclick.com/	•	•	
Television Broadcast	http://www.tvbroadcast.com/	•	•	
Video Systems	http://www.videosystems.com/	•	•	
Wireless Review	http://www.telecomclick.com/		•	Supplier directory
World Broadcast Engineering	http://www.wbnonline.com/html/ HomeSet1.htm		•	Conference directory
World Radio Online	http://www.wr6wr.com/		•	

RAILROAD TOPICS

PR practitioners will find some news sites and enormous resources. Railroading topics are mixed between industry news (sparse) and fan news (plentiful). There are hundreds of links sites (too many to list), and

almost are all fan or model railroading related. There are dozens of
railroad forums, almost all fan-related. Newsgroups are well represented too—rec.models.railroad, misc.transport.rail.americas, uk.rail-
way, alt.railroad.

Publication/Medium	URL	Daily news	Archive news	Resources
Eastern Railroad News	http://www.eastrailnews.com/	•	•	Railroading east of the Mississippi; subscriber only
Locomotive Engineers Journal	http://www.ble.org/	•	•	Member services
Railpace	http://www.railpace.com/	•		Photo gallery
Railroadinfo	http://www.railroadinfo.com/			Large links site, discussion group, photo gallery
Railway Age	http://www.railwayage.com/	•	•	Large industry links site; industry reports
Trains	http://www.trains.com/trains/	•	•	Selected archival stories, webcam, links section
Transource	http://www.transource.org/		•	Transportation environmental resource center

REAL ESTATE AND BUILDING MAINTENANCE
TOPICS

Real estate has a huge online presence in both news and resources,
and PR practitioners should have a strategy for incorporating online
into publicity efforts. In spite of the numbers of sites listed here, there
are dozens more print magazines and local/regional publications that
are not represented. Many of these do not have Web sites. There are
dozens of real estate link and forum sites. Many are of little use to
practitioners. There are at least three newsgroup sites—alt.invest.real-
estate, misc.invest.real-estate, alt.real-estate-agents.

Publication/Medium	URL	Daily news	Archive news	Resources
AOL (America Online)			•	Maintains real estate advice and listing section
Area Development	http://www.area-development.com/		•	Development site directory
Brownfield News	http://www.brownfieldnews.com/		•	Industry calendar, links, and listserv
Building Operating Management	http://www.facilitiesnet.com/fn	•	•	Active bulletin board; includes Maintenance

Publication/Medium	URL	Daily news	Archive news	Resources
				Solutions, Energy Decisions and Facilities Management and Technology magazines
Buildings	http://www.buildings.com/	•	•	News aggregated from various sources; directories, industry calendar
Business Facilities	http://www.facilitycity.com/		•	Location directory
Cleanfax	http://www.cleanfax.com/	•	•	Identical to www.facility-maintenance.com (Cleaning & Maintenance Management)
Commercial Investment Real Estate Journal	http://www.ccim.com/		•	Links, calendar of events
Commercial Property News	http://www.cpnrenet.com/	•	•	Calendar of events
Common Ground	http://www.caionline.org/		•	
Condo Management	http://condomgmt.com/		•	
Facility Management Journal	http://www.ifma.org/		•	Subscribers only
Florida Realtor	http://fl.realtorplace.com/	•	•	
FM Data Monthly	http://www.fmdata.com/			Subscribers only; forum, reports, conferences, tools
Habitat Magazine	http://www.habitatmag.com/		•	Recent building loans, management changes, and property improvements; chat room; profiles of attorneys and property managers
Institutional Real Estate Newsline	http://www.ire-net.com/		•	Industry calendar
Maintenance supplies	http://www.jansan.com/		•	Buyers guide, calendar, industry links
Midwest Real Estate News Magazine	http://www.mwrenonline.com/	•	•	Sourcebook, news channels
Multifamily Executive	http://www.multifamilyexecutive.com/		•	
National Real Estate Investor	http://industryclick.com		•	News divided by 18 channels; sourcebook, links, calendar
National Relocation & Real Estate Magazine	http://www.rismedia.com/news/top/	•		

Publication/Medium	URL	Daily news	Archive news	Resources
New England Real Estate Journal	http://www.rejournal.com/			Events, property listings, chat room, mortgage bureau, workshops, professional association listings
Office and Industrial Properties Magazine	http://www.multifamilyexecutive .com/		•	
Pest Control	http://www.pestcontrolmag.com/		•	Industry products, industry links
Pest Control Technology	http://www.pctonline.com/	•	•	Active bulletin board, product reviews, e-mail newsletter
Plants, Sites & Parks	http://www.bizsites.com/	•	•	Regional reviews
Real Estate Intelligence Report	http://www.reintel.com/		•	
Realtor magazine	http://www.realtor.com/	•	•	Part of massive Realtor portal, which provides real estate listings and homeowner help nationwide; special section devoted to realtors
Realty Times	http://realtytimes.com/	•	•	
Sanitary Maintenance	http://www.cleanlink.com/		•	
Shopping Center World	http://www.scwonline.com/	•	•	Sourcebook, news channels
Site Selection	http://www.sitenet.com/	•	•	Videos, GeoFacts library, industry calendar
The Crittenden Report	http://www.crittendennews.com/	•	•	Subscriber only
The Real Estate Forum of New York	http://www.servenet.com/ reforum/			Bulletin board and chat rooms
Today's Facility Manager	http://www.tfmgr.com/		•	Products and services directory

RECREATION, OUTDOOR

This category is poorly covered online. The numbers of print publications outweigh Web sites of merit. PR practitioners working in this segment are better off with a print strategy. On the other hand, there are a number of newsgroups that merit investigation, including rec.outdoor, rec.backcountry, and rec.climbing.

Publication/Medium	URL	Daily news	Archive news	Resources
All Outdoors	http://www.alloutdoors.com/		•	
American Snowmobiler	http://www.amsnow.com/ amdefault.asp	•	•	Much of the site is members only

Publication/Medium	URL	Daily news	Archive news	Resources
Backpacker	http://www.backpacker.com/		•	Forum, clubs, events calendar, photo gallery
Bodyboarding	http://www.bodyboardingweb.com/		•	
Bowhunter	htt://www.bowhunter.com/		•	
California Diving News	http://www.saintbrendan.com/		•	
Climbing	http://www.climbing.com/		•	Reviews, calendar of events
Diver (Canadian)	http://www.divermag.com/		•	
Explore (Canadian)	http://www.explore-mag.com/		•	Calendar of events, product reviews
Florida Sportsman	http://floridasportsman.com/		•	
Fly Fisherman	http://www.flyshop.com/		•	
Great Outdoor Recreation Page	http://www.gorp.com/		•	Links, discussion boards, experts, travel, gear
Great Outdoors	http://www.greatoutdoors.com/		•	Combines magazines from adventure travel, climbing, cycling, destinations, diving, fly fishing, hiking/camping, mountain biking, paddling, skiing, snow boarding, and water sports
Imoutdoor.com	http://www.imoutdoor.com/			Link site to outdoor sites
In-fisherman	http://in-fisherman.com/		•	TV, Radio
Krause Outdoor	http://www.krause.com/outdoors/		•	Includes Deer & Deer Hunting, Turkey & Turkey Hunting, The Trapper & Predator Caller, Wisconsin Outdoor Journal, and Whitetail Business
Midwest Outdoors	http://www.midwestoutdoors.com/home.asp		•	Message board, links
Outdoor Retailer	http://www.outdoorbiz.com/	•	•	
Outdoor Times	http://www.outdoortimes.com/		•	
Outfitter	http://www.outfittermag.com/		•	
Outside	http://www.outsidemag.com/	•	•	
Raghorn News (Indiana outdoors)	http://www.raghorn.com/		•	
Recreation Resources	http://www.rec-net.com/	•	•	Links
Ski Canada	http://www.skicanadamag.com/		•	
Snowest	http://www.snowest.com/		•	
Snowmobile News	http://snowmobilenews.rivals.com/	•	•	Message board, chat, videos

Publication/Medium	URL	Daily news	Archive news	Resources
Splash	http://www.splashweb.com/index2.html		•	
Sport Diver	http://www.sportdiver.com/newFrontdoor/		•	
Surfer	http://www.surfermag.com/	•	•	Web features, videos
Trailblazer	http://www.trailblazermagazine.net/		•	Selected editorial
Waterski	http://www.waterskimag.com/		•	
Wind Surfing	http://www.windsurfingmag.com/		•	

RESTAURANT AND CLUB TRADE

PR Practitioners will find that this is a poorly covered segment and that using print media is the better way to go. Many of the industry publications have no Web sites. In addition, finding anything in the industry is complicated by consumer sites, such as restaurant links and newsgroups run for and by dining enthusiasts. Resources are relatively abundant, but it takes a fair amount of searching to find them.

Publication/Medium	URL	Daily news	Archive news	Resources
Chain Leader	http://www.chainleader.com/		•	Event calendar, industry links
Chef Magazine	http://www.chefmagazine.com/index.htm		•	Selected snippets of editorial
Club Management	http://www.club-mgmt.com/		•	Bulletin board
Empire State Foodservice News	http://www.theheadtable.com/		•	
FEDA News & Views	http://www.feda.com/		•	
Food & Beverage News	http://www.fbnews.com/		•	
Food Service Equipment and Supplies	http://www.fesmag.com/	•	•	News aggregated from various sources; product directory; events and links
Food Service Equipment Reports	http://www.fermag.com/		•	Buyer's guide, company directory, service suppliers guide, calendar, association listings
Food Service News (part of restaurant-ville.com—Texas Restaurant Assocation)	http://www.restaurantville.com/FSN/	•	•	Aggregated news from various sources
Foodservice.com	http://www.foodservice.com/	•		Aggregated news from various sources, active

Publication/Medium	URL	Daily news	Archive news	Resources
				forums, product finder, market reports, trade show listings
Fresh Cup	http://www.freshcup.com/		•	Selected editorial, calendar
Nation's Restaurant News	http://www.nrn.com/	•	•	Links, industry reports, product directory, dining guide
Nightclub & Bar Magazine	http://www.nightclub.com/		•	
Restaurant Business (includes Food Service Director and ID Online)	http://www.restaurantbiz.com/	•	•	Daily e-mail newsletter, industry links, conferences
Restaurant News	http://restaurantnews.com/	•		
Restaurant Report	http://www.restaurantreport.com/		•	Buyer's guide
Restaurants and Institutions	http://www.rimag.com/	•	•	
Southeast Food Service News and Southwest Food Service News	http://www.sfsn.com/		•	

ROCK AND CEMENT/MASONRY TRADE TOPICS

There is little for the PR practitioner in this segment. Even resources are scant. It is better to remain with print media.

Publication/Medium	URL	Daily news	Archive news	Resources
Concrete Construction (includes Masonry Construction and Concrete Producer)	http://www.worldofconcrete.com/HomePage/		•	Buyer's guide
Aggregates Manager	http://www.aggman.com/	•	•	Links
Concrete Products	http://industryclick.com		•	
Pit & Quarry	http://www.pitandquarry.com/		•	Weekly e-mail newsletter
Rock Products	http://industryclick.com/		•	Buyer's guide
Stone World	http://www.stoneworld.com/		•	Active bulletin board

SCHOOLS AND EDUCATION

The Internet started in universities, and higher education institutions have been linked for decades. Universities and colleges also led in the early development of the Web. On the other hand, secondary and grade schools were relatively late entrants. PR practitioners will find enormous resources related to schools and education. News outlets, however, are another matter. There are few daily news sources of use. In addition to the Web sites listed here, there are many city, state, and regional educational Web sites of varying worth, which practitioners should investigate as appropriate. Link sites are too numerous to cover and many are useful. There are at least two newsgroups—misc.education and k12.chat.teacher. At the postsecondary level, there are many more by speciality. PR practitioners should have an online strategy for the education segment.

Publication/Medium	URL	Daily news	Archive news	Resources
Academe	http://www.aaup.org/acahome.htm		•	
American Federation of Teachers	http://www.aft.org/			Links list to K–12 education resources
American Journal of Physics	http://www.aapt.org/		•	
American School & University	http://industryclick.com/		•	Buyers guide, industry news, calendar
American School Board Journal	http://www.asbj.com/		•	
American School Directory	http://www.asd.com/			Directory to 108,000 U.S. K–12 schools
American Teacher	http://www.aft.org/		•	
Black Issues in Higher Education	http://www.blackissues.com/	•	•	News briefs and selected editorial
Cause/Effect	http://www.educause.edu/		•	
Chronicle of Higher Education	http://www.chronicle.com/	•	•	News divided into 14 sections
College Composition and Communication	http://www.ncte.org/ccc/		•	
College Planning & Management	http://www.cpmmag.com/		•	
Community College Week	http://www.ccweek.com/		•	
Creative Classroom	http://www.creativeclassroom.org/		•	
Curriculum Administrator	http://educatorsportal.com/		•	
Distance Education Clearinghouse	http://www.uwex.edu/disted/denews.htm	•	•	Aggregates news from various sources
Early Childhood News	http://www.earlychildhood.com/		•	Bulletin board
Ednow	http://ednow.com/	•	•	Bulletin board, suppliers, listservs directory for educators, links lists, search engines
Education Daily	http://www.educationdaily.com/	•	•	Subscriber only; e-mail version
Education Leadership	http://www.ascd.org/		•	Selected editorial

Publication/Medium	URL	Daily news	Archive news	Resources
Education Week	http://www.edweek.org/	•	•	Aggregates daily news from various sources, e-mail newsletter
Education World	http://www.education-world.com/education_news/	•	•	Aggregates daily news; news channels, databases, message board, calendar, world school directory
Educational Researcher	http://www.aera.net/		•	Calendar of events
English Journal	http://www.cc.ysu.edu/tej/		•	
International Reading Association	http://www.reading.org/			Links list to literacy sites
ISTE Update	http://www.iste.org/			Subscriber only
Iteachnet	http://members.iteachnet.org/webzine/	•	•	e-zine
Lingua Franca	http://www.linguafranca.com/		•	
Media & Methods	http://www.media-methods.com/		•	Selected editorial; Buyers guide
NEA Today	http://www.nea.org/		•	Events, meetings calendar
NSTA Reports	http://www.nsta.org/reports/		•	
On Campus	http://www.aft.org/		•	
Scholastic Teacher	http://teacher.scholastic.com/index.htm	•	•	Lesson plans, professional resources, authors & books, online curriculum projects, research tools, software and book clubs, reading programs
School Administator	http://www.aasa.org/		•	
School Planning & Management	http://www.spmmag.com/		•	
Schoolarts	http://www.davis-art.com/schoolarts/			
Schoolnet (Canadian)	http://www.schoolnet.ca/home/e/			Abundant links resources
Science Netlinks	http://www.sciencenetlinks.com/index.html			Comprehensive link resource for science teachers
Special Education News	http://www.specialednews.com/		•	Resource library
Syllabus	http://www.syllabus.com/		•	Selected editorial
T.H.E. Journal	http://www.thejournal.com/		•	Presentation products, infrastrucuture, road map to the Web, EdTech conference listings

Publication/Medium	URL	Daily news	Archive news	Resources
Teacher Magazine	http://www.teachermagazine.org/tm/tm.cfm	•	•	News aggregated from various sources; calendar, products and services
Teaching Tolerance	http://www.splcenter.org/teachingtolerance/tt-index.html		•	
Tech Directions	http://www.techdirections.com/		•	
The Academy	http://www.sport.ussa.edu/pubsplit.htm		•	
The American Mathematical Monthly	http://www.maa.org/		•	Abstracts
Today's Catholic Teacher	http://www.catholicteacher.com/		•	
University Business	http://www.universitybusiness.com/	•	•	Consultants directory, products/services directory
Weekly Reader	http://www.weeklyreader.com/	•	•	Links; sections for parents, teachers, and children

SCIENCE

The science sector is difficult for PR practitioners. There are dozens, if not hundreds, of small-circulation journals by specialty. Many of these are abstracted online or reprinted in full, often in pdf image formats. As a result, we have covered just large-circulation Web sites here. There are more than 300 newsgroups on specific science topics, and science link sites are too numerous to cover. Many of them are useful. Daily news sites are plentiful too, which means that practitioners should have an online strategy for the science sector.

Publication/Medium	URL	Daily news	Archive news	Resources
American Chemical Society	http://www.pubs.acs.org/		•	Editorial from 35 journals
American Scientist	http://www.amsci.org/amsci/		•	
American Society for Microbiology	http://www.journals.asm.org/		•	Selected editorial from 10 journals
Archaeology	http://www.archaeology.org/		•	Interactive digs
Artigen Science news	http://www.artigen.com/newswire/scitech.html	•		Aggregated from various sources
Astronomy	http://www.astronomy.com/astro/		•	Weekly news; sky calendar, Deep Sky e-zine, product catalog
Bulletin of the Atomic Scientists	http://www.bullatomsci.org/		•	
Cell	http://www.cell.com/		•	
Discover	http://www.discover.com/	•	•	

Publication/Medium	URL	Daily news	Archive news	Resources
Fate	http://www.fatemag.com/		•	
Geological Society of America	http://www.geosociety.org/ pubs/journals.htm		•	Three publications—Geology, Bulletin, and GSA Today
Geotimes	http://www.geotimes.org/ current/		•	
InScight	http://www.apnet.com/inscight/	•		
ISC Pubs	http://www.iscpubs.com/		•	Selected editorial from 13 laboratory journals; buyer's guide; calendar
Issues in Science and Technology	http://www.nap.edu/issues/		•	
Laboratory Equipment	http://www.labequipmag.com/		•	Supplier directory, product directory
MIT's Technology Review	http://www.techreview.com/		•	
NASA Space Science News	http://www.science-news.com/	•	•	
Nature Biotechnology	http://www.nature.com/nbt/		•	
New Scientist	http://www.newscientist.com/		•	
Physics Today	http://www.aip.org/pt/		•	Buyer's guide, calendar
Popular Science	http://www.popsci.com/	•	•	Forums, Q&A
ScienceaGoGo	http://www.scienceagogo.com/	•		
Science Daily	http://www.sciencedaily.com/ index.htm	•		
Science Magazine	http://www.sciencemag.org/	•	•	Forum
Science Matters	http://www.sciencematters.com/		•	
Science News	http://www.sciencenews.org/		•	
Science Spectra	http://www.gbhap.com/ scispectra/		•	Selected editorial
Scientific American	http://www.sciam.com/		•	Ask the experts
Sky & Telescope	http://www.skypub.com/	•		Links, club directory, calendar of events
Spectroscopy	http://www.spectroscopymag .com/		•	Buyer's guide, products directory, expert advice
The Scientist	http://www.the-scientist.com/		•	
Unisci	http://unisci.com/	•	•	
Whyfiles	http://www.whyfiles.news.wisc.ed u/	•	•	Science behind news stories

SECURITY TRADES (NOT COMPUTER-RELATED)

The security trades are limited online and mostly reprinted content. PR practitioners do not need an online publicity strategy for the segment, although they should be aware of the news outlets. There are hundreds of link sites, but most are not useful for practitioners.

Publication/Medium	URL	Daily news	Archive news	Resources
Access Control and Security Systems Integration	http://industryclick.com/		•	
The Security Information Management Online Network	http://www.simon-net.com/	•		Extensive resources
Security Magazine and Security Distributing and Marketing (Cahners)	http://www.securitymagazine .com/	•		News is aggregated from various sources; extensive resources
Security Sales	http://www.securitysales.com/ main.cfm	•		
The Securities Industry Association	http://www.siaonline.org/	•		Links site to other security associations

SPORTS AND SPORTING GOODS

This is a huge category, and PR practitioners should have an online strategy for sports news in general and specific sports as well. There are hundreds of sports news sites and thousands of forum and links sites. What is presented here is a fraction of what is available. Some sports are not well-covered and require a print stategy. In addition, there are at least 33 newsgroups under rec.sport.

Publication/Medium	URL	Daily news	Archive news	Resources
American Football Monthly	http://www.www .americanfootballmonthly.com/		•	Subscribers only
AOL (America Online)				Active sports news and scores site, forums
Aqua (for spa and pool professionals)	http://www.aquamagazine.com/		•	
Aquatics International	http://www.aquaticsintl.com/		•	Industry calendar, links
Athletic Business	http://www.athleticbusiness.com/			Buyer's guide, links
ATV News	http://atvnews.rivals.com/	•	•	Message board, chat, videos
Baseball Weekly	http://www.usatoday.com/ bbwfront.htm		•	
Bicycling	http://www.bicyclingmagazine .com/	•	•	Forum, contest
Bowhunter	http://www.bowhunter.com/		•	
Bowlers Journal International	http://www.bowlersjournal.com/	•	•	Tutorials, links

Publication/Medium	URL	Daily news	Archive news	Resources
Buckmasters	http://www.buckmasters.com/		•	Chat room, message board, video
CBS Sportsline	http://www.sportsline.com/	•	•	Audio, video, e-mail newsletters
City Sports Magazine (Includes Competitor Magazine)	http://www.citysportsmag.com/ and http://www.competitor.com/	Cal endar		
Colorado Golf	http://www.coloradogolf.com/		•	
CompuServe				Active sports news and scores site, forums
Crittenden Golf Inc.	http://www.crittendengolfinc.com/	•	•	Subscribers only
Daily Racing Form	http://www.drf2000.com/	•	•	
Dirt Rag (for mountain bikers)	http://www.dirtragmag.com/		•	Product reviews
ESPN	http://espn.go.com/	•	•	Everything about sports; forums, chats, fantasy games, contests, careers, webcasting
Field & Stream (includes Outdoor Life)	http://www.fieldandstream.com/		•	Forums, chat
Fish Sniffer (West Coast fishing)	http://fishsniffer.rivals.com/		•	Message boards, chats, videos
Fitness World	http://www.fitnessworld.com/index_main.html		•	
Florida Sports	http://www.floridasports.com/		•	
Florida Sportsman	http://www.flsportsman.com/		•	
Fly Fisherman	http://www.flyshop.com/		•	Bulletin board, chat room
Fly Rod & Reel	http://www.fttn.com/		•	Bulletin board
Golf Course News	http://www.golfcoursenews.com/		•	Buyer's guide, resources
Golf.com (includes Golf Digest)	http://www.golf.com/	•	•	Readers forum, audio
Golfer's Guide	http://www.golfersguide.com/		•	Contests, tutorial
Golf Illustrated	http://www.golfillustrated.com/index.asp	•	•	
Golf Magazine (includes Golfweek)	http://www.golfonline.com/	•	•	Chat
Golfweb	http://www.golfweb.com/	•	•	Audio, tutorials
Gulf Coast Fisherman	http://www.gulffishing.com/		•	
Gungames	http://www.gungames.com/	•	•	Calendar of events, product review
Hawaii Fishing News	http://www.hawaiifishingnews.com/		•	
Indians Ink (Cleveland Indians)	http://indians.rivals.com/	•	•	Message board, chats, video
Inside Triathlon	http://www.greatoutdoors.com/auto_docs/insidetri/		•	

Publication/Medium	URL	Daily news	Archive news	Resources
International Figure Skating	http://www.ifsmagazine.com/		•	Chat
International Gymnast	http://www.intlgymnast.com/	•	•	Event calendar, tutorials
Metrosports Boston	http://www.metrosportsboston.com/		•	
Metrosports DC	http://www.metrosportsdc.com/		•	
Metrosports New York	http://www.metrosportsny.com/		•	
Motorcycle Report	http://motorcyclereport.rivals.com/	•	•	Message board, chat, videos
Mountain Bike	http://www.mountainbike.com/		•	Product reviews
Musky Hunter	http://www.muskyhunter.com/		•	
New Jersey Angler	http://newjerseyangler.rivals.com/		•	Message board, chat, video
Paddler	http://www.acanet.org/acanet.htm	•	•	Bulletin board, buyer's guide
Pro Football Weekly	http://www.profootballweekly.com/		•	
Running Network	http://www.runningnetwork.com/			Calendar of events, links
Runner's World	http://www.runnersworld.com/	•	•	
Salt Water Sportsman	http://www.saltwatersportsman.com/		•	Forums
Ski Net	http://www.skinet.com/		•	Forums, snow reports
Ski Racing International	http://www.skiracing.com/		•	
Snowboarding-online.com	http://www.twsnow.com/	•	•	Forum, chat; combines Snowboarding, Snowboarding Life, and Snowboarding Business
Snowboarder	http://www.snowboardermag.com/		•	
Soccer America	http://www.socceramerica.com/		•	Chat
Sport Fishing	http://www.sportfishingmag.com/		•	
Sporting Clays	http://sportingclays.rivals.com/		•	Message board, chat, videos
Sporting Goods Business	http://www.sgblink.com/	•	•	Message boards, product reviews
Sporting Goods Dealer	http://www.sgdealer.com/	•	•	Trade show calendar, new products
Sporting News	http://www.sportingnews.com/	•	•	Chat rooms, message boards, fanatasy games, contests
Sports Afield	http://www.sportsafield.com/		•	
Sports Arizona	http://www.sportsaz.com/	•		Message board, calendar
Sports Business Journal	http://www.www.sportsbusinessjournal.com/		•	

Publication/Medium	URL	Daily news	Archive news	Resources
Sports Etc.	http://www.sportsetc.com/		•	
Sports IIIlustrated for Kids	http://www.sikids.com/	•	•	Video, fanatasy sports
Sports Illustrated (in cooperation with CNN)	http://sportsillustrated.cnn.com/	•	•	Message boards, fanatasy games
Sports Trend	http://www.sportstrend.com/	•	•	Trade show calendar, new products
Student Sports	http://studentsports.rivals.com/	•	•	
Swim (includes Swimming Technique and Swimming World & Junior Swimmer)	http://www.swiminfo.com/	•	•	Tutorials
Team Licensing Business	http://www.tlbmag.com/		•	Buyer's guide
Tennis	http://www.tennis.com/	•	•	Bulletin board
Tennis Directory	http://www.tennisindustry.com/		•	Events calendar, directory
The Hockey News	http://www.thn.com/servlet/thn	•	•	Forum
The Olympian	http://www.olympic-usa.org/	•		Calendar of events
The Sports Network	http://www.sportsnetwork.com/home.asp	•	•	
Transworld Skateboarding	http://www.twskate.com/		•	
Triathlete	http://www.triathletemag.com/		•	Message board, e-mail newsletter
Velo News	http://www.greatoutdoors.com/auto_docs/velonews/index.html		•	
Volleyball	http://www.volleyballmag.com/		•	
World Boxing	http://www.world-boxing.com/shtml/index. shtml		•	Audio, video

STUDENT AND CAREER

There are hundreds of campus newspapers online, far more than could be covered here, and hundreds of college and university student forums and newsgroups. These do not include the dozens of career sites that also carry archival editorial, such as Monster.com. The PR practitioner's best bet is to use link sites to find particular newspapers and forums. Practitioners working in student and career topics need an online strategy.

Publication/Medium	URL	Daily news	Archive news	Resources
American Cheerleader	http://www.americancheerleader.com/		•	Chat, message board

Publication/Medium	URL	Daily news	Archive news	Resources
Black College	http://www.black-collegian.com/		•	Careers, scholarships, calendar, music reviews, job bank
Campus Life	http://www.christianityonline .com/campuslife/current/		•	AOL chat boards
Careers & Colleges	http://www.careersandcolleges .com/		•	
Career Journal	http://www.careerjournal.com/		•	The Wall Street Journal's career site with editorial
College Bound	http://www.collegebound.net/		•	
College News	http://www.collegenews.com/ index.htm		•	Links to college newspapers
Florida Leader (for college students in Florida)	http://www.floridaleader.com/		•	
Link	http://www.linkmag.com/		•	Movie, music reviews
Monster.com	http://www.monster.com/		•	Career, job site with archival editorial
Saludos Hispanos	http://www.saludos.com/ saludosmagazine.html		•	Careers, jobs
Student Leader	http://www.studentleader.com/		•	
Study Breaks	http://www.studybreaks.com/		•	
The Next Step	http://www.nextstepmagazine .com/		•	
U Magazine	http://www.colleges.com/		•	

TELECOMMUNICATIONS AND NETWORKING

Telecommunications and networking are covered in depth online with plenty of daily news sites and other resources. PR practitioners should have an online strategy for this segment. Newsgroups are more difficult to isolate. Telecommunications and networking issues are covered under a variety of newsgroups including comp.dcom.telecom. CompuServe has several forums as well dedicated to telecommunications topics. Practitioners may need to build their own lists for specific topic areas. There are plenty of link sites, but most are not useful to PR practitioners.

Publication/Medium	URL	Daily news	Archive news	Resources
America's Network	http://www.americasnetwork .com/		•	E-mail newsletter, Web features, supplier directory, calendar of events, organization directory

Publication/Medium	URL	Daily news	Archive news	Resources
Broadband Bob Report	http://www.catv.org/frame/bbb.html		•	
Business Communications Review	http://www.bcr.com/		•	
Cabling Installation and Maintenance	http://im.pennnet.com/home/home.cfm	•	•	Product guide, calendar of events
Call Center Magazine (part of CommWeb)	http://www.callcentermagazine.com/	•	•	Daily news aggregated from Information Week; product info, association directory
China Telecommunications News	http://www.chinatelecomnews.com/		•	
Cisco world	http://www.ciscoworldmagazine.com/index.htm		•	E-mail newsletter, trade show calendar, web papers, vendor directory
Communications & Networking (Canadian)	http://www.plesman.com/cn/		•	
Communications News	http://www.comnews.com/		•	Buyer's guide, events calendar, e-mail newsletter
Communications Systems Design	http://www.csdmag.com/		•	Buyer's guide, glossary
Computer Telephony (part of CommWeb)	http://www.computertelephony.com/	•	•	Daily news aggregated from Information Week; product info, association directory
Global Wireless	http://www.rcrnews.com/	•	•	
Intele-card News	http://www.intelecard.com/home.htm		•	
Network Computing	http://www.networkcomputing.com/		•	Technology guides, events calendar
Network Magazine	http://www.networkmagazine.com/	•	•	Tech center, chats, tutorials, guides
Network World	http://www.nwfusion.com/	•	•	Buyer's guide, reviews, technology primer, vendor profiles, forums, white papers, e-mail newsletters
Networking News	http://networkingnews.org/		•	Message board
Outside Plant	http://www.ospmag.com/	•	•	E-mail newsletter
Phone+	http://www.phoneplusmag.com/	•	•	Events calendar, directory
Portable Design	http://pd.pennnet.com/home/home.cfm	•	•	Product guide, consultant directory
RCR News	http://www.rcrnews.com/	•	•	
Security Advisor	http://www.advisor.com/		•	Incorporates 13 magazines on

Publication/Medium	URL	Daily news	Archive news	Resources
				various technical subjects, several of them not network related
Sounding Board	http://www.soundingboardmag.com/		•	Buyer's guide
Tele.com (part of CMPnet)	http://www.teledotcom.com/	•	•	Calendar of events, company profiles, encyclopedia
Telecom Daily	http://www.faulkner.com/telecom/default.htm	•		
Telecom Reseller	http://www.telecomreseller.com/		•	
Telecom Update (Canada)	http://www.angustel.ca/update/up.html		•	
Telecom Web	http://www.telecomweb.com/		•	E-mail newsletter
Telecommunications	http://www.telecoms-mag.com/		•	
Telecommunications links worldwide	http://www.questus.co.uk/links.htm			Links
Telecommunications Reports (includes 15 separate newsletters)	http://www.tr.com/	•	•	Subscriber only sections
Teleconnect (part of CommWeb)	http://www.teleconnect.com/	•	•	Daily news aggregated from Information Week; product info, association directory
Telephony	http://telecomclick.com/	•	•	Supplier directory, newsletters
TMCnet	http://www.tmcnet.com/	•	•	Includes Communications Solutions, Internet Telephony, and C@ll Center CRM Solutions; events calendar; link library
Wireless Click	http://wirelessclick.com/	•	•	Buyer's guide, dictionary
Wireless Design & Development	http://www.wirelessdesignmag.com/		•	New products, buyer's guide, events
Wireless Systems Design	http://www.wsdmag.com/		•	Links
WirelessWeek	http://www.wirelessweek.com/	•		Buyer's guide, industry directory
X-Change	http://www.x-changemag.com/	•	•	Reprints press releases; trade show calendar; links

TEXTILE TRADE

This is a poorly covered category on the Web in terms of news and even link sites are sparse. It is noteworthy that two of the sites that carry news are located outside of the U.S. PR practitioners working in this segment should stay with a print strategy.

Publication/Medium	URL	Daily news	Archive news	Resources
ATI America's Textiles International	http://www.atimag.com/		•	
Home Textiles Today	http://www.hometextilestoday.com/		•	
International Fiber Journal	http://www.ifj.com/		•	Selected editorial
Nonwovens Market	http://www.nonwovens.com/		•	
Southern Textile News	http://www.textilenews.com/		•	
Textile News (Spanish)	http://www.bemarnet.es/textilenews/	•	•	
Textile World	http://industryclick.com/		•	Buyer's guide; Industry calendar

TOBACCO TOPICS

There are three publications with an online presence in this category. There are hundreds of links, but most are not useful for PR practitioners. Newsgroups include alt.smokers, under which there are separate sections for cigars and pipes.

Publication/Medium	URL	Daily news	Archive news	Resources
Cigar Aficionado	http://www.cigaraficionado.com/		•	
Cigar News	http://www.cigarnews.com/		•	
Smoke	http://www.smokemag.com/		•	Contests, reviews

TOYS, CRAFTS, ARTS, AND HOBBIES

This is a difficult category for PR practitioners. There are hundreds of toys, crafts, arts, and hobbies in known and obscure areas. Many are not well represented online, or they are covered in small Web sites that are not easy to find. There is little news as well. Most magazines offer reprinted features or tutorials and how-to's. Many major crafts, games, and hobbies publishers do not have an online presence beyond a listing of their magazines. Newsgroups are abundant and are generally located under the rec forum area. CompuServe has a large forum for model railroaders, and America Online (AOL) has more than 30 forums on various hobbies. Still, PR practitioners working in this area are better off remaining with print publications.

Publication/Medium	URL	Daily news	Archive news	Resources
Action Figure Times	http://www.aftimes.com/	•	•	

Publication/Medium	URL	Daily news	Archive news	Resources
Art Papers	http://www.artpapers.org/		•	Selected editorial
Bead and Button	http://www.beadandbutton.com/		•	
Butterick	http://www.butterick.com/index2 .html		•	
Classic Toy Trains	http://www.classtrain.com/			Product reviews
Country Quilts	http://www.quiltmag.com/		•	Selected editorial
Craft ideas	http://www.craftideas.com/		•	Newsletters, messageboards, chat
Craftrends	http://www.craftrends.com/		•	
Finescale Modeler	http://www.finescale.com/			Product reviews
Linn's Stamp News	http://www.linns.com/		•	
Lost Treasure	http://www.losttreasure.com/		•	Clubs directory, events calendar
Model Railroader Magazine	http://www.modelrailroader.com/		•	Events and clubs directory, forum
Quilters Village	http://www.mccallsquilting.com/		•	Message boards
RTM	http://www.toymania.com/news/	•	•	
S&E Modeler	http://www.sailplanemodeler .com/contents.html		•	
Sew News	http://www.sewnews.com/		•	
The Crafts Report	http://www.craftsreport.com/		•	Artist listings, forum, directories to organizations
Toysource.com	http://www.toysource.com/menu .htm			Worldwide toy product, manufacturer directory

TRAFFIC, TRANSPORTATION, AND SHIPPING TOPICS

Traffic, transportation, and shipping topics are poorly covered online in terms of news. There are hundreds of links but most belong to individual shippers and are not of much use to PR practitioners. This category should be searched under "logistics" as well when assembling resources. There is at least one newsgroup under misc.transport. Overall, PR practitioners are better off using a print strategy in this segment.

Publication/Medium	URL	Daily news	Archive news	Resources
Air Cargo News	http://www.air-cargo-news.com/		•	
American Journal of Transportation	http://www.ajot.com/	•	•	
Subscriber only				
Cargoweb (Dutch)	http://www.cargoweb.nl/asp/ default.asp		•	

Publication/Medium	URL	Daily news	Archive news	Resources
Distribution Channels	http://www.distributionchannels.org/	•	•	Daily news aggregated from various sources; bulletin board
Food Logistics	http://foodlogistics.com/		•	Industry calendar, trade association listing
GSE Today	http://www.gsetoday.com/		•	
Inbound Logistics	http://www.inboundlogistics.com/			Links
Inside Self-Storage	http://www.insideselfstorage.com/		•	
Journal of Commerce	http://www.joc.com/	•	•	
Logistics Management & Distribution Report	http://www.manufacturing.net/magazine/logistic/	•	•	Buyer's guide
Logistics World	http://www.logisticsworld.com/			Links
Loglink	http://www.loglink.net/			Links for logistics
Mailing Systems Technology	http://www.mailingsystemsmag.com/	•		Parts are subscriber only
Marine Publishing	http://www.marinelink.com/	•	•	Includes Maritime Reporter, Maritime Week, and Maritime News; parts are subscriber only; e-mail newsletter
Parcel Shipping & Distribution	http://www.psdmag.com/	•		Parts are subscriber only
SchedNet	http://www.schednet.com/schedule/			Online shipping schedules, links
Traffic World	http://www.trafficworld.com/		•	Calendar of events and conferences
Transport News	http://www.transportnews.com/		•	Aggregates news from various sources
Transportation & Distribution	http://www.tdmagazine.com/		•	Trade Assocations listing
Warehouse Management	http://www.warehousemag.com/		•	Buyer's guide, industry links

TRAVEL AND TOURISM

Travel and tourism are difficult topics because there are so many Web sites. PR practitioners working in this segment need to develop their own lists by specialty. Hundreds of sites are tied to locations and hundreds more to specific vendors in these locations. News outlets are another matter. This area has many print publications that do not necessarily have an equivalent on the Web—for example, the American Automobile Association (AAA) magazines. Further, almost all news is republished from print publications. PR practitioners can safely stay with a print strategy in this field. The listing given here is a fraction of what is available, and it does not include travel columns in newspapers and other general circulation media.

Publication/Medium	URL	Daily news	Archive news	Resources
American Way	http://www.americanair.com/away/		•	Selected editorial
Arthur Frommer's Budget Travel	http://www.frommers.com/		•	
Best Fares	http://www.bestfares.com/	•	•	
Business Travel News	http://www.btonline.com/		•	
Caribbean Travel and Life	http://www.caribbeantravelmag.com/		•	
Conde Nast Traveler	http://www.cntraveler.com/		•	Forums
Cruise Industry News	http://www.cruiseindustrynews.com/articles.html		•	
Diversion	http://www.diversionmag.com/		•	
eTravel.org	http://www.etravel.org/	•	•	Daily news aggregated from variouse sources
Group Travel Leader	http://www.grouptravelleader.com/		•	
Historic Traveler	http://www.thehistorynet.com/		•	
International Travel News	http://www.intltravelnews.com/		•	Forum
Islands	http://www.islandsmag.com/		•	Selected editorial
Jax Fax Travel Marketing Magazine	http://www.jaxfax.com/		•	
Leisure Travel News	http://www.ttgweb.com/		•	Trade show listings, forum
Marco Polo	http://www.travelroads.com/		•	
Meeting News	http://www.meetingnews.com/		•	Listserv, trade show list
National Geographic Traveler	http://www.nationalgeographic.com/traveler/index.html		•	E-mail newsletter
Online City Guide	http://www.olcg.com/			Links
Open World	http://www.openworld.co.uk/			Links to worldwide hotel sites
Outpost	http://www.outpostmagazine.com/		•	
Pathfinders Travel	http://www.pathfinderstravel.com/		•	Selected editorial
RCM Travelsite	http://rcmtravelsite.com/	•	•	Forums
Travel and Leisure	http://www.pathfinder.com/travel/TL/		•	Bulletin boards, chat
Travel and Leisure Golf	http://www.tlgolf.com/		•	
Travel Asia	http://www.travel-asia.com/	•	•	
Travel Base	http://www.travelbase.com/		•	
Travel Facts	http://www.travelfacts.com/		•	Includes magazines for Charlotte, Kansas City, and Orlando;

Publication/Medium	URL	Daily news	Archive news	Resources
				has archival news for all Caribbean destinations, Colorado-Utah and Florida
Travel Holiday	http://www.travelholiday.com/		•	Forum, e-mail newsletter
Travel News	http://www.travelagents.com/	•	•	Daily news aggregated from various sources
Travel Search	http://travelsearch.com/	•		Daily news aggregated from various sources; links, forum, chats
Travel Weekly	http://www.twcrossroads.com/findme.asp		•	Forums
Travelmag (United Kingdom)	http://www.travelmag.co.uk/		•	
Travel.org	http://www.travel.org/index2.html			Links
Travel Trade	http://www.traveltrade.com/		•	E-mail newsletter
Trips	http://www.tripsmag.com/		•	
Underground Travel	http://www.undergroundtravel.com/		•	Links
Where Magazines	http://www.wheremagazine.com/		•	Local magazines for 45 cities and destinations; some destinations have separate "Where" Web sites, and some do not
World Travel Directory	http://www.tuttinsieme.it/			Links
World Travel Guide	http://www.wtgonline.com/navigate/world.asp			Links

TV LISTING GUIDES

PR practitioners should have little difficulty identifying times when programs run on network, cable, satellite, and digital satellite television anywhere in the United States, Canada, and much of the world. Nearly every local TV station maintains a Web site with locally produced news and editorial and listings. All broadcasters maintain listings, both domestically and internally. In addition, listing services are abundant. Editorial, however, is sparse.

Publication/Medium	URL	Daily news	Archive news	Resources
AOL (America Online)				Comprehensive listings, ratings

Publication/Medium	URL	Daily news	Archive news	Resources
				from Entertainment Weekly
Broadcasters on the Web	http://archive.comlab.ox.ac.uk/publishers/broadcast.html			Listing of broadcaster Web sites worldwide
Cableview	http://www.cableview-online.com/			Cable listings
ClickTV	http://www.clicktv.com/	•	•	
Compuserve		•	•	Comprehensive listings for TV and radio; news aggregated from variety of sources
Directv	http://www.directv.com/		•	Listings for Directv digital TV service
Gist TV	http://www.gist.com/tv/	•	•	
Satellite Direct	http://directmagazine.com/		•	For digital satellite systems
Satellite Orbit	http://www.orbitmagazine.com/	•	•	For users of C-band and KU-band satellite dish owners
TV Grid	http://www.tvgrid.com/			Listings
TV Guide	http://www.tvguide.com/	•	•	
TV Show	http://www.tvshow.com/			TV station and program listings worldwide
TV Times Online	http://www.tvtimesonline.com/		•	Canadian TV listings
Yahoo! Broadcast	http://www.broadcast.com/			Listings
Zap2It	http://tvlistings.zap2it.com/register.asp			Listings

WASTE MANAGEMENT AND POLLUTION CONTROL

Waste managemement and pollution control are not well covered online. Most news is republished from print media. Resources, on the other hand, are good with major link sites. There is at least one newsgroup under sci.environment. PR practitioners can safely stay with a print stategy.

Publication/Medium	URL	Daily news	Archive news	Resources
EeLink (Environmental Education)	http://eelink.net/			Links
Environews	http://www.environews.com/		•	
Environmental Industry	http://www.environmentalindustry.com/			Links
Environmental Protection	http://www.eponline.com/		•	Events calendar

Publication/Medium	URL	Daily news	Archive news	Resources
Erosion Control	http://www.forester.net/ec.html		•	
Governing.com	http://www.governing.com/env.htm			Links
Hazardous Materials Magazine	http://www.hazmatmag.com/		•	
Industrial Hygiene	http://www.rimbach.com/home/ihnpage/news/news1.htm		•	
MSW Management	http://www.forester.net/msw_current_toc.html			
Pollution	http://www.pollution.com/	•	•	Links
Pollution Engineering	http://www.pollutionengineering.com/main.html	•	•	Web links, calendar of events
Pollution Equipment News	http://www.rimbach.com/home/penpage/pen.htm		•	Trade shows, suppliers directory
Recycling Today	http://www.recyclingtoday.com/		•	Online features, bulletin boards
Small Flows	http://www.estd.wvu.edu/nsfc/SFQ/SFQhome.html		•	
Soil & Groundwater Cleanup	http://www.sgcleanup.com/		•	
Solid Waste & Recycling (Canada)	http://www.solidwastemag.com/		•	Selected editorial
U.S. Water News	http://www.uswaternews.com/homepage.html		•	
Ultrapure Water	http://www.talloaks.com/		•	
Waste Age	http://industryclick.com/	•		Combines World Wastes
Waste News	http://www.wastenews.com/	•	•	Events calendar
Waste Water Info Center	http://www.waterinfocenter.com/w/	•	•	Combines Water Engineering and Management, Water & Wastes Digest, and Water Quality Products; products and suppliers directories
Water Conditioning and Purification	http://www.wcp.net/home.htm		•	Product reviews, buyer's guide
Water World	http://www.ww.pennnet.com/home/home.cfm	•	•	Product guide, calendar of events
Water links	http://www.awwa.org/asp/links.asp			Links
Water Links	http://www.worldwater.org/links.htm			Links

WEARING APPAREL INDUSTRY

The wearing apparel trade industry is not well covered online. Resources are moderately available, but there is the one news bible of the industry, Women's Wear Daily. There is at least one newsgroup that touches on fashion topics—Alt.fashion. Overall, PR practitioners can remain with a print-based strategy.

Publication/Medium	URL	Daily news	Archive news	Resources
Bobbin	http://www.bobbin.com/BOBBINGROUP/BOBBINMAG/index.html		•	
California Apparel News	http://www.apparelnews.net/		•	Events calendar, trade show calendar, links
Embroidery News	http://www.embmag.com/EMBnew/index.html		•	Selected editorial
Footwear News	http://www.footwearnews.com/		•	
Just Style	http://www.just-style.com/	•	•	Events, resources, e-mail newsletter
Style.com (Advance Publications)	http://www.style.com/	•	•	Forums, e-mail newsletter, Web video
Textile World	http://www.textileworld.com/	•	•	Selected archival editorial; Buyer's guide, shows/events calendar, industry reports
Women's Wear Daily	http://www.wwd.com/	•	•	Online subscription

WOMEN'S TOPICS

Publishers of women's magazines have done a poor job to date in establishing Web sites that are of use to PR practitioners. However, since women have reached parity in online usage, we expect that better Web sites will appear soon. Several of the most popular women's magazines have pages on other Web sites, especially on women.com. In almost all cases, content is republished from a print version. PR practitioners should watch this category. We expect publishers to become more Web savvy. Until then, follow a print strategy. There are dozens of women-related newsgroups, but they are hard to find.

Publication/Medium	URL	Daily news	Archive news	Resources
Chatelaine (Canada)	http://www.chatelaine.com/		•	Many how-to articles and advice columns
Chickclick	http://www.chickclick.com/	•	•	
Cosmopolitan (part of Women.com)	http://www.cosmomag.com/		•	Selected editorial
Digital Women	http://www.digital-women.com/		•	

Publication/Medium	URL	Daily news	Archive news	Resources
Elle			•	Forum; members-only section; America Online (AOL)
Flare (Canadian)	http://www.flare.com/home.html		•	Calendar of events
Femina	http://www.femina.cybergrrl.com/			Links
The Glass Ceiling	http://www.theglassceiling.com/		•	
Gurl	http://www.gurl.com/	•	•	E-mail newsletter, events calendar
Herspace	http://www.herspace.com/		•	
iVillage	http://www.ivillage.com/	•	•	News aggregated from various sources; many how-to articles and advice columns; bulletin boards, chat
Ladies' Home Journal	http://www.lhj.com/		•	Selected editorial, forums
Latina	http://www.latina.com/		•	Selected editorial
Lilith	http://www.lilithmag.com/		•	Selected editorial
Marie Claire (part of Women.com)	http://www.marieclaire.com/		•	
Martha Stewart	http://www.marthastewart.com/		•	Bulletin boards, chat, how-to's
Mode	http://www.modestyle.com/		•	
Modern Bride	http://www.modernbride.com/		•	Local resources, planning help and tools, e-mail newsletter, Yahoo-based chats
Pageantry	http://www.pageantrymagazine.com/		•	
Redbook (part of Women.com)	http://www.redbookmag.com/		•	
Self	http://www.phys.com/self/home.html		•	Forums
Today's Arizona Woman	http://www.taw.com/		•	Chat, calendar of events
Underwire	http://underwire.msn.com/Underwire/Cover.asp		•	Chat, events calendar
Victoria (part of Women.com)	http://www.victoriamag.com/		•	
Woman's Day			•	On America Online (AOL); chat, messages, e-mail newsletter
Women Inc	http://www.womeninc.com/		•	E-mail newsletter, calendar of events
Women.com	http://women.com/index.html		•	Many how-to articles and advice columns; bulletin boards, chat

Publication/Medium	URL	Daily news	Archive news	Resources
Women's Forum	http://www.womensforum.com/		•	100+ partner sites on broad range of topics; e-mail newsletters
Womens Net	http://www.womensnet.net/	•	•	
Women's News Bureau	http://www.womensnewsbureau.com/SiteMap.htm	•	•	News from women entrepreneurs
Working Woman	http://www.workingwomanmag.com/		•	
Wwwomen	http://www.wwwomen.com/			Links
Y2K Moms	http://www.y2kmoms.com/		•	

WOODWORKING

Most of the information in this segment is republished from printed material. There is little daily news. Forums are active, however, in some of the publications and are worth monitoring. There are hundreds of woodworking link sites, most of which are not of use to PR practitioners. At least one newsgroup is devoted to woodworking at rec.woodworking.

Publication/Medium	URL	Daily news	Archive news	Resources
American Woodworker	http://www.americanwoodworker.com/		•	Event listings, tutorials
Fine Homebuilding	http://www.taunton.com/fh/		•	Forums, tutorials
Fine Woodworking	http://www.taunton.com/fw/		•	Forums, tutorials
Industrial Strength Woodworking (includes Custom Woodworking)	http://www.iswonline.com/		•	
Modern Woodworking	http://www.modernwoodworking.com/		•	Manufacturers listing, forum
Popular Woodworking	http://www.popularwoodworking.com/		•	Selected editorial, product reviews, tutorials
Wood	http://www.woodmagazine.com/		•	Tutorials, forums, club listings
Woodnet	http://www.woodnet.net/		•	Product reviews, forums, links, tutorials
Woodworker's Journal	http://www.woodworkersjournal.com/		•	Links, tutorials

Index

ABOUT THE AUTHOR

James L. Horton is a Senior Director at Robert Marston and Associates, New York. He is also the founder and Web master of one of the best-known PR source sites on the Web—Online-PR.com. He counsels clients on corporate strategy and product positioning, crisis communications, and the use of online media in public relations. Mr. Horton is the author of numerous articles and studies and a book: *Integrating Corporate Communications* (Quorum, 1995).